EMERALD GEMS

New Perspectives in Global Environmental Disasters

EMERALD GEMS

New Perspectives in Global Environmental Disasters

Emerald

United Kingdom • North America • Japan
India • Malaysia • China

Emerald Group Publishing Limited
Howard House, Wagon Lane, Bingley BD16 1WA, UK

First edition 2015

British Library Cataloguing in Publication Data
A catalogue record for this book is available from the British Library

ISBN: 978-1-78560-809-4

Printed and bound by CPI Group (UK) Ltd, Croydon, CR0 4YY

ISOQAR certified Management System, awarded to Emerald for adherence to Environmental standard ISO 14001:2004.

ISOQAR REGISTERED

Certificate Number 1985
ISO 14001

INVESTOR IN PEOPLE

Contents

Preface

New Perspectives in Global Environmental Disasters is a unique collection of articles that represent the very highest level of scholarship in the sphere of environmental management research. The articles published in this collection identify some emergent themes that have subsequently established themselves as key issues among academics in the field. These include the following:

- Community-based disaster management
- AHP based decision support systems
- Crisis management
- Emergency planning

This new collection provides an unparalleled insight into the world of disaster risk and reduction management, and will enable readers to access the most important 'thinkers' active in this arena today.

A Fuzzy AHP Based Decision Support System for Disaster Center Location Selection and a Case Study for Istanbul

Banu Tuğba Turğut, Gamze Taş, Ahmet Herekoğlu, Hakan Tozan and Ozalp Vayvay

Abstract

Purpose – The purpose of this paper is to propose a disaster logistics center location selection decision support system, based on analytic hierarchy/fuzzy analytic hierarchy process methods, which will serve to fulfill the needs of disaster victims and rescue teams after a possible earthquake, and to implement the proposed systems for Istanbul.

Design/methodology/approach – Determining the appropriate location from among the possibilities by taking many sophisticated and inter-related processes and parameters into consideration under stringent constraints is one of the keystones of logistics. Disaster logistics center location selections are extremely complex and vital. In this paper, analytic hierarchy/fuzzy analytic hierarchy process methods are used to compose a decision support system for determining the location of disaster logistics centers. The criteria and the weighting for the criteria that are used are determined via a questionnaire technique applied to specialists working in the Istanbul Center of Disaster Coordination.

Findings – Results gathered from the implementation of the proposed models to the chosen case illustrate that systems successfully determine the location, and both models point out the same result with different weights.

Originality/value – The paper introduces two disaster logistics center location selection decision support systems (fuzzy and crisp) and presents an empirical case study of the proposed models for Istanbul. The proposed model and outcomes from the application may shed light on future work, especially in the field of disaster logistics management.

Keywords: Disasters; Emergency response; Emergency logistics; Location selection; Fuzzy AHP; Analytical hierarchy process; Decision support systems

Reprinted from *Disaster Prevention and Management*
Vol. 20 No. 5, pp. 499–520 (2011). doi:10.1108/09653561111178943

1. Introduction

In recent years, both frequent natural and anthropogenic disasters have brought serious losses to human beings (Yuan and Wang, 2009). For effective emergency preparedness, managerial and organizational discussions keep their severity (Rebmann *et al.*, 2006). Logistics support is one of the main activities in emergency preparedness against disasters (Ozdamar *et al.*, 2004; Yuan and Wang, 2009). A quick response for the urgent needs of support in affected areas is a critical issue in emergency logistics (Sheu, 2007). Necessities such as food, shelter, medicine, etc., have to be sent from supply centers to disaster areas as quickly as possible (Yuan and Wang, 2009).

Emergency logistics is different from business logistics as the uncertainty as to logistics requirements is higher in emergency logistics (Sheu, 2007). This chaotic nature of emergency logistics necessitates the development of special precautions, requisiteness and means for emergency logistics. One of the means of emergency preparedness is to utilize disaster logistics centers. Disaster logistics centers can be defined simply as distribution centers supplying urgent requirements such as aid supplies, search and rescue equipment, food, beverages, blankets, tents, etc., to normalize living conditions at the time of and after disasters. The locations of these centers are vitally important since they provide basic necessities for people in the case of emergencies. In addition, possible impacts of disasters on these centers (which are related to the type and characteristics of disasters such as earthquake, famine, fires, hurricanes, or a combination thereof) requires decision makers to be very careful regarding the selection of their location. Although there are many studies regarding the selection of location in the literature, especially in the business area, studies that directly focuses on disaster logistics center location selection decision making models are scarce (Ozdamar *et al.*, 2004; Chang *et al.*, 2007). Hence the main motivation of this paper.

Most multi-criteria decision-making approaches focus on model human judgment/inference and try to implement them into decision models (Anagnostopoulos *et al.*, 2008). This paper mainly concentrates on developing a decision support system (DSS) in a fuzzy environment for disaster logistics center location selection. The methodology of both analytic hierarchy process (AHP) and fuzzy AHP, based on Chang's (1996) extent analysis, are preferred as an evaluation tool.

This paper is organized as follows. In section 2, same basic methods for location selection problems are outlined. The background and research methods of the paper including fuzzy set theory, AHP and fuzzy AHP (Zhu *et al.*, 1999) are introduced in section 3. In section 4, the proposed disaster logistics center location selection DSS (based on AHP and fuzzy AHP) is introduced, the criteria determination process of the study is explained and an empirical case study of the model for Istanbul (the biggest city in Turkey) is presented. Finally, conclusions and further recommendations are highlighted in the last section.

2. Location Selection

Location selection is a significant part of strategic management activities (Tabari *et al.*, 2008). Studies on location selection have a long research history related to many different research fields, such as operations research, industrial engineering, geography, economics, computer science, mathematics, marketing, electrical engineering and urban planning (Cheng and Li, 2004; Drezner, 1995). Also, many methods have been developed for this vital subject (Chou *et al.*, 2008). The basic methods that are used in location selection can be summarized as (Chou *et al.*, 2008; Kahraman *et al.*, 2003):

- factor rating (Chase and Aquilano, 1995);
- center of gravity (Chase and Aquilano, 1995);
- analytic Delphi method (Chase and Aquilano, 1995);
- analog approach (Applebaum, 1968);
- AHP (Badri, 1999);
- multiple regression analysis (Nobuaki *et al.*, 1998; Nicolau, 2002);
- artificial neural networks; and
- mathematical programming methods, including dynamic programming (Canel *et al.*, 2000), integer programming (Melkote and Daskin, 2001), non-linear programming (Nanthavanij and Yenradee, 1999) and quadratic programming (Comley, 1995).

3. Research methods: AHP and Fuzzy AHP

As a decision support tool, AHP and fuzzy AHP methods are used individually. In this section the AHP methodology, fuzzy set theory (background of fuzzy AHP) and fuzzy AHP are explained briefly.

3.1 Analytic Hierarchy Process (AHP)

AHP, introduced by Saaty in the 1970s, is one of the most widely used and strongest multi-criteria decision making tools (Kahraman *et al.*, 2008). It is a mathematical theory for deriving ratio scale priority vectors from positive reciprocal matrices with entries built up by paired comparisons (Saaty and Hu, 1998; Vijayvargiya and Dey, 2010) and a decision making tool that can help general decision activity by decomposing a complex problem into a multi-level hierarchical structure including objectives, criteria, sub-criteria and alternatives (Saaty, 1995; Sharma *et al.*, 2008).

AHP enables decision makers to structure complex problems in a simple hierarchical form and to evaluate a large number of factors in a systematic way, whether they are quantitative or qualitative (Lee *et al.*, 2008). It can also be used in complex and unstructured decision-making procedures containing multiple attributes that may involve conflict between themselves (Saaty, 1995). Furthermore, it offers the opportunity of breaking down problems in a logical manner and

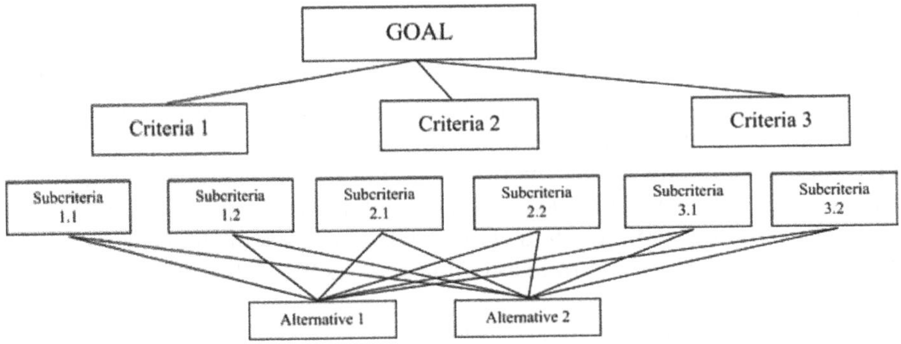

Figure 1: The hierarchical structure

connecting the judgments from lower levels to upper levels of the hierarchical structure (Al-Harbi, 2001).

The process of AHP can be summarized in four main steps (Saaty, 1995; Lee *et al.*, 2008; Shin *et al.*, 2007):

- *Step 1: Definition of the problem and determination of its goal* – In this step, decision makers determine the evaluation criteria and alternatives (see Figure 1).
- *Step 2: Establishment of each factor for the pair-wise comparison matrix* – In this step, the elements of pairwise comparison values are determined (by experts, questionnaires, etc.). First, the criteria are compared according to the main goal. If there are sub-criteria, these sub-criteria are compared with pairwise comparison with respect to the criteria that they belong to. Then, the alternatives are compared with respect to the criteria. Consequently, the comparison matrix of the decision model is constructed.
- *Step 3: Calculation of eigenvalue and eigenvector* – The comparison matrix with n criteria is an $n \times n$ square matrix A. The elements of matrix A are a_{ij}, which illustrates the value of the comparison of the ith criteria over the jth criteria, and element a_{ij}, which illustrates the reverse as $1/a_{ji}$. Matrix W is calculated by dividing each column of A to its column sum. Then $\lambda_{\max}$ the principal eigenvalue of the matrix, can be found using the mathematical relation $AW = \lambda_{\max} W$.
- *Step 4: Determination of the appropriate alternative(s)* – Using the weights of the eigenvector the convenient alternative(s) is (are) determined.

3.2 *Fuzzy Set Theory*

In contrast to many cases that involve human judgment, crisp sets divide the given universe of discourse in to basic two groups:

(1) members, which definitely belong to the set; and
(2) non-members, which definitely do not.

This delimitation, which arises from their mutually exclusive structure, enforces the decision maker to set a clear-cut boundary between the decision variables and alternatives. However, in the real world, it is very hard to extract precise data from human judgment and reasoning to numerical measurement indicators, as human preferences include a degree of uncertainty. In addition, decision makers may very well be reluctant or unable to assign crucial numerical values to compare judgments. Fuzzy set theory, which was introduced in the pioneering work of Zadeh in 1965, deals with ambiguous or not well-defined conditions (Kahraman *et al.*, 2008). It uses approximate rather than precise reasoning (Saaty and Tran, 2007) and has the brilliant capability of data processing using partial set membership functions. This characteristic, including the ability to assign intermediate values between expressions mathematically, turns fuzzy logic into a strong device for impersonating ambiguous and uncertain linguistic knowledge, and offers a robust framework for model designers dealing with systems that contain high uncertainty (Aguilar-Lasserre *et al.*, 2009).

3.3 Fuzzy AHP

The fuzzy AHP method is based on the concept of Zadeh's fuzzy set theory (Celik *et al.*, 2009). Studies regarding this method can be tracked back to the study of Van Laarhoven and Pedrycz in the 1980s (Van Laarhoven and Pedrycz, 1983). In 1985 Buckley proposed fuzzy ratios in calculations for pair-wise comparisons (Buckley, 1985; Kahraman *et al.*, 2008). Then Mikhailov suggested a fuzzy preference programming method (Mikhailov, 2003). One of the latest approaches to fuzzy AHP is Chang's extent analysis (Shin *et al.*, 2007). As extent analysis is found to be simple to computate (Wang and Chin, 2008), easy to understand and has the ability to use both qualitative and quantitative data (Tabari *et al.*, 2008) it has a broad variety of applications, such as the prioritization of customer requirements in quality function deployment (QFD), the prioritization of human capital measurement indicators, building a ranking system for semiconductor fabrication, etc. (Aguilar-Lasserre *et al.*, 2009).

As stated above, in this study Chang's extent fuzzy AHP is selected and utilized. The steps of Chang's extent analysis can be summarized as follows (Tabari *et al.*, 2008; Chang, 1996; Çakir *et al.*, 2010).

Let $X=\{x_1, x_2, x_3, \ldots, x_n\}$ be an object set, and let $G=\{g_1, g_2, g_3, \ldots, g_n\}$ be a goal set. Here, extent analysis for each goal must be performed respectively, so that for each object $M_{gi}^{1}, M_{gi}^{2}, \ldots, M_{gi}^{m}$, $i=1, 2, \ldots, n$ (where M_{gi}^{j} $(j=1, 2, \ldots, m)$ are all triangular fuzzy numbers (TFN)), m extent analysis values can be obtained.

Step 1: The value of fuzzy synthetic extent with respect to the *i*th object is defined as:

$$S_i = \sum_{j=1}^{m} M_{gi}^{j} \otimes \left[\sum_{i=1}^{n} \sum_{j=1}^{m} M_{gi}^{j} \right]^{-1} \tag{1}$$

where $[\sum_{j=1}^{n}\sum_{j=1}^{m} M_{gi}^{j}]^{-1}$is computed via equations (2) and (3) as follows:

$$\sum_{j=1}^{m} M_{gi}^{j} = \left(\sum_{j=1}^{m} l_j, \sum_{j=1}^{m} m_j, \sum_{j=1}^{m} u_j\right), \tag{2}$$

$$\left[\sum_{i=1}^{n}\sum_{j=1}^{m} M_{gi}^{j}\right]^{-1} = \left(\frac{1}{\sum_{i=1}^{n} u_i}, \frac{1}{\sum_{i=1}^{n} m_i}, \frac{1}{\sum_{i=1}^{n} l_i}\right). \tag{3}$$

Step 2: The degree of possibility of $M_2=(l_2, m_2, u_2)\geq M_1=(l_1, m_1, u_1)$ can be defined as:

$$V(\tilde{M}_2 \geq \tilde{M}_1) = \sup_{y\geq x} [\min(\mu_{\tilde{M}_1}(x), \mu_{\tilde{M}_2}(y))], \tag{4}$$

where $\tilde{M}_1=(l_1, m_1, u_1)$ and $\tilde{M}_2=(l_2, m_2, u_2)$ are triangular fuzzy numbers The intersection between M_1 and M_2 is shown in Figure 2.

Equation (4) can be equivalently expressed as follows:

$$V(\tilde{M}_2 \geq \tilde{M}_1) = hgt(\tilde{M}_1 \cap \tilde{M}_2) = \mu_{M_2}(d) = \begin{cases} 1, & \text{if } m_2 \geq m_1, \\ 0, & \text{if } l_1 \geq u_2, \\ \dfrac{l_1 - u_2}{(m_2 - u_2) - (m_1 - l_1)} & \text{otherwise.} \end{cases} \tag{5}$$

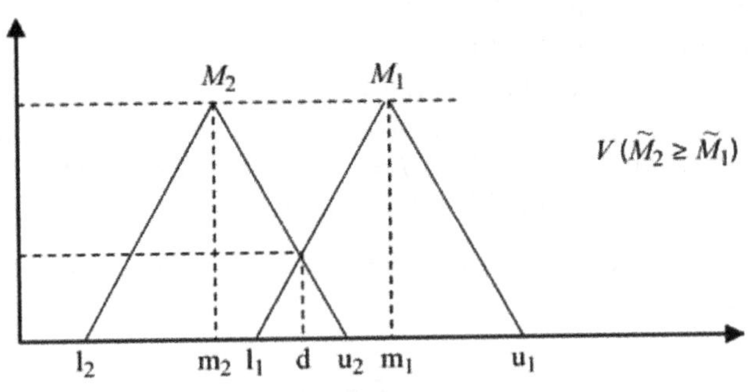

Source: Çakır (2009)

Figure 2: The intersection between M_1 and M_2 (Çakır, 2009)

Step 3: The degree of possibility for a convex fuzzy number to be greater than k convex fuzzy numbers M_i can be found as:

$$V(M \geq M_1, M_2, \ldots, M_k) = V[(M \geq M_1) \text{ and } (M \geq M_2) \text{ and} \ldots \text{and} \\ (M \geq M_k)] = \min V(M \geq M_i), \tag{6}$$

where $i=1, 2, 3, \ldots, k$.

Assuming $d(A_i)$=min $V(S_i \geq S_k)$ for $k=1, 2, \ldots, n$; $k \neq i$, where $A_i=(i=1, 2, \ldots, n)$ are n elements, the weight vector can be given as:

$$W' = [d'(A_1), d'(A_2), \ldots, d'(A_n)]^T. \tag{7}$$

Step 4: Finally, the normalized weight vectors can be computed as:

$$W = [d(A_1), d(A_2), \ldots, d(A_n)]^T, \tag{8}$$

where the weight W is non-fuzzy.

4. Proposed DSS and a Case Study for the City of Istanbul

4.1 Proposed DSS

Earthquakes are among the most destructive of natural disasters. Through human history, people living in countries on seismic belts (like Turkey) have faced the devastating impact of earthquakes many times. Each time, the vital importance of a disaster logistics centers and their location have been realized by the authorities. But, more is the pity, realizing the importance after disasters claims many lives. From this point of view, the main purpose of the proposed DSS is to determine the criteria for selecting the location of disaster logistics centers for massive cities like Istanbul. These centers will mainly be constructed to fulfill the needs of disaster victims and rescue teams after a possible earthquake.

Determination of the criteria and sub-criteria for the proposed DSS was done via a questionnaire filled in by specialists working in the Istanbul Center of Disaster Coordination (ICDC), deep discussions with experts, and making use of the study of Fernandez and Ruiz (2009). The location alternatives for the case study (i.e. Istanbul) were determined based on suggestions from the ICDC experts. After the criteria and location alternatives were determined, the specialists from ICDC were asked to state the importance of each criterion, and this was then used in the proposed model. Figure 3 illustrates the skeleton of the proposed hierarchical model including criteria, sub-criteria and alternatives.

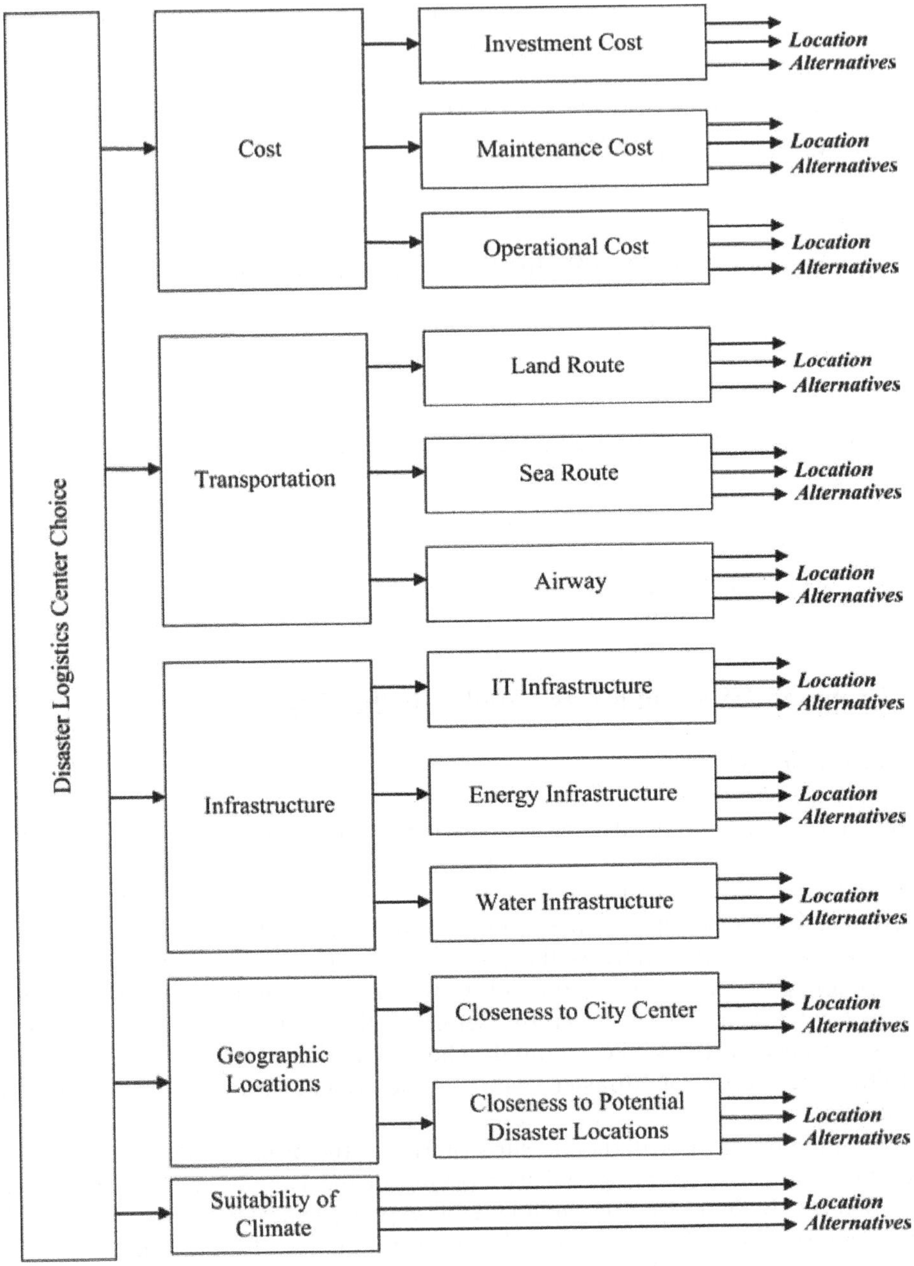

Figure 3: The hierarchical structure of the disaster logistics center location selection DSS model

4.2 A Case Study for the City of Istanbul

The possible locations for the disaster logistics center determined by the specialists working in ICDC were Halkalı, Kartal and Tuzla. Figure 4 illustrates the hierarchical structure of the proposed DSS model for the case study.

In the questionnaires designed for the crisp and the fuzzy AHP, five linguistic values are used. The linguistic values and the fuzzy scale are illustrated in Table I. For the application of Saaty's AHP (crisp), the fundamental scale of Saaty (1994, p. 73) was used. Based on the aforementioned scales, Saaty's AHP method and Chang's fuzzy AHP methods were applied. Due to its simplicity and the fact that it is used extensively, Microsoft Excel VBA was used to compute the results.

4.2.1 Location selection with AHP

According to the answers of specialists the pair-wise comparison matrix for main goal is constructed as illustrated in Table II. In Table III, Table IV, Table V, Table VI, Table VII, Table VIII, Table IX, Table X, Table XI, Table XII, Table XIII, Table XIV, Table XV, Table XVI, Table XVII, Table XVIII, the sub-attributes and alternatives are compared with each other and the weight vectors are calculated. In Table XIX the summary of the calculations and the selected best option with respect to the main goal is illustrated.

The weight calculated according to Table II is:

$$W = (0.067, 0.481, 0.265, 0.149, 0.037),$$

with a consistency ratio (CR) of 0.06.

Table XIX illustrates the summary of all processes and their results described above. As a result, Kartal is selected as the most suitable location for the disaster logistics center according to crisp AHP, with a weight of 0.468 and an overall CR of 0.04.

4.2.2 Location selection using fuzzy AHP

Similarly to the application of crisp AHP described in the previous section, with respect to the answers from specialists to the questionnaire designed in linguistic values for fuzzy AHP, the fuzzy evaluation matrix for the main goal was constructed using VBA as illustrated in Table XX. In the following tables, the sub-attributes and alternatives are compared with each other and all weight vectors gathered from these matrices are used to select the best option with respect to main goal. Table XXI illustrates the synthetic extent values. By using these vectors the degree of possibilities are obtained and can be seen in Table XXII. Thus, the weight vector from Table XXII is computed as $W=(0, 0.84, 0.07, 0.09, 0)$. The weight vector for Table XXIII is $W=(0.29, 0.05, 0.66)$. The weight vector for Table XXIV is $W=(1, 0, 0)$. The weight vector for Table XXV is $W=(0.42, 0.58, 0)$. The weight

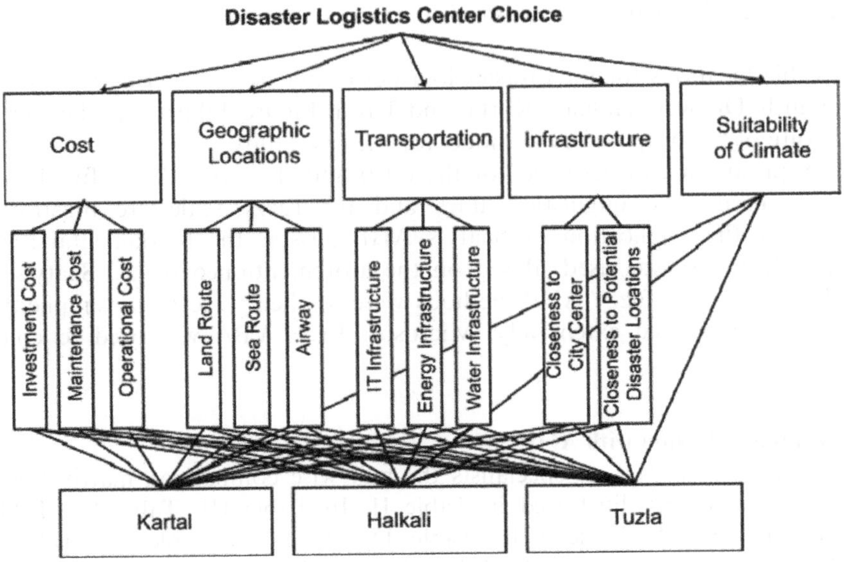

Figure 4: The hierarchical structure of the disaster logistics center location selection DSS model for the case study

Table I: The scale for crisp and fuzzy AHP

Verbal judgment	Fuzzy scale
Equal	(1, 1, 1)
Weak	(2/3, 1, 3/2)
Fairly strong	(3/2, 2, 5/2)
Very strong	(5/2, 3, 7/2)
Absolute	(7/2, 4, 9/2)

Table II: Pairwise comparison matrix with respect to main goal

	Cost	Transportation	Infrastructure	Geographic location	Suitability of climate
Cost	1.000	0.143	0.200	0.333	3.000
Transportation	7.000	1.000	3.000	3.000	9.000
Infrastructure	5.000	0.333	1.000	3.000	5.000
Geographic location	3.000	0.333	0.333	1.000	5.000
Suitability of climate	0.333	0.111	0.200	0.200	1.000
Sum	16.333	1.920	4.733	7.533	232
CR	0.06				

Table III: Pairwise comparison matrix of sub criteria with respect to cost

	Investment cost	Maintenance cost	Operational cost
Investment cost	1.000	3.000	0.333
Maintenance cost	0.333	1.000	0.143
Operational cost	3.000	7.000	1.000
Sum	4.333	11.000	1.476
CR	0.006		

Note: $W = (0.24, 0.09, 0.67)$

Table IV: Pairwise comparison matrix of sub criteria with respect to transportation

	Land route	Sea route	Airway
Land route	1.000	5.000	9.000
Sea route	0.200	1.000	1.000
Airway	0.111	1.000	1.000
Sum	1.311	7.000	11.000
CR	0.04		

Note: $W = (0.77, 0.13, 0.10)$

Table V: Pairwise comparison matrix of sub criteria with respect to infrastructure

	IT infrastructure	Energy infrastructure	Water infrastructure
IT infrastructure	1.000	0.333	5.000
Energy infrastructure	3.000	1.000	7.000
Water infrastructure	0.200	0.143	1.000
Sum	4.200	1.476	13.000
CR	0.06		

Note: $W = (0.28, 0.65, 0.07)$

Table VI: Pairwise comparison matrix of sub criteria with respect to geographic location

	Closeness to city center	Closeness to potential disaster locations
Closeness to city center	1.000	0.333
Closeness to potential disaster locations	3.000	1.000
Sum	4.000	1.333
CR	0.00	

Note: $W = (0.25, 0.75)$

Table VII: Pairwise comparison matrix of alternatives with respect to investment cost

	Halkalı	Kartal	Tuzla
Halkalı	1.000	3.000	3.000
Kartal	0.333	1.000	1.000
Tuzla	0.333	1.000	1.000
Sum	1.667	5.000	5.000
CR	0.00		

Note: $W = (0.6, 0.2, 0.2)$

Table VIII: Pairwise comparison matrix of alternatives with respect to maintenance cost

	Halkalı	Kartal	Tuzla
Halkalı	1.000	1.000	3.000
Kartal	1.000	1.000	3.000
Tuzla	0.333	0.333	1.000
Sum	2.333	2.333	7.000
CR	0.00		

Note: $W = (0.43, 0.43, 0.14)$

Table IX: Pairwise comparison matrix of alternatives with respect to operational cost

	Halkalı	Kartal	Tuzla
Halkalı	1.000	0.333	3.000
Kartal	3.000	1.000	5.000
Tuzla	0.333	0.200	1.000
Sum	4.333	1.533	6.000
CR	0.04		

Note: $W = (0.26, 0.64, 0.10)$

Table X: Pairwise comparison matrix of alternatives with respect to land route

	Halkalı	Kartal	Tuzla
Halkalı	1.000	1.000	3.000
Kartal	1.000	1.000	3.000
Tuzla	0.333	0.333	1.000
Sum	2.333	2.333	7.000
CR	0.00		

Note: $W = (0.43, 0.43, 0.14)$

Table XI: Pairwise comparison matrix of alternatives with respect to sea route

	Halkalı	Kartal	Tuzla
Halkalı	1.000	0.143	0.200
Kartal	7.000	1.000	3.000
Tuzla	5.000	0.333	1.000
Sum	13.000	1.476	4.200
CR	0.06		

Note: $W = (0.07, 0.65, 0.28)$

Table XII: Pairwise comparison matrix of alternatives with respect to airway

	Halkalı	Kartal	Tuzla
Halkalı	1.000	3.000	3.000
Kartal	0.333	1.000	1.000
Tuzla	0.333	1.000	1.000
Sum	1.667	5.000	5.000
CR	0.00		

Note: $W = (0.60, 0.20, 0.20)$

Table XIII: Pairwise comparison matrix of alternatives with respect to IT infrastructure

	Halkalı	Kartal	Tuzla
Halkalı	1.000	0.333	0.333
Kartal	3.000	1.000	1.000
Tuzla	3.000	1.000	1.000
Sum	7.000	2.333	2.333
CR	0.00		

Note: $W = (0.14, 0.43, 0.43)$

Table XIV: Pairwise comparison matrix of alternatives with respect to energy infrastructure

	Halkalı	Kartal	Tuzla
Halkalı	1.000	0.333	0.333
Kartal	3.000	1.000	1.000
Tuzla	3.000	1.000	1.000
Sum	6.000	2.333	2.333
CR	0.00		

Note: $W = (0.14, 0.43, 0.43)$

Table XV: Pairwise comparison matrix of alternatives with respect to water infrastructure

	Halkalı	Kartal	Tuzla
Halkalı	1.000	0.200	1.000
Kartal	5.000	1.000	3.000
Tuzla	1.000	0.333	1.000
Sum	7.000	1.533	5.000
CR	0.03		

Note: $W = (0.16, 0.66, 0.19)$

Table XVI: Pairwise comparison matrix of alternatives with respect to closeness to city center

	Halkalı	Kartal	Tuzla
Halkalı	1.000	0.200	1.000
Kartal	5.000	1.000	3.000
Tuzla	1.000	0.333	1.000
Sum	7.000	1.533	5.000
CR	0.03		

Note: $W = (0.16, 0.66, 0.19)$

Table XVII: Pairwise comparison matrix of alternatives with respect to closeness to potential disaster locations

	Halkalı	Kartal	Tuzla
Halkalı	1.000	0.333	1.000
Kartal	3.000	1.000	3.000
Tuzla	1.000	0.333	1.000
Sum	5.000	1.667	5.000
CR	0.00		

Note: $W = (0.2, 0.6, 0.2)$

Table XVIII: Pairwise comparison matrix of alternatives with respect to suitability of climate

	Halkalı	Kartal	Tuzla
Halkalı	1.000	0.333	0.333
Kartal	3.000	1.000	1.000
Tuzla	3.000	1.000	1.000
Sum	7.000	2.333	2.333
CR	0.00		

Note: $W = (0.14, 0.43, 0.43)$

Table XIX: Process summary for AHP (crisp)

Sub-criteria	Weight	Halkalı	Alternatives Kartal	Tuzla
Weight of cost criteria				
Investment cost	0.243	0.6	0.2	0.2
Maintenance cost	0.088	0.429	0.429	0.143
Operational cost	0.669	0.258	0.637	0.105
Composite weight		0.356	0.513	0.131
Weight of transportation criteria				
Land route	0.769	0.429	0.429	0.143
Sea Route	0.127	0.072	0.649	0.279
Airway	0.104	0.6	0.2	0.2
Composite weight		0.401	0.433	0.166
Weight of infrastructure criteria				
IT infrastructure	0.279	0.143	0.429	0.429
Energy infrastructure	0.649	0.143	0.429	0.429
Water infrastructure	0.072	0.156	0.659	0.185
Composite weight		0.144	0.445	0.411
Weight of geographic location criteria				
Closeness to city center	0.25	0.156	0.659	0.185
Closeness to possible disaster location	0.75	0.2	0.6	0.2
Composite weight		0.189	0.615	0.196
Pairwise comparison with respect to main goal				
Cost	0.067	0.356	0.513	0.131
Transportation	0.481	0.401	0.433	0.166
Infrastructure	0.265	0.144	0.433	0.411
Geographic location	0.143	0.189	0.615	0.196
Suitability of climate	0.037	0.143	0.429	0.429
Composite weights		0.289	0.468	0.243

vector for Table XXVI is $W=(0.5, 0.5)$. The weight vector for Table XXVII is $W=(0.30, 0.35, 0.35)$. The weight vector for Table XXVIII is $W=(0.35, 0.35, 0.30)$. The weight vector for Table XXIX is $W=(0.30, 0.35, 0.35)$. The weight vector for Table XXX is $W=(0.35, 0.35, 0.30)$ The weight vector for Table XXXI is $W=(0, 0.5, 0.5)$. The weight vector for Table XXXII is $W=(0.33, 0.33, 0.33)$. The weight vector for Table XXXIII is $W=(0.30, 0.35, 0.35)$. The weight vector for Table XXXIV is $W=(0.22, 0.22, 0.56)$. The weight vector for Table XXXV is $W=(0.20, 0.40, 0.40)$. The weight vector for Table XXXVI is $W=(0.20, 0.40, 0.40)$. The weight vector for Table XXXVII is $W=(0.35, 0.30, 0.35)$. The weight vector for Table XXXVIII is $W=(0.30, 0.35, 0.35)$.

As a result, similarly to the crisp method, Kartal is again selected as the most suitable location for a disaster logistics center according to Chang's fuzzy AHP, but this time with a weight of 0.346. Table XXXIX illustrates a summary of the whole process.

Table XX: Fuzzy evaluation matrix with respect to goal

	Cost	Transportation	Infrastructure	Geographical location	Suitability of climate
Cost	(1, 1, 1)	(2/7, 1/3, 2/5)	(2/7, 1/3, 2/5)	(2/3, 1, 3/2)	(2/3, 1, 3/2)
Transportation	(5/2, 3, 7/2)	(1, 1, 1)	(7/2, 4, 9/2)	(3/2, 2, 5/2)	(7/2, 4, 9/2)
Infrastructure	(5/2, 3, 7/2)	(2/9, 1/4, 2/7)	(1, 1, 1)	(2/5, 1/2, 2/3)	(5/2, 3, 7/2)
Geographical location	(2/3, 1, 3/2)	(2/5, 1/2, 2/3)	(3/2, 2, 5/2)	(1, 1, 1)	(5/2, 3, 7/2)
Suitability of climate	(2/3, 1, 3/2)	(2/9, 1/4, 2/7)	(2/7, 1/3, 2/5)	(2/7, 1/3, 2/5)	(1, 1, 1)

Table XXI: Synthetic extent values of main attribute

S_cost	(0.068, 0.102, 0.160)
$S\_transportation$	(0.282, 0.391, 0.532)
$S\_infrastructure$	(0.156, 0.216, 0.298)
$S\_geographical\_location$	(0.143, 0.209, 0.305)
$S\_suitability\_of\_climate$	(0.058, 0.081, 0.119)

Table XXII: The comparison of degree of possibilities of main attributes

$V(S\_cost > S\_transportation)$	0.000
$V(S\_cost > S\_infrastructure)$	0.033
$V(S\_cost > S\_geographical\_location)$	0.137
$V(S\_cost > S\_suitability\_climate)$	1.000
$V(S\_transportation > S\_cost)$	1.000
$V(S\_transportation > S\_infrastructure)$	1.000
$V(S\_transportation > S\_geographical\_location)$	1.000
$V(S\_transportation > S\_suitability\_climate)$	1.000
$V(S\_infrastructure > S\_cost)$	1.000
$V(S\_infrastructure > S\_transportation)$	0.082
$V(S\_infrastructure > S\_geographical\_location)$	1.000
V(S_infrastructure > S_suitability_climate)	1.000
$V(S\_geographical\_location > S\_cost)$	1.000
$V(S\_geographical\_location > S\_transportation)$	0.111
$V(S\_geographical\_location > S\_infrastructure)$	0.955
$V(S\_geographical\_location > S\_suitability\_climate)$	1.000
$V(S\_suitability\_climate > S\_cost)$	0.709
$V(S\_suitability\_climate > S\_transportation)$	0.000
$V(S\_suitability\_climate >$ S_infrastructure)	0.000
$V(S\_suitability\_climate >$ S_geographical_location)	0.000

Table XXIII: Evaluation of sub attributes with respect to cost

	Investment cost	Maintenance cost	Operational cost
Investment cost	(1, 1, 1)	(2/3, 1, 3/2)	(2/3, 1, 3/2)
Maintenance cost	(2/3, 1, 3/2)	(1, 1, 1)	(2/7, 1/3, 2/5)
Operational cost	(2/3, 1, 3/2)	(5/2, 2, 7/2)	(1, 1, 1)

Table XXIV: Evaluation of sub-attributes with respect to transportation

	Land route	Sea route	Airway
Land route	(1, 1, 1)	(7/2, 4, 9/2)	(3/2, 2, 5/2)
Sea route	(2/9, 1/4, 2/7)	(1, 1, 1)	(1, 1, 1)
Airway	(2/5, 1/2, 2/3)	(1, 1, 1)	(1, 1, 1)

Table XXV: Evaluation of sub-attributes with respect to infrastructure

	IT infrastructure	Energy infrastructure	Water infrastructure
IT infrastructure	(1, 1, 1)	(2/3, 1, 3/2)	(3/2, 2, 5/2)
Energy infrastructure	(2/3, 1, 3/2)	(1, 1, 1)	(5/2, 3, 7/2)
Water infrastructure	(2/5, 1/2, 2/3)	(2/7, 1/3, 2/5)	(1, 1, 1)

Table XXVI: Evaluation of sub attributes with respect to geographic location

	Closeness to city center	Closeness to potential disaster locations
Closeness to city center	(1, 1, 1)	(2/3, 1, 3/2)
Closeness to potential disaster locations	(2/3, 1, 3/2)	(1, 1, 1)

Table XXVII: Evaluation of locations with respect to investment cost

	Halkalı	Kartal	Tuzla
Halkalı	(1, 1, 1)	(2/3, 1, 3/2)	(2/3, 1, 3/2)
Kartal	(2/3, 1, 3/2)	(1, 1, 1)	(1, 1, 1)
Tuzla	(2/3, 1, 3/2)	(1, 1, 1)	(1, 1, 1)

Table XXVIII: Evaluation of locations with respect to maintenance cost

	Halkalı	Kartal	Tuzla
Halkalı	(1, 1, 1)	(1, 1, 1)	(2/3, 1, 3/2)
Kartal	(1, 1, 1)	(1, 1, 1)	(2/3, 1, 3/2)
Tuzla	(2/3, 1, 3/2)	(2/3, 1, 3/2)	(1, 1, 1)

Table XXIX: Evaluation of locations with respect to operational cost

	Halkalı	Kartal	Tuzla
Halkalı	(1, 1, 1)	(2/3, 1, 3/2)	(2/3, 1, 3/2)
Kartal	(2/3, 1, 3/2)	(1, 1, 1)	(1, 1, 1)
Tuzla	(2/3, 1, 3/2)	(1, 1, 1)	(1, 1, 1)

Table XXX: Evaluation of locations with respect to land route

	Halkalı	Kartal	Tuzla
Halkalı	(1, 1, 1)	(1, 1, 1)	(2/3, 1, 3/2)
Kartal	(1, 1, 1)	(1, 1, 1)	(2/3, 1, 3/2)

Table XXXI: Evaluation of locations with respect to sea route

	Halkalı	Kartal	Tuzla
Halkalı	(1, 1, 1)	(2/7, 1/3, 2/5)	(2/5, 1/2, 2/3)
Kartal	(5/2, 3, 7/2)	(1, 1, 1)	(2/3, 1, 3/2)
Tuzla	(3/2, 2, 5/2)	(2/3, 1, 3/2)	(1, 1, 1)

Table XXXII: Evaluation of locations with respect to airway

	Halkalı	Kartal	Tuzla
Halkalı	(1, 1, 1)	(2/3, 1, 3/2)	(2/3, 1, 3/2)
Kartal	(2/3, 1 3/2)	(1, 1, 1)	(2/3, 1, 3/2)
Tuzla	(2/3, 1, 3/2)	(2/3, 1, 3/2)	(1, 1, 1)

Table XXXIII: Evaluation of locations with respect to IT infrastructure

	Halkalı	Kartal	Tuzla
Halkalı	(1, 1, 1)	(2/3, 1, 3/2)	(2/3, 1, 3/2)
Kartal	(2/3, 1, 3/2)	(1, 1, 1)	(1, 1, 1)
Tuzla	(2/3, 1, 3/2)	(1, 1, 1)	(1, 1, 1)

Table XXXIV: Evaluation of locations with respect to energy infrastructure

	Halkalı	Kartal	Tuzla
Halkalı	(1, 1, 1)	(2/3, 1, 3/2)	(1, 1, 1)
Kartal	(2/3, 1, 3/2)	(1, 1, 1)	(1, 1, 1)
Tuzla	(1, 1, 1)	(1, 1, 1)	(1, 1, 1)

Table XXXV: Evaluation of locations with respect to water infrastructure

	Halkalı	Kartal	Tuzla
Halkalı	(1, 1, 1)	(2/5, 1/2, 2/3)	(1, 1, 1)
Kartal	(3/2, 3, 5/2)	(1, 1, 1)	(2/3, 1, 3/2)
Tuzla	(1, 1, 1)	(2/3, 1, 3/2)	(1, 1, 1)

Table XXXVI: Evaluation of locations with respect to closeness to city center

	Halkalı	Kartal	Tuzla
Halkalı	(1, 1, 1)	(2/5, 1/2, 2/3)	(1, 1, 1)
Kartal	(3/2, 2, 5/2)	(1, 1, 1)	(2/3, 1, 3/2)
Tuzla	(1, 1, 1)	(2/3, 1, 3/2)	(1, 1, 1)

Table XXXVII: Evaluation of locations with respect to closeness to possible disaster areas

	Halkalı	Kartal	Tuzla
Halkalı	(1, 1, 1)	(2/3, 1, 3/2)	(1, 1, 1)
Kartal	(2/3, 1, 3/2)	(1, 1, 1)	(2/3, 1, 3/2)
Tuzla	(1, 1, 1)	(2/3, 1, 3/2)	(1, 1, 1)

Table XXXVIII: Evaluation of locations with respect to suitability of climate

	Halkalı	Kartal	Tuzla
Halkalı	(1, 1, 1)	(2/3, 1, 3/2)	(2/3, 1, 3/2)
Kartal	(2/3, 1, 3/2)	(1, 1, 1)	(1, 1, 1)
Tuzla	(2/3, 1, 3/2)	(1, 1, 1)	(1, 1, 1)

Table XXXIX: Process summary for fuzzy AHP

		Alternatives		
	Weight	Halkalı	Kartal	Tuzla
Weights of alternatives with respect to sub attribute of cost				
Investment cost	0.29	0.297	0.352	0.352
Maintenance cost	0.048	0.352	0.352	0.297
Operational cost	0.663	0.297	0.352	0.352
Alternative priority weight		0.3	0.351	0.349
Weights of alternatives with respect to sub attribute of transportation				
Land route	1	0.352	0.352	0.297
Sea route	0	0	0.5	0.5
Airway	0	0.333	0.333	0.333
Alternative priority weight		0.352	0.352	0.297
Weights of alternatives with respect to sub attribute of infrastructure				
IT infrastructure	0.418	0.297	0.352	0.352
Energy infrastructure	0.582	0.22	0.22	0.56
Water infrastructure	0	0.208	0.396	0.396
Alternative priority weight		0.252	0.275	0.473
Weights of alternatives with respect to sub attribute of geographical location				
Closeness to city center	0.5	0.208	0.396	0.396
Closeness to potential disaster locations	0.5	0.352	0.297	0.352
Alternative priority weight		0.28	0.346	0.374
Weights of alternatives with respect to main goal				
Cost	0	0.3	0.352	0.349
Transportation	0.838	0.352	0.352	0.297
Infrastructure	0.069	0.252	0.275	0.473
Geographical location	0.093	0.28	0.346	0.374
Suitability of climate	0	0.297	0.352	0.352
Alternative priority weight		0.338	0.346	0.316

4.2.3 Comparison of results from both methods

Results gathered from both methods illustrate that the best location for a disaster logistics center is Kartal, with a weight of 0.468 in the crisp method and a weight of 0.346 in the fuzzy method, respectively.

In fuzzy method, due to their relatively lower weights than other criteria, the degree of importance of cost and suitability of climate criteria on the whole system can be neglected. In both methods, the highest weight is given to transportation.

5. Conclusion

In every logistics system (whether in the area of business, the military or state enterprise) one of the most important decisions that has to be dealt with is determining the location of logistics facilities due to their functions. Of these, the selection of the location of disaster logistics centers is extremely complex and vitally important. In this paper AHP and fuzzy AHP based DSSs for the selection of the location of a disaster logistics center to be used for quick response to the needs of disaster victims and rescue teams after a possible earthquake are proposed, and an empirical case study is performed with the proposed models for Istanbul (Turkey's biggest city). A fuzzy AHP model is used to cope with the possible uncertainties that might arise from the nature of human judgment. Criteria for the models and weights that represent the rate of importance for those criteria were identified via questionnaires given to specialists from ICDC, deep discussions with experts, and making use of past studies. Microsoft Excel VBA was used to compute the results of each model. Finally, the results gathered from both models were discussed briefly.

The results gained from the application of the proposed DSS models to the chosen case illustrate that both methods point out the same alternative, albeit with different weights. In the crisp model, all main attributes are still valid even when they have lower weights, and Kartal is selected as the appropriate location for the disaster logistics center with a weight of 0.468. The fuzzy model also pointed out the same location with relatively a similar weight of 0.346.

Further research using different methods such as fuzzy ELECTRE, fuzzy TOPSIS, fuzzy axiomatic design and ANFIS based systems could be performed in order to develop the proposed DSS models.

References

Aguilar-Lasserre, A.A., Bautista, M.A.B., Ponsich, A. and Huerta, M.A.G. (2009), "An AHP-based decision-making tool for the solution of multiproduct batch plant design problem under imprecise demand", *Computers & Operations Research*, Vol. 36, pp. 711–36.

Al-Harbi, K.M.A.S. (2001), "Application of the AHP in project management", *International Journal of Project Management*, Vol. 19, pp. 19–27.

Anagnostopoulos, K., Doukas, H. and Psarras, J. (2008), "A linguistic multicriteria analysis system combining fuzzy sets theory, ideal and anti-ideal points for location site selection", *Expert Systems with Applications*, Vol. 35, pp. 2041–8.

Applebaum, W. (1968), "The analog method for estimating potential store sales", in Kornblau, C. (Ed.), *Guide to Store Location Research*, Addison-Wesley, Reading, MA.

Badri, M.A. (1999), "Combining the analytic hierarchy process and goal programming for global facility location allocation problem", *International Journal of Production Economics*, Vol. 62 No. 3, pp. 237–48.

Buckley, J. (1985), "Fuzzy hierarchical analysis", *Fuzzy Sets and Systems*, Vol. 17, pp. 233–47.

Çakır, E. (2009), "Logistics outsourcing and selection of third party logistic service provider (3PL) via fuzzy AHP", Master's thesis, Bahçeşehir University, Istanbul.

Çakır, E., Tozan, H. and Vayvay, O. (2010), "A method for selecting third party logistic service provider using fuzzy AHP", *Journal of Naval Science and Engineering*, Vol. 5, pp. 38–54.

Canel, C., Khumawala, B.M., Law, J. and Loh, A. (2000), "Algorithm for the capacitated, multi-commodity multi-period facility location problem", *Computers and Operations Research*, Vol. 28 No. 5, pp. 411–27.

Celik, M., Er, I.D. and Ozok, A.F. (2009), "Application of fuzzy extended AHP methodology on shipping registry selection: the case of Turkish maritime industry", *Expert Systems with Applications*, Vol. 36, pp. 190–8.

Chang, D.Y. (1996), "Applications of the extent analysis method on fuzzy AHP", *European Journal of Operational Research*, Vol. 95, pp. 649–55.

Chang, M.S., Tseng, Y.L. and Chen, J.W. (2007), "A scenario planning approach for flood emergency logistics preparation problem under uncertainty", *Transportation Research Part E*, Vol. 43, pp. 737–54.

Chase, R.B. and Aquilano, N. (1995), *Production and Operations Management*, Irwin, Chicago, IL.

Cheng, E.W.L. and Li, H. (2004), "Exploring quantitative methods for project location selection", *Building and Environment*, Vol. 39, pp. 1467–76.

Chou, T., Hsu, C.L. and Chen, M.C. (2008), "A fuzzy multi-criteria decision model for international tourist hotels location selection", *International Journal of Hospitality Management*, Vol. 27, pp. 293–301.

Comley, W.J. (1995), "Location of ambivalent facilities: use of a quadratic zero-one programming algorithm", *Applied Mathematical Modeling*, Vol. 19 No. 1, pp. 26–9.

Drezner, Z. (1995), *Facility Location: A Survey of Applications and Method*, Springer, New York, NY.

Fernandez, I. and Ruiz, M.C. (2009), "Descriptive model and evaluation system to locate sustainable industrial areas", *Journal of Cleaner Production*, Vol. 17, pp. 87–100.

Kahraman, C., Ruan, D. and Doğan, I. (2003), "Fuzzy group decision-making for facility location selection", *Information Sciences*, Vol. 157, pp. 135–53.

Kahraman, C., Demirel, N.C., Demirel, T. and Ates, N.Y. (2008), "A SWOT-AHP application using fuzzy concept: e-government in Turkey", in Kahraman, C. (Ed.), *Fuzzy Multi-Criteria Decision Making, Theory and Applications with Recent Developments*, Springer, New York, NY, pp. 85–118.

Lee, S.K., Mogi, G., Kim, J.W. and Gim, B.J. (2008), "A fuzzy analytic hierarchy process approach for assessing national competitiveness in the hydrogen technology sector", *International Journal of Hydrogen Energy*, Vol. 33, pp. 6840–8.

Melkote, S. and Daskin, M.S. (2001), "Capacitated facility location/network design problems", *European Journal of Operational Research*, Vol. 129 No. 3, pp. 481–95.

Mikhailov, L. (2003), "Deriving priorities from fuzzy pairwise comparison judgements", *Fuzzy Sets and Systems*, Vol. 134, pp. 365–85.

Nanthavanij, S. and Yenradee, P. (1999), "Predicting the optimum number, location, and signal sound level of auditory warning devices for manufacturing facilities", *International Journal of Industrial Ergonomics*, Vol. 24 No. 6, pp. 569–78.

Nicolau, J.L. (2002), "Assessing new hotel opening through an even study", *Tourism Management*, Vol. 23, pp. 47–54.

Nobuaki, S., Akira, U., Atsushi, D., Akira, O., Seiji, S. and Satoshi, H. (1998), "Commercial facility location model using multiple regression analysis", *Computers Environment and Urban Systems*, Vol. 22 No. 3, pp. 219–40.

Ozdamar, L., Ekinci, E. and Kucukyazici, B. (2004), "Emergency logistics planning in natural disasters", *Annals of Operations Research*, Vol. 129, pp. 217–45.

Rebmann, T., Judith, F. and Carrico, R. (2006), "Disaster preparedness lessons learned and future directions for education: results from focus groups conducted at the APIC Conference", *American Journal of Infection Control*, Vol. 35 No. 6, pp. 374–81.

Saaty, T.L. (1994), *Fundamentals of Decision Making and Priority Theory with AHP*, Vol. 5, RWS Publications, Pittsburgh, PA.

Saaty, T.L. (1995), *Decision Making for Leaders*, RWS Publications, Pittsburgh, PA.

Saaty, T.L. and Hu, G. (1998), "Ranking by eigenvector versus other methods in the analytic hierarchy process", *Applied Mathematics*, Vol. 11 No. 4, pp. 121–5.

Saaty, T.L. and Tran, L.T. (2007), "On the invalidity of fuzzifying numerical judgments in the analytic hierarchy process", *Mathematical and Computer Modeling*, Vol. 46, pp. 962–75.

Sharma, M.J., Moon, I. and Bae, H. (2008), "Analytic hierarchy process to assess and optimize distribution network", *Applied Mathematics and Computation*, Vol. 202, pp. 256–65.

Sheu, J.B. (2007), "An emergency logistics distribution approach for quick response to urgent relief demand in disasters", *Transportation Research Part E*, Vol. 43, pp. 687–709.

Shin, K.C.O., Yoo, S.H. and Kwak, S.J. (2007), "Applying the analytic hierarchy process to evaluation of the national nuclear R&D projects: the case of Korea", *Progress in Nuclear Energy*, Vol. 49, pp. 375–84.

Tabari, M., Kaboli, A., Aryanezhad, M.B., Shahanaghi, K. and Siadat, A. (2008), "A new method for location selection: a hybrid analysis", *Applied Mathematics and Computation*, Vol. 206, pp. 598–606.

Van Laarhoven, P. and Pedrycz, W. (1983), "A fuzzy extension of Saaty's priority theory", *Fuzzy Set and Systems*, Vol. 11, pp. 229–41.

Vijayvargiya, A. and Dey, A.K. (2010), "An analytical approach for selection of a logistics provider", *Management Decision*, Vol. 48, pp. 403–18.

Wang, Y.M. and Chin, K.S. (2008), "A linear goal programming priority method for fuzzy analytic hierarchy process and its applications in new product screening", *International Journal of Approximate Reasoning*, Vol. 49, pp. 451–65.

Yuan, Y. and Wang, D. (2009), "Path selection model and algorithm for emergency logistics management", *Computers & Industrial Engineering*, Vol. 56, pp. 1081–94.

Zhu, K.J., Jing, Y. and Chang, D.Y. (1999), "A discussion on extent analysis method and applications of fuzzy AHP", *European Journal of Operational Research*, Vol. 116, pp. 450–6.

Further Reading

Ross, T.J. (2004), *Fuzzy Logic with Engineering Applications*, 2nd ed., Wiley, Hoboken, NJ, pp. 178–211.

About the Authors

Banu Tuğba Turğut entered the Management Faculty of Istanbul Technical University in 2000. She received the degree of Bachelor of Science in Management Engineering in 2004. She graduated from the Management Engineering Program at Istanbul Technical University in 2007. In 2008, she started PhD studies at the Institute of Applied Sciences, Marmara University, in the Industrial Engineering Program, and continues as a PhD candidate.

Gamze Taş graduated from the Industrial Engineering Department of Yıldız Technical University in 2005. She has been studying in the Industrial Engineering Master's Program at Marmara University since 2008.

Ahmet Herekoğlu graduated from the Industrial Engineering Department of Istanbul Technical University in 2005. He has been studying in the Industrial Engineering Master's Program at Marmara University since 2008.

Assistant Professor Dr Hakan Tozan currently works at the Turkish Naval Academy and is also a Visiting Professor in the Industrial Engineering Department at Marmara University. His current research interests include fuzzy logic, artificial intelligence, supply chain optimization, and operations management. Hakan Tozan is the corresponding author and can be contacted at: htozan@marmara.edu.tr

Özalp Vayvay, PhD, works in the Industrial Engineering Department at Marmara University. He is currently the Chairman of the Engineering Management Department at Marmara University. His current research interests include supply chain management, technology and innovation management, business process reengineering, and operations management.

Challenges of Disaster Vulnerability Reduction in Lagos Megacity Area, Nigeria

Eziyi Offia Ibem

Abstract

Purpose – The aim of this research is to identify the factors responsible for the inability of authorities in rapidly growing megacities in developing countries to integrate disaster risk vulnerability reduction strategies effectively with their development plans.

Design/methodology/approach – The study followed a qualitative research strategy. A survey research approach with pre-tested questionnaires as key data collection instrument was used in eliciting responses from 135 randomly selected built environment professionals in academics and disaster management practitioners in government and non-governmental organizations in Lagos Megacity Area, Nigeria.

Findings – A number of factors militating against the adoption of effective disaster vulnerability reduction strategies in the area were identified. The most critical were faltering institutions and governance, weak infrastructure base and a low level of disaster education.

Research limitations/implications – The sample population comprised mainly built environment professionals in academics and disaster managers across the city. Therefore, the views presented in the paper may not be considered generalizable within the context of multiplicity of stakeholders in disaster studies. However, the research presents the perception of experts and key stakeholders in disaster vulnerability reduction in the study area.

Practical implications – The findings can form the basis for addressing these challenges, most particularly in generating and adopting new approaches to policy formulation and implementation by the public and private sectors.

Originality/value – Research on this subject-matter is very limited in Nigeria. It is, however, very relevant in efforts at addressing the challenges of sustainable development in developing countries from the human and policy dimensions.

Keywords: Disasters; Environmental and safety engineering; Risk management; Cities; Nigeria

Reprinted from *Disaster Prevention and Management*
Vol. 20 No. 1, pp. 27–40 (2011). doi:10.1108/09653561111111063

1. Introduction

Although all countries are vulnerable to disaster impacts, there are indications that parts of less developed continents of Africa, Asia and South America and the poorest people living in them are the most exposed and least equipped to adapt, and thus, the most vulnerable to disaster impacts (Diagne, 2007; Douglas *et al.*, 2008). The frequency and intensity of physical, social, economic, psychosocial and political impacts (WHO, 1995; Walter, 2006) resulting from disaster occurrence suggest that the reduction of risks associated with natural and human-induced events such as floods, earthquakes, hurricanes, tornadoes, storms, tsunamis, wildfire, terrorism, armed conflicts, transport and industrial accidents (Gustin, 2004; Howie, 2007) constitute a critical challenge to achievement of the millennium development goals (MDGs) by 2015, particularly in countries in sub-Saharan Africa that are already faced with problems of poverty, hunger, killer diseases, environmental degradation and underdevelopment (Levay in Bergen, 1999; Olokesusi, 2005).

Over the years, the impacts of hydrological and geological disasters have consumed global attention and were perceived to be the "acts of God" (Cannon, 1994), which can only be managed through post-impact and rehabilitation efforts (UN, 2001a). But recent developments indicate that damage and losses associated with development – induced disaster impacts pose serious threats to sustainable development in most countries in sub-Saharan Africa (Nwokoro, 2004; UNDP, 2004; Abang, 2005). Therefore, emphasis on pro-active measures to prevent the occurrence and mitigate the impacts of hazards in the built environment is receiving global attention (Nakajima, 1991; Yodmani, 2001).

Despite this paradigm shift, the ECOWAS (2006) observed that much of the efforts in disaster risk management in the West African sub-region tended to focus on response, recovery and rehabilitation with little done in reducing vulnerability to disaster and hazards in the sub-region. In a rapidly urbanizing country like Nigeria where about 50 percent its 140 million people live in urban areas (OMP, 2004; Nwaka, 2005), increasing population without corresponding economic growth, physical development challenges, global climate change (Huq *et al.*, 2007) as well as inability of her institutions to integrate disaster preparedness, prevention and mitigation strategies into its national development plans and programs have been identified as responsible for increasing vulnerabilities in urban areas in this country (UNDAC, 2002; Abang, 2005). As a result of this, vulnerability to hazards and disaster impacts has added to the growing number of urban challenges confronting the Nigerian people (National Planning Commission, 2004), which is a serious threat to national development and achievement of vision of Nigeria becoming among the top 25 economies by 2020.

It is against this background that this paper seeks to investigate the factors militating against the adoption of disaster risk vulnerability reduction strategies in Nigerian cities using Lagos Mega City Area as a case study. This study focuses mainly on development-induced disasters such as floods, fire, transport and industrial accidents as well as political motivated conflicts that are due to human actions and inactions in the built environment. This is based on evidence that indicates that biological (human-induced) disasters have resulted in the death of more people than hydrological and geological disasters in the African continent between 1991 and 2005. The paper explores ways of reducing vulnerability of the built environment to human-induced disasters, and thus, provides pathways to achieving environmental sustainability in Nigeria.

2. Disaster Risk Management and Vulnerability Reduction

According to Tierney *et al.*(2001), different theoretical perspectives and conceptual frameworks have been engaged in the study of hazards and disasters impacts. As a result of this, disaster risk management and vulnerability reduction have been viewed from diverse perspectives and defined in various ways. Globally, disasters are natural or human-induced incidents or occurrences (Carter, 1991; UNDP, 2004) resulting in widespread ecological, social and economic damages or losses as well as disruption of the normal functioning of a community (WHO, 1995; Carter, 1998). Disasters are mostly attributed to natural or human-induced events meeting vulnerable conditions in the environment (Nwokoro, 2004; Awosedo, 2005; Cannon, 2008). This definition suggests that disaster impacts manifest whenever there are vulnerability conditions in the environment.

Vulnerability in this context refers to the susceptibility of human society to hazards and disaster impacts (Cross, 2001, Smit and Wandel, 2006) as well as the degree to which a system or part thereof may react adversely to the occurrence of a hazardous event (Kasperson *et al.*, 2001). Tierney *et al* (2001, p. 5) noted that vulnerability is a product of natural events, built and human environment systems while Kasperson *et al* (2001, p. 5) asserted that vulnerability is a function of variability and distribution in physical and socio-economic systems and limited human capacity to cope with accumulating hazards and the socio-economic constraints that limits this capacity. Obiegbu (2005, p. 130) however submitted that the root cause of urban disaster and vulnerability are human actions as a result of shortsighted over use of natural resources and widespread environmental degradation. Viewed from another perspective, several authors (Bankoff *et al.*, 2004; Diagne, 2007; Douglas *et al.*, 2008; Cannon, 2008) indicated that physical and economic development activities that are out of context with established procedures and standards but are used as basis for determining the relative position various socio-economic class or groups, occupy on the socio-economic, political and spatial strata of the society play often-neglected role in generating vulnerabilities. This conception buttresses the fact that the misapplication of science, technological and political control may increase vulnerability or even create new and unanticipated risks (Kasperson *et al.*, 2001). This appears to be consistent with the notion in (DFID, 2002; Bankoff *et al.*, 2004; Douglas *et al.*, 2008; Cannon, 2008) indicating that vulnerabilities generated by development challenges are functions of human activities, as well as socio-economic, demographic, cultural, and environmental factors, which play significant role in determining the level of exposure of the built environment to disaster risks as well as developing and adopting human capacity to cope with them. From these submissions, one can infer that increasing vulnerability of human settlements to disaster impacts across has strong links to socio-economic and political circumstances that are intertwined with environmental degradation, rapid urbanization and development challenges.

Carter (1998) and Yodmani (2001) noted that disaster risk vulnerability reduction has in the last few decades witnessed transformations in perceptions and in policy framework. Yodmani (2001) attributed this to the evolving knowledge and experience in the field. Kasperson *et al.* (2001) and Becker *et al.* (2008) were of the view that vulnerability can be overcome by science, technology, political control and the application of indigenous knowledge. Hence, current paradigm shift in vulnerability reduction which emphasizes the need for adoption of disaster risk management strategies with potentials of addressing poverty, social inequality, infrastructure provision, environmental resources depletion and reduction in environmental degradation (WHO, 1990; UN-HABITAT, 1992; UN, 2001b). As well, the integration of multi-sectoral and interdisciplinary-based vulnerability reduction approaches, resources and techniques with local and national development plans, programs and policies have also been advocated (Annan, 1998; Hartmann *et al.*, 2004; Ajayi, 2005; UNISDR and World Bank, 2006). Within the context of emerging knowledge, the variety of research efforts in disaster risk management in various disciplines encompasses the theory and practice of disaster prevention, preparedness, mitigation and emergency response as well as the reconstruction of disaster affected systems (Abang, 1997; Carter, 1991). The three-phase inter-linked cyclic process of pre-disaster, disaster and post- disaster phases have been identified (Carter, 1991; Obiegbu, 2005, MDPS, 2007). However, the pre-disaster phase of preparedness, prevention and mitigation is particularly important to this study as evidence in literature (Yodmani, 2001; ECOWAS, 2006; Cannon, 2008) suggests that this phase of disaster risk reduction and management is grossly neglected in sun-Sharan Africa.

It is worthy of note that increasing research activities in disaster and hazard vulnerability reduction have given rise to different approaches and concepts such as resistance (ability to absorb impacts and remain functioning), resilience (ability to maintain a system and recover from impact) and exposure (the presence of a threat in the built environment). In all its ramifications, vulnerability reduction represents the pre-disaster phase of disaster risk management which aims at preventing both natural and human-induced occurrences from assuming catastrophic effects and ensuring that appropriate actions are taken at the right time in reducing the severity of the impacts on society (Carter, 1998; Huq *et al.*, 2007). Three distinct and interrelated components have also been suggested in vulnerability reduction (Yodmani, 2001). The first deals with vulnerability assessment, involving the identification of potential hazards. The second aspect is vulnerability analysis, which is concerned with the estimation of level of exposure of physical structures (building, infrastructure, and critical facilities), human beings (vulnerable groups, livelihoods) as well as the economy to hazards (Hartmann *et al.*, 2004). Finally, there is also capacity building of management ability of the human and environment to cope with disaster impacts. Abang (2005) and Tierney *et al.* (2001) identified vulnerability study, environmental protection, public education and enlightenment, land use zoning, physical development control, early warning systems as well as research, data collation, planning and forecasting as essential components of vulnerability reduction strategies. This suggest that the whole essence of vulnerability reduction is recognizing the potential for danger, developing and adopting appropriate measures for preventing the danger from transforming into disasters and mitigating their impacts on vulnerable components of the built environment. In view of this Quarantelli (1998) noted that what constitutes disaster vulnerability reduction and risk management is a function of the location, pace of development, and nature of settlement as well as the nature of the disaster that are most likely to occur in a place. Therefore, Carter (1991) suggested that individual settlements should draw from the existing disaster risk management framework and adopt vulnerability reduction strategies most suitable to their needs within the context of prevailing socio-economic, political and development circumstances.

3. Research Methodology

Lagos Mega City area comprises the built up area of Lagos State and four local government areas of Ado – Odo/Ota, Ifo, Obafemi Owode and Sagamu in the neighboring Ogun State. Located on the Southwestern coast of Nigeria along the Bight of Benin, it covers an area of about 153,540 hectares. With a population of over 10 million, Lagos is currently the 25th most populated city in the world (Federal Republic of Nigeria, 2007); and going by current population growth rate of between 6 percent and 8 percent, it is estimated that by year 2015 this city will be among the three largest mega cities in the world with a population figure of about 24.5 million behind Mumbai (27.4 million) and ahead of Tokyo (23.7 million) (George, 2002). Lagos, which ceased to be Nigeria's administrative capital in 1991 harbors over 50 percent of the total business and industrial establishments in this country (Samuel, 2004), and it is currently Nigeria's financial, economic and business capital. There is no doubt that the rising status of Lagos as an emerging mega-city and a commercial nerve center in sub-Saharan Africa has come with a number of challenges. Rapidly growing population, high densities, proliferation of slums and environmental degradation are considered as contributing factors to increasing vulnerability in this city. In fact perennial floods, ocean surge, transport accidents, industrial and construction related events are among the development-induced disasters that have assumed an alarming proportion in this city (NEST, 1991; Oyewande, 1992; UNDAC, 2002; Simpson, 2006; Ana *et al.*, 2007).

The primary data used in this paper were derived through a cross-sectional survey conducted between December 2007 and September 2008. The target population was mainly built environment professionals in academics and disaster management practitioners across the city. This choice was based on the fact that the study was to harvest experts' view on the subject matter. For this reason a total of 135 persons representing 20 percent of the sample frame formed the sample size for the survey. Pre-tested questionnaires were administered to randomly selected built environment professionals among faculty members of three Universities, namely: the University of Lagos, Covenant University, Ota, and Olabisi Onabanjo University, Ifo Campus, as well as personnel of disaster management institutions including the Fire Service, Federal Road Safety Corps (FRSC), National Emergency Management Agency (NEMA), Nigerian Red Cross Society (NRCS), Nigerian Air Space Management Agency (NASMA) and Civil Defense Corps. A total of 110 valid questionnaires representing 81.48 percent of the distributed questionnaires were retrieved. This was considered a high response rate. Personnel of disaster management institutions constituted 62 (56.36 percent) of the respondents, while the remaining 48(43.64 percent) of the respondents were built environment professionals in academics (architects, engineers, urban and regional planners, builders and estate managers). Among the key issues the questionnaire elicited responses from the respondents were the most prevalent human-induced disaster in the city, disaster prevention and vulnerability reduction strategies and challenges of vulnerability reduction in the study area.

On the other hand, the secondary data were derived from literature search. Key sources of this category of data were books, journal articles, online databases and news paper reports as well as official bulletins of disaster management organizations. Both descriptive and non-descriptive statistical tools were used for the data analysis. Specifically, descriptive statistics was used in the analysis of quantitative data while content analysis was used for the quantitative data. Cross tabulation was used in the presentation of the result in the subsequent section.

4. Study Findings

4.1 The Most Prevalent Disasters

The respondents were asked to identify the most prevalent human-induced disaster in Lagos. Table I shows the result of the analysis of their views. An examination of the results shows that good proportion (36.36 percent) of the respondents identified transport accidents as the most frequently occurring human-induced disaster, 27.27 percent identified fire disaster, 12.73 percent indicated building collapse (12.73 percent), 14.55 percent said it was flood, 5.45 percent indicated petroleum pipeline explosion, while 3.64 percent of the respondents identified politically motivated conflicts as the most prevalent human-disasters in Lagos Megacity Area. From this result, it can be seen both the built environment professional and disaster managers were in agreement that transport accidents were the most prevalent human–induced disaster in the area. Next, was fire disaster, followed by building collapse and floods respectively. This clearly shows that the four most prevalent human-induced disasters in the Lagos Megacity Area were development related challenges.

Table I: Respondents' view on prevalent disasters in Lagos Megacity region

Disasters	Built environment professionals		Disaster managers		Total	
	n	(%)	*n*	(%)	*n*	(%)
Transport accidents	18	37.5	22	35.48	40	36.36
Fire	14	29.17	16	25.8	30	27.27
Building collapse	4	8.33	10	16.13	14	12.73
Floods	7	14.58	9	14.52	16	14.55
Oil pipeline explosion	3	6.3	3	4.84	6	5.45
Conflicts	2	4.12	2	3.23	4	3.64
Total	48	100	62	100	110	100

Source: Field work (2008)

Table II: Challenges of vulnerability reduction in Lagos Megacity Area

Factors	Built environment professionals		Disaster managers		Total	
	n	(%)	*n*	(%)	*n*	(%)
Institutional failures	14	29.12	12	19.35	26	23.64
Inadequate housing and infrastructure	16	33.3	18	29.03	34	30.91
Socio-economic challenges	4	8.33	9	14.5	13	11.82
Disaster education	12	25.0	20	32.26	32	29.09
Political issues	2	4.12	3	4.84	5	4.55
Total	48	100	62	100	110	100

Source: Field survey (2008)

4.2 Challenges of Disaster Vulnerability Reduction

The respondents identified a number of factors militating against the adoption of effective disaster vulnerability reduction strategies in the study area. The result (Table II) indicates that 30.91 percent of the respondents identified poor housing and infrastructure as the key challenge to vulnerability reduction in the city, 29.09 percent identified lack of disaster education, 23.64 percent indicated that it was institutional failure, 11.82 percent identified socio-economic challenges, while 4.55 percent of the respondents were of the view that political issues were the key factors militating against the adoption of effective disaster vulnerability challenges in the Lagos Megacity Area. It is evident from the result that inadequate housing and infrastructure was the most critical challenge to the adoption of effective vulnerability reduction strategies in the study area. Next was poor disaster education, followed by institutional failures, socio-economic challenges and lastly political issues. Again, these factors are closely associated with physical and socio-economic development challenges in Nigeria.

5. Discussion

The result of the experts' opinion on this subject matter have revealed some vital issues that require detail discussion for possible lesson in addressing the challenges identified in this paper. It is obvious from the result that the most prevalent human-induced disasters in the area are transport related accidents. This is against the general notion that floods are the most prevalent disasters in Lagos. The possible explanation for this result is the need to clearly distinguish between the most prevalent and most expensive disasters in terms of loose of lives and destruction. Evidence in literature (NEST, 1991; Simpson, 2006) suggested that flood was the most expensive disaster in the study area going by the city's low-lying terrain and the number of months of rainfall in the area. By reason of the fact that flood is a seasonal occurrence; it cannot be considered to be the most prevalent in the study area, but rather flood be regarded as the most expensive disaster in Lagos Megacity Area. The result also tends to suggest that disasters such as fire, building collapse, petroleum pipeline explosion and conflicts are occasional occurrences in Lagos. The incidence of transport-related disasters in Lagos is quite understandable going by the rapidly growing population, which is not matched with proportionate improvement in the provision of transport facilities. The poor state of the transport road network, low percentage of roadworthy vehicles and absence of functional alternatives to the road transport system were identified as key factors responsible for increasing road transport-related disasters in the city.

From Table II it is also evident that the five key challenges identified by the experts as militating against the adoption of effective vulnerability reduction strategies in the study area are germane to the current discussion. In fact, development experts and stakeholders will agree that poor housing and infrastructure is a critical challenge that has defiled all previous efforts by governments in Lagos. UN-HABITAT (2006) report indicated that there is no city in Nigeria where infrastructure and housing challenges are more manifest like in Lagos. This is an indication that resident of this city are faced with serious housing and infrastructure shortage. Most neighborhood in the city comprised mainly of unplanned settlements characterized by inadequate supply of both social and economic infrastructure. Sporadic development of buildings and facilities that are not in conformity with building regulations and development controls such as setbacks, easements and fire safety requirements are common features in most neighborhoods across the city. Because of the shortage of housing and lack of access to land, residents of Lagos have resorted to building make-shift and permanent structures in hazard prone areas such as flood plains, rights of ways of high tension power transmission lines and petroleum pipelines. Apart from exposing the users of such structures to dangers of floods and fire disasters, such developments make the coordination of activities of disaster management and physical development control agencies difficult. Therefore, the predominant informal characteristics of the built up area of Lagos Megacity Area is known to have constituted a huge environmental hazard and vulnerabilities to the residents.

Closely related to poor housing condition is lack of functional and integrated communication facilities and data capturing equipments which are necessary for vulnerability assessment/analysis, research and data collation, disaster database development as well as production of disaster risk maps to guide future physical developments and also provide input for policy formulation and implementations. As indicated by most of the respondents from the disaster management institutions, this category of equipments were in short supply in the city. Consequently, the generation of vital data on which policy formulation and program development are based on is fraught difficulties.

Next to poor housing and infrastructure challenge was low level of disaster education. It is common knowledge that vulnerability can be substantially reduced if people are well informed on what activities and practices constitute hazards and potential threat to lives and property. In addition, disaster education enhances the development of culture of preparedness and prevention of potential hazard from becoming disasters and also protecting vulnerable sections of the built environment from the impacts of disasters. The result of the study suggests that most residents were not adequately informed on what constitutes hazards and increases the chances of the built environment to be susceptible to disaster impacts. From the responses, it was gathered that the formal educational system in the city was deficient in disaster education, while the informal disaster education channels (enlightenment campaigns, public awareness seminars, talk shows, workshops and conferences) by responsible institutions have not been effective in commuting the right kind of information on disaster to the residents of Lagos. As a result of this, most residents of the city have continued to engage in practices such as erection of structure on drainage channels and indiscriminate dumping of domestic wastes, which contribute to environmental degradation and increasing vulnerabilities. Also, the perceived poor disaster education constitutes serious impediments to the implementation of vulnerability and disaster reduction policies and programs that requires the co-operation of the citizens in the city.

Federal Republic of Nigeria (FRN, 1991) noted that faltering institutions was a major challenge to the implementation of public policies and programs in Nigeria. From the experts opinion, one can infer that the inability of disaster risk management institutions, environmental protection agencies as well as physical development control authorities to effectively and consistently carry out disaster preparedness and mitigation activities such as public information and enlightenment campaigns, hazards identification, risk assessment, vulnerability studies as well as proper monitoring of physical development activities in Lagos Megacity Area were direct consequences of institutional failures. This was also responsible for lack of research, poor generation and dissemination of disaster and vulnerability related information by disaster management institutions in the study area. The consequences of this has shown manifestation in inadequate enforcement of land use zoning, building codes, bye-laws, regulations and physical development legislations as well road use legislations by responsible agencies, which have contributed to recurrent cases of floods, building collapse, fire outbreaks and the proliferation of overcrowded squatter settlements and road accidents. On factors responsible for the poor performance of the institutions on their statutory responsibilities; evidence from the result indicated that the institutions were faced with challenges of inadequate funding, lack of adequate human resources, operational equipments and poor remuneration of personnel as well as absence of appropriate legislations and harmonized national emergency systems in the city. These had created communication and collaboration barriers among disaster managers, policy makers and urban development experts, and had further weakened the capacity of public institutions to formulate and implement appropriate vulnerability reduction policies and programs in line with the development needs and aspirations of the people in this fast-growing city.

From the foregoing discussion, it is obvious that one cannot isolate the challenges of poor housing and infrastructure, poor disaster education, and faltering institutions in Lagos Megacity Area from political and socio-economic context of Nigeria. Experience has shown that these challenges are traceable to unresolved political and socio-economic issues across the length and breadth of this country. Specifically, bad governance which is as a result of control of the political and economic structures of Nigeria by very few privileged political class and individuals have generated intensive struggle for political power and resources control among various sections of the society, most especially in a multi ethno-religious urban center like Lagos. These struggles most often have resulted in politically motivated civil and armed conflicts. For instance, the respondents cited the incessant clashes between ethnic militia groups such as the O'odua Peoples' Congress (OPC) and social miscreants popularly called "Area Boys" in the city as a result of youth unemployment and poverty and perceived deprivation among the citizens. Such conflicts are inimical to social cohesion, rule of law and peaceful co-existence, which are necessary for economic development and environmental sustainability.

6. Recommendations and Concluding Remarks

This case study on the challenges of disaster vulnerability reduction in Lagos Megacity Area, Nigeria has demonstrated that human factors such as ignorance; errors and carelessness were responsible for vulnerabilities in Lagos. The study identified transport accidents, fire and flooding as the three most prevalent disasters in the area. A number of factors militating against the adoption of effective disaster vulnerability reduction strategies in the area were identified. These include inadequate supply of housing and infrastructure, institutional failures, poor disaster education, socio-economic and political issues. To address these challenges, the following suggestions are made.

First, is the improvement of the provision of housing and transport facilities through collaborative efforts between community-based organizations, non-governmental organizations, government agencies and the commercial private sector organizations. In achieving this all discriminating legislations such as the Land Use Act which prevents proper land administration and limits access to land for housing development should be abolished. Also, the mortgage system should be integrated with the micro-finance banking system to enable the teeming population gain access to housing finance for housing development.

Second, existing legislations on physical development and road use should be strictly enforced. This will check the proliferation of illegal and substandard developments along infrastructure easements, drainage canals, flood plains, and other disasters prone areas. It will also reduce the use of non-road worthy vehicles on Lagos intra-city roads. There might be need to establish physical development monitoring unit compressing of professionals in both the public and private sectors. This unit can be funded through partnership arrangement between the government and organized private sector. The Lagos Mega City Development Authority should also develop and adopt both short- and long-term measures in evolving strategic development plans that take into consideration anticipated disaster impacts in the area. Such measures may include the establishment of more strategic (satellite) towns that would distribute the population away from already congested and most vulnerable areas of the city.

Third, the use of building standards and materials that can withstand anticipated disaster impacts such as flooding, fire and structural failure should be promoted. For example, buildings could be designed and constructed with reliable materials, elevated above the ground level in flood prone areas and with minimum set-backs and easements to avert loss of lives and property to floods and fire outbreaks respectively. It is imperative to sensitize the public on the necessity to engage qualified professionals (e.g. architects, engineers, builders and estate surveyors etc.) in the design and construction of building and other infrastructural facilities. This will promote the use of environmentally friendly approaches and materials in ensuring that minimum safety standards are not compromised. To this end, one must comment the current efforts of the Nigerian Institutes of Architects (NIA) in re-training her members and embarking on public awareness campaign through the "Archi-built" and colloquium events.

To address the problem of institutional failures, all legal constraints militating against the smooth operations of disaster and environmental management agencies should be urgently addressed. Specifically, the disaster and emergency management act which is expected to address policy, institutional and legal constraints at the local, state and national levels should be implemented. In the like manner, the activities of disaster risk management institutions should be decentralized through the establishment of functional offices at state, local government and community levels. This will encourage community participation and also provide a broad-based platform for the implementation of disaster vulnerability reduction programs in the study area.

Another possibility within the framework of partnership is private sector participation in disaster vulnerability reduction activities. Non-governmental and charity organizations, multinationals, professional bodies and community-based organizations should be encouraged to collaborate with disaster management organizations in the areas of funding, staff development and technical assistance. This can be achieved through the sponsorship of conferences, workshops, seminars and disaster related researches as well as in the acquisition of equipment and materials. These will encourage professionalism and provide the organizations access to requisite human and physical infrastructure that engenders development and adoption of effective disaster vulnerability reduction strategies.

Furthermore, awareness on disaster impacts is necessary in inculcating into the citizens the culture of disaster preparedness, prevention and mitigation. Therefore, both formal and informal approaches to disaster education are advocated. Public information and enlightenment campaigns in print and electronic media and through community-based organizations (e.g. women and youth associations, neighborhood organizations, market/trade and religious organizations) should be vigorously pursued. Also, disaster management studies should be incorporated into the educational curriculum at all levels in Nigeria with emphasis on disaster vulnerability reduction. This will among other benefits produce qualified professionals, policy makers and managers required to meet the human resources need of disaster management organizations and enhance the capacity of the agencies to formulate the right policies needed for effective vulnerability reduction strategies.

Finally, good governance, religious and ethnic tolerance and the adoption of effective conflict management mechanism within the Nigerian polity as well as the creation of job opportunities will reduce civil conflicts and associated vulnerability in the city. It is hoped that the implementation of the foregoing suggestions will assist in providing the basis for the integration of disaster vulnerability reduction with development plans and programs in Lagos Megacity Area in particular and urban area in sub-Saharan Africa in general.

References

Abang, B.E. (1997), "Disaster management in Nigeria: the role of the military in an integrated search, rescue evacuation organization", lecture of NAMCS Training, Lagos.

Abang, B.E. (2005), "Threats to the built environment in Nigeria by possible disaster event at Lake Nyos and the Cumbre Vieja volcano", in Alabi, A.S. and Sam-Epelle, A.O. (Eds), *Proceedings of the 1st National Built Environment Summit Organized by the Nigerian Institute of Architects and the Nigeria Institute of International Affairs, Victoria Island, Lagos, 8-10 February 2005*, Nigerian Institute of Architects, Lagos, pp. 17–28.

Ajayi, T.A. (2005), "Disaster management in built environment", in Alabi, A.S. and Sam-Epelle, A.O. (Eds), *Proceedings of the 1st National Built Environment Summit Organized by The Nigerian Institute of Architects and the Nigeria Institute of International Affairs, Victoria Island, Lagos, 8-10 February 2005*, Vol. 2005, Nigerian Institute of Architects, Lagos, pp. 10–16.

Ana, G.R.E.E., Sridhar, M.C.K., Olankunle, E.O. and Gregory, A.U. (2007), "Bomb explosions, environment and health: a Nigerian experience", *Disaster Prevention and Management*, Vol. 16 No. 1, pp. 6–14.

Annan, K. (1998), "Message on world disaster reduction day 1998", *National Disaster Response Plan*, Vol. 1.

Awosedo, R. (2005), "Building against disasters: a developer's perspective", in Alabi, A.S. and Sam-Epelle, A.O. (Eds), *Proceedings of the 1st National Built Environment Summit*

Organized by The Nigerian Institute of Architects and the Nigeria Institute of International Affairs, Victoria Island, Lagos, 8-10 February 2005, Nigerian Institute of Architects, Lagos, pp. 137–42.

Bankoff, G., Frerks, G. and Hilhorst, T. (Eds) (2004), *Mapping Vulnerability: Disasters, Development and People*, Earthscan, London.

Becker, J., Johnson, D., Lazarus, H., Crawford, G. and Nelson, D. (2008), "Use of traditional knowledge in emergency management for tsunami hazard: a case study from Washington State, USA", *Disaster Prevention and Management*, Vol. 17 No. 4, pp. 488–502.

Bergen, M. (Ed.) (1999), "Disaster – how cities can prepare for the worst", *Urban Age – The Global City Magazine*, Summer, pp. 16–17.

Cannon, T. (1994), "Vulnerability analysis and the explanation of natural disasters", in Varley, A. (Ed.), *Disaster, Development and Environment*, John Wiley & Sons, Chichester, pp. 13–30.

Cannon, T. (2008), "Vulnerability, innocent disasters and the imperative of cultural understanding", *Disaster Prevention and Management*, Vol. 17 No. 13, pp. 350–7.

Carter, N.W. (1991), *Disaster Management: A Disaster Manager's Hand Book*, Asian Development Bank, Manila.

Carter, N.W. (1998), *Disaster Management: A Disaster Manager's Hand Book*, Asian Development Bank, Manila.

Cross, J.A. (2001), "Megacities and small towns: different perspectives on hazard vulnerability", *Environmental Hazards*, No. 3, pp. 63–80.

DFID (2002), "Making connections: infrastructure for poverty reduction", Department for International Development, available at: www.dfid.gov.uk (accessed February 2007).

Diagne, K. (2007), "Governance and natural disasters: addressing flooding in Saint Louis, Senegal", *Environment & Urbanization*, Vol. 19 No. 2, pp. 552–62.

Douglas, I., Alam, K., Maghenda, M., McDonnell, Y., McLean, L. and Campbell, J. (2008), "Unjust waters: climate change, flooding and the urban poor in Africa", *Environment & Urbanization*, Vol. 20 No. 1, pp. 187–204.

Economic Communities for West African States (ECOWAS) (2006), "ECOWAS policy framework for disaster risk reduction", available at: www.unisdr.org (accessed August 2007).

Federal Republic of Nigeria (FRN) (1991), *National Housing Policy*, Federal Government Press, Lagos.

George, C.K. (2002), *Basic Principles and Methods of Urban and Regional Planning*, Libro-Gem Books, Lagos.

Gustin, J.F. (2004), *Disaster and Recovery Planning: A Guide for Facility Managers*, 3rd ed., Marcel Dekker, London.

Hartmann, J., Okada, N. and Levy, J.K. (2004), "Integrated disaster risk management strategy to prevent exposure to hazardous substance due to inundation triggered release: a concept for Japan", *Journal of Natural Disaster Science*, Vol. 26 No. 2, pp. 87–93.

Howie, L. (2007), "The terrorism threat and managing workplaces", *Disaster Prevention and Management*, Vol. 16 No. 1, pp. 70–8.

Huq, S., Kovats, S., Reid, H. and Satterthwaite, D. (2007), *Reducing Risks to Cities from Climate Change: An Environmental or Development Agenda? Brief for April 2007 Issues of Environment and Urbanization*, International Institute for Environment and Development (IIED), London.

Kasperson, R.E., Kasperson, J.X., Dow, K., Ezcurra, E., Liverman, D.M., Mitchell, J.K., Samuel, J.R., O'Riordan, T. and Timmerman, P. (2001), "Introduction: global environmental risk and society", in Kasperson, J.X. and Kasperson, R.E. (Eds), *Global Environmental Risk*, United Nations University Press, Tokyo, pp. 1–48.

MDPS (2007), *Minnesota Disaster Management Handbook*, Minnesota Department of Public Safety Homeland Security and Emergency Management, Saint Paul, MN, available ar: www.dps.state.mn (accessed May 14, 2007).

Nakajima, H. (1991), "World Health Day: should disaster strike – be prepared", *World Health Journal*, January-February.

National Planning Commission (2004), *National Economic Empowerment and Development Strategy (NEEDS)*, National Planning Commission, Abuja.

Nigeria Environmental Study/Action Team (NEST) (1991), *Nigeria's Threatened Environment: A National Profile*, Interface Printers, Ibadan.

Nwaka, G.I. (2005), "The urban informal sector in Nigeria: towards economic development, environmental health and social harmony", *Global Urban Development Magazine*, Vol. 1 No. 1, May.

Nwokoro, V.N. (2004), "Mitigating effects of environmental hazards in settled areas", in Mba, H.C., Uchegbu, S.N., Udeh, C.A. and Muoghalu, L.N. (Eds), *Management of Environmental Problems and Hazards in Nigeria*, Ashgate Publishing, Aldershot, pp. 161–70.

Obiegbu, M.A. (2005), "Panacea for natural disaster in built environment", in Alabi, A.S. and Sam-Epelle, A.O. (Eds), *Proceedings of the 1st National Built Environment Summit Organized by The Nigerian Institute of Architects and the Nigeria Institute of International Affairs, Victoria Island, Lagos, 8-10 February 2005*, Nigerian Institute of Architects, Lagos, pp. 128–36.

Olokesusi, F. (2005), "Financing disaster mitigation in Nigeria: the imperative of public-private partnership", *Disaster Reduction in Africa – ISDR Informs*, No. 6, December, pp. 17–19.

Oxford Management Policy (OMP) (2004), *DFID Rural and Urban Development Case Study – Nigeria*, DFID, London.

Oyewande, B. (1992), "A research for quality in the construction industry", *Builders Magazine*, June/July.

Quarantelli, E. (1998), "Where we have been and where we might go", in Quarantelli, E.L. (Ed.), *What Is a Disaster?*, Routledge, London, pp. 146–59.

Samuel, I.O. (2004), "Urbanization and transportation development in metropolitan Lagos", in Adejugbe, M.A. (Ed.), *Industrialization, Urbanization and Development in Nigeria: 1959-1999*, Concept Publishers, Lagos.

Simpson, A. (2006), "Sustainable strategies for combating the problem of floods in Lagos: pointer from a Csi-UNESCO culture based project", in Okewole, I.A., Daramola, S.A., Ajayi, C.A., Ogunba, O.A. and Odusami, K.T. (Eds), *International Conference Proceedings on the Built Environment: Innovation Policy and Sustainable Development, Department of Architecture, Covenant University, Ota, Nigeria, 24-26 January, 2006*, Department of Architecture, Covenant University, Ota, pp. 165–72.

Smit, B. and Wandel, J. (2006), "Adaptation, adaptive capacity and vulnerability", *Global Environmental Change*, No. 16, pp. 282–92.

Tierney, K.J., Lindell, M.K. and Perry, R.W. (2001), *Facing the Unexpected: Disaster Preparedness and Response in the United States*, Joseph Henry Press, New York, NY.

UNDAC (2002), *Munitions Depot Explosion: Environmental and Humanitarian Assistance Report*, UNDAC Mission to Lagos, January 31-February 7, available at: Reliefweb.int/ochaunep/edr/NigeriaUNDACReport (accessed July 2006).

UN-HABITAT (1992), "Promoting sustainable settlement development agenda 21", document agreed at the United Nations Earth Summit, Rio de Janeiro.

UN-HABITAT (2006), *National Trends in Housing Production Practices Volume 4: Nigeria*, United Nations Centre for Human Settlement, Nairobi.

UNISDR and World Bank (2006), "Global facility for disaster reduction and recovery progress report 1", available at: www.unisdr.org.

United Nations (UN) (2001a), "Secretary General's message on World Disaster Reduction Day on 4th October 1998", *Monthly Highlights*, Vol. 1, January.

United Nations (UN) (2001b), *Road Map towards the Implementation of the United Nations*, Millennium Declaration Document No. A/56/326, UN, New York, NY.

United Nations Development Programme (UNDP) (2004), *Reducing Disaster Risk: A Challenge for Development*, UNDP, Geneva.

Walter, J. (2006), "What on earth's happening?", *Developments – The International Development Magazine*, No. 33.

World Health Organization (WHO) (1990), "Towards a less hazardous world in the 21st century", *Proceedings of the International Decade for Natural Disaster Reduction (IDNDR), International Conference, Yokohama, Japan.*

World Health Organization (WHO) (1995), *World Health Organization Coping with Emergencies: WHO Strategies and Approaches to Humanitarian Action*, WHO, Geneva.

Yodmani, S. (2001), "Disaster risk management and vulnerability reduction: protecting the poor", paper presented at The Social Protection Workshop 6: Protecting Communities – Social Funds and Disaster Management, Asian Development Bank, Manila, February 5-9, available at: www.adb.org/poverty/forum/pdf/Yodmani.pdf (accessed February 8, 2008).

Further Reading

Bulama, M. (2005), "The Nigerian built environment challenges", in Alabi, A.S. and Sam-Epelle, A.O. (Eds), *Proceedings of the 1st National Built Environment Summit Organized by The Nigerian Institute of Architects and The Nigeria Institute of International Affairs, Victoria Island, Lagos, 8-10 February 2005*, Vol. 2005, Nigerian Institute of Architects, Lagos, pp. 197–205.

Federal Republic of Nigeria (FRN) (2007), *Official Gazette on the Breakdown of the National and State Provisional Totals 2006 Census*, SI No. 23 of 2007, (24).94, Federal Government Press, Lagos, May 15.

Onah, G. (2006), "200 people died in pipeline explosion at Sarki Iloda, Lagos", Vanguard Newspapers, Lagos, May 25.

Onibokun, A.G. and Faniran, A. (1995), *Community Based Organizations in Nigerian Urban Centres: Critical Evaluation of Their Achievements and Potentials as Agents of Development*, Monograph Series 7, Centre for African Settlement Studies and Development (CASSAD), Ibadan.

United Nations (UN) (2007), "Disaster risk reduction 2007: global review (consultation edition)", available at: www.unisdr.org/eng/about (accessed September 2007).

United Nations/ISDR (2007), "International strategy for disaster reduction: platform for the promotion of early warning", available at: www.Unisdr.org/.

About the Author

Eziyi Offia Ibem is Registered Architect and Member of the Nigerian Institute of Architects. He is a Lecturer in the Department of Architecture, Covenant University, Ota, Nigeria, where he is also doing a PhD in Architecture. His areas of research interest include urban environment, infrastructure and housing. Eziyi Offia Ibem can be contacted at: eziyioffia@yahoo.com

Emerald Gems: New Perspectives in Global Environmental Disasters

Community Preparedness for Tsunami Disaster: A Case Study ☆

Aini Mat Said, Fakhru'l-Razi Ahmadun, Ahmad Rodzi Mahmud and Fuad Abas

Abstract

Purpose – The main objective of this study is to develop a tsunami emergency response plan for a coastal community by adopting a community-based disaster preparedness approach.

Design/methodology/approach – A multi-strategy research design utilizing both quantitative and qualitative methods was used. The weaknesses and strengths of the different agencies involved in responding to the 2004 tsunami disaster were identified through a focus group discussion. A survey was used to assess the preparedness of the community. Tsunami awareness and education were imparted through lectures, sermons, radio talk shows, informal briefings, workshops and printed materials. Tsunami evacuation routes, safe zones, warning protocols and evacuation plans were finalized through a consultation process with the community. A tsunami evacuation plan was verified during a table-top exercise and was tested through a drill.

Findings – It is evident from the study that a community-based approach (where the local community is taken as the primary focus of attention in disaster reduction) to tsunami mitigation and preparedness is viable. This process has provided an opportunity for tapping traditional organizational structures and mechanisms (including formal and informal community leaders) and capability-building activities with the community disaster committees and volunteers.

Originality/value – Tsunami 2004 is the first ever tsunami disaster experienced in the country and thus the study provides significant lessons learned from the

☆This study was funded by the Ministry of Science, Technology and Innovation (MOSTI), through the Malaysian Meteorology Department (MMD) and coordinated by the Academy of Sciences Malaysia (ASM). The authors would also like to express their sincere gratitude and appreciation to Universiti Putra Malaysia (UPM), National Security Council (NSC), JICA, ADRC, all participating agencies and the target communities in the study area for their excellent cooperation.

Reprinted from *Disaster Prevention and Management*
Vol. 20 No. 3, pp. 266–280 (2011). doi:10.1108/09653561111141718

event. The community-based approach to disaster preparedness is not the current practice in the country. Thus, the study demonstrates that the approach is a viable tool to enhance community preparedness to tsunami and other types of disasters as well.

Keywords: Tsunami; Emergency response; Disasters; Community preparedness; Evacuation routes; Malaysia

Introduction

December 26, 2004 is one of the most deadly dates in modern history when more than 288,000 people in a dozen countries, including Malaysia, died as a result of the Sumatra earthquake and the resulting tsunami (Collins, 2005). According to the report by the Malaysian Drainage and Irrigation Department, the first tsunami wave that hit the Malaysian coast was detected in Langkawi Island between 12.00 to 12.30 in the afternoon and between 1.00 to 1.30 pm (local time) in the coastal areas of the southern states of Kedah, Penang and Perak. The resulting tsunami affected 200 kilometers of the Malaysian coastline from Perlis to Selangor, caused 68 deaths, 6 declared missing, 91 hospitalized and 276 were treated as out-patients and 10,564 people evacuated. Geographically, Malaysia lies outside the Pacific Rim of Fire and is thus relatively free from any severe ravages and destruction caused by natural disasters such as earthquake, typhoons and volcanic eruptions. However, the recent tsunami had caught Malaysians unprepared for such a disaster. The incident was very significant although the death toll was very much less than its neighboring countries, as it was the first time Malaysia had ever encountered a tsunami disaster.

The Malaysian government has undertaken various measures to enhance prevention, mitigation, response, relief and recovery of natural and man-made disasters in the country. The measures include:

- amendments to existing acts, laws and regulations;
- establishment of forecasting and early warning systems;
- disaster alert system;
- mitigation structures;
- public awareness and education;
- national disaster relief fund;
- development of standard operating procedures;
- development programs by Town and Country Planning Department; and
- bilateral, regional and international cooperation with various nations and agencies.

The National Security Council Directive No. 20 is a decree that provides guidelines on the management of land disasters including the responsibilities and functions of the various agencies under an integrated emergency management system. The main purpose of the Directive 20 is to put in place a comprehensive emergency management program which seeks to mitigate the effects of various hazards, to prepare for measures which will preserve life and minimize damage to the environment, to respond during emergencies and provide assistance, and to establish a recovery system to ensure that the affected community will return to normalcy as soon as possible. Nevertheless, tsunami is not included under the decree and as such no preparedness was formulated for the disaster.

Malaysia was stunned by the after-effects of the earthquake, trapped by ignorance of tsunami and there was no single warning issued by the authorities to minimize the impacts the disaster. It is now necessary for Malaysia to be vigilant for future similar events and it is therefore a priority for the country to put in place an integrated tsunami emergency plan for better protection of future generations. Consequently, the Government has undertaken various measures to enhance mitigation and preparedness for future tsunami disasters. The Government had established a Malaysian National Tsunami Early Warning System (MNTEWS) just after the tsunami 2004 (MMD, 2008). It enables a provision for timely and effective early warning to the public in the event of the occurrence of a tsunami generated over the Indian Ocean, South China Sea, Sulu Sea or the Pacific Ocean that will affect Malaysia. It is an integral part of the Indian Ocean Tsunami Warning System and the Northwest Pacific Advisory System coordinated by the Intergovernmental Oceanographic Commission, UNESCO. The tsunami early warning system and infrastructure include 15 seismic stations, three technologically advanced deep sea buoys, 16 tidal gauges, and four off-shore cameras. Deep Ocean Tsunami Buoys located at strategic locations in the seas surrounding Malaysia will form a network of ocean level observing stations. Coastal cameras have been installed at strategic locations along the Malaysian coastline. A total of 13 tsunami public sirens were also installed at high-risk areas throughout the country. This will enable a real-time continuous monitoring of earthquake occurrences and tsunami on a 24-hour basis.

In addition, the Ministry of Science, Technology and Innovation (MOSTI) set up an Inter-Agency Committee for Earthquake and Tsunami Risk Management (IACETRM). IACETRM endorsed a comprehensive "Seismic and Tsunami Hazards and Risk Study in Malaysia" on 5 September 2005 with an allocation of RM 4 million (USD 1.2 million). There were a total of seven projects, and they were being conducted by various agencies and local universities. This paper reports the findings of one of the above projects that was commissioned by the agency and coordinated by the Academy of Sciences Malaysia (ASM).

Literature Review

Preparedness is defined as actions taken in advance of an emergency to develop operational capabilities and to facilitate an effective response in the event an emergency occurs (Godschalk, 1991). Preparedness is important and essential because effective preparedness helps saves lives, reduce injuries, limit property loss and minimize all sorts of disruptions that disasters cause (Mileti, 1999). This is evident in the case of 2004 tsunami whereby, despite a lag of almost three hours between the earthquake and the impact of the first tsunami on the Malaysian shores, all the victims and the authorities were taken completely by surprise. Most of the victims might have been able to evacuate safety had they received sufficient warning from the authority and they themselves were prepared for such an event (Aini *et al.*, 2008).

Preparedness are anticipatory activities such as planning, resource identification, warning system, training, risk communication, public awareness and education, and exercising which are undertaken to improve the safety and effectiveness of a community's response during a disaster. Primary responsibility for preparedness planning and response originates with the local community (Simpson, 2008). This is sensible since the public have to take the initial responsibility for themselves and their neighborhoods when a disaster strikes. Disaster preparedness that starts at the local level and adopting a consensus building approach is essential to foster local resiliency to and responsibility for disaster (Simpson, 2001). This community based disaster preparedness (CBDP) approach is being adopted worldwide. It differs from the traditional approach to disaster preparedness that is "top to bottom" approach where the citizens tend to place the sole responsibility of disaster preparedness and response to the government. Currently, the country has in place a comprehensive disaster management and relief operation mechanism that was formulated in 1994 (known as Directive 20). The system has successfully responded to emergencies and provides assistance to affected populations but there is minimal participation of the local community in the preparedness activities. Realizing that CBDP would enhance local resiliency and preparedness to disasters, the government has taken some initiatives to embrace its approach.

Despite considerable efforts and expenditure on public disaster education, levels of preparedness remained low (Lindell and Whitney, 2000; Paton *et al.*, 2000). Studies have found that although people may be aware of the disaster hazards that they faced, there were many misconceptions regarding preparedness and that households were found to be unprepared (King, 2000; Kapucu, 2008). Having an appropriate infrastructure such as early warning system in place also does not guarantee that the masses will respond accordingly to a disaster. In a study conducted by Nakamura (2006), it was found that the people in the surrounding areas were not aware of the tsunami risk, did not know what the siren is for and there were no designated tsunami evacuation zones and evacuation routes for them although the Malaysian Government had installed tsunami sirens in the region.

Another important aspect that has to be considered in order to facilitate preparedness is that disaster communication and education strategy must acknowledge heterogeneity in community characteristics (Paton and Johnson, 2001). Differences with respect to demographics (age, ethnic, education level), cultural (beliefs, custom, norms) and resources (funding, facilities, infrastructure) must therefore be considered by researchers and planners in their approach to facilitate community preparedness. In order to accommodate heterogeneity in community characteristics and roles, the population of the study selected was segmented into local residents (villagers), community leaders, students, teachers and the Langkawi District Disaster Management and Relief Committee (DDRC) members.

Besides the negative consequences of these disasters to the community and environment, they have also led to some positive outcomes as a result of lessons learnt from them. Some of those disasters have resulted in the evolution and formation of various legislations and safety practices at the national and international levels. Therefore, it is important that a learning system from disasters is incorporated in an organization where hindsight gained from previous accidents within organizations and of others (Bogner, 2002; Turner, 1978) is assimilated. Lessons from past events could be utilized by governments and enterprises to design organizational structures that will help improve response and preparedness to future disasters. As such, it is imperative that lessons from the landmark event of Tsunami 2004 have to be extracted in order to learn from it.

A recent seismotectonic study conducted by the Department of Mineral and Geosains Malaysia (DMGM) concluded that Northwestern Peninsular Malaysia faces a greater risk of tsunami from the Andaman-Nicobar Islands area and Northwestern Sumatran area (ASM and MMD, 2009). Hence, the report recommended that resilience of the nation and communities to disaster through a people-centered approach whereby a culture of disaster prevention and resilience is fostered at all levels – individual, local society and national. There is a need to increase the level of awareness and preparedness of the communities living in the coastal areas of Malaysia. Accordingly, a study was commissioned by IACETRM to utilize the CBDP approach in developing an integrated tsunami emergency plan for the local community of Langkawi. This will also ensure a systematic command, control, and coordination of all emergency response agencies in managing future tsunami events. This process would constitute a platform to institute similar community preparedness programs for other tsunami hazard prone areas in the country.

Methodology

The location of the study comprised of three villages, namely: Kampong Kuala Teriang, Kampong Kuala Melaka and Kampong Batu Ara of Padang Maksirat District, Langkawi Island. It was estimated that there were 375 families residing in the three villages. Langkawi consists of 99 islands, situated on the North West of Malaysian Peninsular with a land area of 487 km^2 and a population of 62,000. The three sites were affected by the 2004 Tsunami disaster with a wave height of about 2 m above sea level. Although there was only one death, there was substantial damage to the houses, fishing boats and properties.

The main objective of the study is to enhance community preparedness and a formulation a tsunami emergency response plan for the study area. The study utilized a multi-strategy research design that employed both quantitative and qualitative research methods in parallel. It entails making decision about which kinds of research question are best answered using a quantitative research method and which by a qualitative research method. In addition, the multi-strategy research approach was undertaken for triangulation and complementarily of the findings. Triangulation refers to the use of quantitative research to substantiate qualitative research findings or vice versa and complementarily is the utilization of both methods in order that different aspects of an investigation can be merged. (Hammersley, 1996).

The following methodologies were developed for the four specific objectives of the study:

(1) *Evaluation and assessment of awareness, preparedness and weaknesses of the community and local and state agencies in responding to the tsunami of 2004.* In order to gauge the level of awareness, preparedness and weaknesses of the community, local and state agencies in facing tsunami, focus group discussion and cross-sectional research design utilizing survey method were used. The focus group discussion (FGD) was specifically conducted to identify the strength and weaknesses of the different responding agencies involved in responding to 2004 tsunami disaster. FGD is a preferred method to individual interview or survey as it enables in depth exploration of the theme topic and the outcome of the group's interaction and joint construction of the subject matter. A list of guided questions was developed prior to the discussion. Listed below are sample questions for the FGD:
   - describe your experiences in responding to 2004 tsunami;
   - identify the strength and weaknesses of the tsunami 2004 emergency response and suggest ways for improvement;
   - explain the roles and responsibilities of your agency in handling the 2004 tsunami disaster. What is your opinion on inter- and intra-agency co-ordination and communication during the disaster?
   - how do you rate your agency in terms of level of preparedness to disaster response in general and which areas need to be enhanced?
   - give your opinion on the comprehension and implementation of directive 20 in disaster response and relief efforts; and
   - describe efforts undertaken by your agency in enhancing public awareness to disaster and suggest ways to achieve it.

   A cross-sectional research design utilizing survey method was used to gauge the risk perception, risk communication and preparedness to tsunami disaster of the samples. The samples were segmented into four types namely local residents (of three the villagers); students (primary school children); teachers; and the key members of the local community (village leaders, response agencies, local government agencies and non-governmental organizations The questionnaires used were adopted and adapted from the Urgent Study of the Great Sumatera Earthquake and Tsunami Disaster: Report of the Survey on Tsunami Awareness in Sri Lanka which was developed by the Asian Disaster Reduction Centre (ADRC, 2005). Four sets of questionnaires were developed with slight variations tailored to the respective samples of the study. Interview survey was used for data collection among all respondents except for teachers where drop and collect method was utilized. A total of 122 households (from total of 375) and 30 respondents representing 17 different local agencies and community leaders, 236 year four of primary school children (aged 10 years) and 37 and 48 teachers from primary and secondary schools respectively responded to the survey. Data was analyzed using Statistical Package for Social Science (SPSS) version 11.0. Descriptive statistics such as frequency distribution, measures of central tendency and variability were computed to explore, summarize and describe the findings.

(2) *Identification of evacuation routes and safe evacuation zones.* Listed below are specific activities that were undertaken to map the inundation zones and consequently to ascertain the evacuation routes and safe evacuation zones for the community:
- compilation of maps and attributes of the existing geographic features, e.g. road width, condition and speed limit;
- identification of existing road signage;
- identification of hilly areas, slopes and routes leading to them;
- classification of areas into several zones;
- demographic data for each of the zone;
- identification of available community centers in each zones;
- identification of most prone areas; and
- identification of substantial buildings (minimum three-storeys high).

(3) *Enhancement of public awareness through education of community.* Information obtained from multiple sources such as the internet (web sites of international disaster agencies), books, journals and local institutions were synthesized into a coherent education and training materials to suit various 6 target groups. Multiple approaches of education methods such as public lecture, seminar, workshops, and training of trainers were adopted in enhancing their awareness to tsunami disaster and preparedness.

(4) *Formulation of a tsunami evacuation plan and observation and evaluation of a simulated tsunami drill.* Tsunami evacuation plan was developed through participation and consultation with representatives from various groups in the community. A workshop was organized to discuss, deliberate and endorse the plan. A table top exercise was performed to test its suitability and practicality. At the end of the study, a simulated tsunami drill was conducted to evaluate the overall accomplishment and effectiveness of the current project on enhancing community preparedness to tsunami disaster.

Findings and Discussion

4.1 Interfacing Activities

In preparation for the project, research visits were organized to the selected tsunami affected areas in West Malaysia, namely Balik Pulau (Penang), Kuala Muda (Kedah), Langkawi (Kedah), and tsunami risk areas such as Sandakan, Lahad

Datu, Semporna, Pulau Mabul, Tawau and Kota Kinabalu (all in the state of Sabah, East Malaysia). These visits provided information on the profile of the tsunami prone areas, indicate the level of awareness of local population, and gave a glimpse of the hardware facilities available to help in tsunami early warning. In addition, a tour of the Malaysian Meteorological Department (MMD) stations at Bukit Kledang, Ipoh, Pasir Panjang (Penang), Kuala Muda (Kedah), Awana Porto Malai and Pantai Chenang in Langkawi (Kedah) were made. These visits involved the participation of two Japanese experts from the Japanese Meteorological Agency (JMA) and one from the Asian Disaster Reduction Centre (ADRC).

Personal contacts were made with key authorities such as the Director of National Security Council, Director of the Kedah State Security Council and the District Officer of Langkawi. Permission was obtained from the Ministry of Education to carry out research among the school teachers and students in the project zone thus enabling the researchers to gain access to schools via the Langkawi District Education Office. The groups initial visit and interview with the Kuala Teriang community leaders, and subsequent community meetings, had enabled the researchers to obtain the full commitment and support from the villagers under study. These personal relationships developed with relevant government agencies and local community has paved the way for cooperation and support from them for the subsequent programs and activities conducted.

4.2 *Focus Group Discussion*

A focus group discussion was conducted among the Langkawi District Disaster Management and Relief Committee (DDRC) members and key community leaders in order to obtain feedbacks on the 2004 Tsunami. Suggestions and opinions with regards to approaches to tsunami education and preparedness of the community were also solicited. This was the first formal activity that was conducted prior to the survey and other activities mentioned below. A total of 19 participants attended the session that lasted for two hours. The discussion was video and audio taped after permission was sought from the participants.

The conclusions from the FGD are as follows:

- The initial response to the 2004 tsunami disaster and initiatives to evacuate were taken by the residents themselves and were led by the Village Security Committee where they forced their entry into the Kuala Teriang Primary School, which was used as an evacuation center. The police of Kuala Teriang were themselves victims as the police station there was inundated with water. They realized that this initial response is crucial, as it will take time for the response agencies to arrive to the scene.
- The residents realized that they are on an island and they have to fend for themselves, as it will take more than two hours to wait for help from the mainland. Therefore, they as a community should be prepared for any disasters or eventualities that may occur in the future.

- It was agreed that all levels of community should be involved in the tsunami preparedness programs ranging from agencies, community leaders, hoteliers, taxi drivers, business associations and local residents.
- Directive 20 was not fully understood by all stakeholders and thus let to unsatisfactory inter agency communication and coordination. This may be due to the fact that Directive 20, which is supposed to be a public document, is however, classified as a restricted document. Hence, relatively few members of the stakeholders knew of its existence. There were lack of concerted efforts by the authority to expound the purpose and application of the document.
- It was also observed that ineffective inter agency coordination is due to lack of stakeholder meeting and exercise. There is a need to identify a contact person or liaison officer who is involve or in charge of disaster from every organization.
- All agencies need to enhance their own disaster preparedness through enhancing awareness and knowledge of their members, logistic adequacy, training and exercises.
- Application of multiple approaches and methods for public awareness and education on tsunami disaster: exhibitions in various program such as trade shows campaigns; printed materials; television and radio programs; electronic media such as internet and CDs; and other community activities. All agencies should participate and involve in organizing these awareness and educational activities to the public.

4.3 Survey

Among the key findings of the survey on villagers, teachers and key members of the local community are:

- *Tsunami awareness and knowledge*. Prior to the 2004 tsunami disaster very few respondents knew about tsunami. Some of them did not know about what may cause tsunami and how to response appropriately to the disaster. The residents indicated that they lack understanding with regards to tsunami warning and safe routes.
- *Sources of tsunami disaster information*. The agencies and residents indicated that television is the most effective mean of raising public tsunami awareness and knowledge.
- *Essential preparedness elements*. The respondents rated all 17 preparedness aspects as very important in order to improve disaster preparedness of the community particularly with respect to the development and improvement of physical infrastructures (such as warning system, wave breaker, evacuation center etc), risk communication (hazard zones identification and dissemination, and warning protocol) and public awareness and education.
- *Tsunami risk perception*. Of the 11 types of disaster listed, tsunami was perceived as posing the highest risk to Langkawi Island. This would motivate the community to enhance their preparedness to tsunami disaster.

- *Tsunami evacuation center*. The residents were of the view that a specially built tsunami shelter would be the most appropriate evacuation venue as compared to other building structures such as school, mosque and offices.
- *Early warning tsunami and evacuation communication channel*. The agencies indicated that the best method to warn the public of impending tsunami disaster is through television, radio, public address system and patrol car. The same methods were deemed effective for evacuation notification.
- *Post-disaster information*. The residents and teachers viewed that information regarding food aids, evacuation centers and utilities are of higher priority as compared to other aspects such as damages, victims and casualties.

The main survey findings among the students are as follows:

- *Tsunami awareness and knowledge*. Majority of the students (78 percent) noted that they were taught about various types of disaster in school and they rated themselves as having a good comprehension of the issues. Nevertheless, when they were asked what could cause tsunami, they could not answer them correctly. About 50 percent of the students indicated that they were both taught by the school and their families on how to respond to a tsunami disaster.
- *Response to tsunami disaster*. When they were asked what they would do if they face a tsunami disaster, majority (78 percent) stated that they would go to higher grounds. A total of 7 percent of them thought that they should stay put, climb trees or go home, while 5 percent did not know what to do. Generally they have good survival instinct.
- *Approaches to disaster education in school*. The students were asked to rate the level of effectiveness of 12 different approaches to disaster education in school. They rated in order of descending level of effectiveness as follows: video; internet; campaigns; school curriculum; education TV; co-curriculum; special disaster day; competition (e.g. essay); text book; magazines; pictorial books and brochures.
- *Disaster risks*. The students perceived that all the 11 listed disaster as posing a relatively high risk to Langkawi. Tsunami disaster was rated as the highest risk followed by earthquake, typhoon, and ferry accidents.

4.4 Identification of Evacuation Routes and Safe Evacuation Zones

Spatial data in the form of topographic map of the area plotted from field survey work was obtained from the Drainage and Irrigation Department. Further field data collection and verification were done and added to the map. The area of study was divided into several zones, using the boundaries of the existing villages. Identification of existing road networks for evacuation routes was done based on the existing road networks, location of physical structures, and identifying strategic positions to place the evacuation signage. The locations were identified along roadways and pathways to indicate the direction inland or to higher ground. In some places, there was more than one direction leading to reach the safer areas. These routes were marked with several signs showing additional options for evacuation. An exercise was subsequently conducted where the community representatives were asked to identify safe evacuation routes and evacuation zones for the respective villages. At the end of the exercise, five evacuation zones and suitable evacuation routes were identified and mapped.

The evacuation refuge centers must fulfill certain specification based on vertical (> 5 m) and horizontal evacuation (> 1000 m). If there is an absence of existing structure/the area that meets the criteria, purpose built safety structures (tower/building > 3 storey) would be proposed for safe refuge. In the study, two hilly areas, one high bridge, one horizontal evacuation zone and one purpose built safety structures were proposed as evacuation centers. A ground thruthing were done with the community leaders and response agencies to confirm the suitability of the identified locations for use as tsunami evacuation centers.

4.5 Enhancement of Public Awareness through Education of Community

Enhancement of public awareness involves producing and disseminating information and training materials to the target groups in the local population, training of selected personnel and public lectures through local platforms. In addition to these primary activities, interfacing activities had to be carried out in order to secure smooth running of the education programs, such as visits to local government agencies and institutions, networking with local groups, and organizing and attending briefing sessions and informal meetings. Discussed below are educational and training activities that were conducted through the course of the study.

Seminars and workshops. There were five seminars/workshops organized by the study group for the purpose of special group education and training. The seminar on "Evacuation Route Planning for Tsunami' was organized to introduce to all key stakeholders in Langkawi to this project. It was attended by key officers from the MMD, the Police, Fire and Rescue Department, and the local authorities. A One Day Workshop on "Emergency Response Plan for Tsunami Disaster" was held to present and discuss the project plan.

Fundamental principles of tsunami preparedness were also presented in order to attain the commitment of the key target groups. The participants included the Director of NSC of Kedah State, representatives of the Public Works Department, Fire and Rescue Services, Police, Local Authority, Langkawi Radio, Langkawi Airport, National Power, Drainage and Irrigation Department, Health Department, District Office, and local community. The program also provided an opportunity for the stakeholders to meet and greet. The interaction strengthened rapport between the community leaders and authority representatives of the various local organizations and government departments. The participation and open discussions between the participants had contributed to enhancing the awareness on the needs for preparedness and planning in facing future tsunamis.

Another workshop was organized with the aim of imparting the principles and guide to the development of a tsunami response plan. They attendees included some of those who had participated in Seminar 2 and other community representatives including teachers, women groups, local mosque and the village security committee. An exercise to identify safety evacuation route was conducted. The participants were asked to identify possible evacuation routes and evacuation zones for their respective villages. At the end of the exercise, five evacuation zones and suitable evacuation routes were identified. The meeting provided opportunities for a wide spectrum of nearly 40 participants to appreciate the need for tsunami preparedness, and the preparations required at local level. Their participation also gave a sense of ownership to the evacuation plan. A final seminar was conducted to reinforce the understanding and commitment of the community leaders, responding agencies, and supporting groups towards creating the tsunami evacuation plan. The participants had the opportunity of experiential learning through visiting the selected study sites and related tsunami warning infrastructure.

Education materials and posters prepared by the group were presented and discussed for feedbacks. Participants were taken to the study areas and shown the selected evacuation routes, safe evacuation centers, coastal cameras and tsunami sirens.

Public lectures. Altogether, six sessions of public lectures were organized. The primary aim was to educate members of the public in the affected villages on tsunami and to increase their awareness. The target groups were villagers, school children and teachers. Talks for the school children and teachers were organized at the respective schools. Prior to the presentations, surveys were administered among the school children with the help of their teachers. The talks for the women were held at either the local mosque or community centers. The public lectures delivered were made simple with audio-visual materials to support. Further, the places chosen had to be comfortable and at ease to the audience, and logistically convenient. Most of these lectures targeted women from the households in the affected villages while the men were catered through the Friday Sermons (Almost 100 percent of the villagers are Muslims). Through them, the understanding and awareness can easily reach the houses and family members. The lectures at the schools on the other hand catered for the children of families from the affected villages.

Friday sermons. Two Friday sermons were delivered by a team member on two different occasions, but at the same mosque. The pulpit was chosen as the platform to convey the message in order to emphasize the importance of disaster preparedness in general and tsunami in particular, besides adding a spiritual dimension to the "earthly" program to face tsunami hazards. The said mosque is the gathering place for Friday prayer for all the men folk of the study area. Thus, information on tsunami was conveyed to all heads of the households. It was emphasized that making preparations to face tsunami is a religious obligation. In addition to the sermons, leaflets containing a summary of the sermon text were also distributed to those who came. In this way the message was also carried back to the houses in the study areas. Both sermons discussed the basic nature of tsunami and the need to prepare to face it. However the first one focused on the understanding and obligation, but the second included an appeal to respond to the drill being planned.

Langkawi radio exclusive slot. An arrangement was made with Langkawi Radio to have talk shows on the weekly exclusive slot in order to disseminate information on tsunami. With full cooperation from the management of the radio station, two sessions of one-hour talk shows were transmitted. The subject matter discussed centers around understanding the nature of tsunami, its threat, and how to prepare to face it. The second session discusses the tsunami evacuation plan and tsunami evacuation drill being prepared in December 2007. The talk shows further widened the information coverage on tsunami to the general population.

4.6 Formulation of Tsunami Evacuation Plan and Procedures

Tsunami evacuation plan has been formulated to assist coastal residents and visitors in locating safe refuge in case of tsunami. Fulfillment of some of the safe evacuation zone criteria is difficult to meet in some geographical areas primarily as a result of private property issues and the relatively flat land. In addition, there were some restrictions to get access to the identified location. For that reason, residents who may be impacted by tsunami have worked together to develop an evacuation plan within their neighborhood or community. The neighborhood plan had address property access issues, evacuation routes, and what might be expected in terms of the numbers of people needing to access a locally organized congregation area.

In formulating strategic procedures for the evacuation procedures the following issues were identified and reconciled:

- Warning protocol;
- Emergency Operation Center (EOC) activation guidelines and procedures;
- hazard zone mapping with evacuation routes and evacuation centers;
- identification of substantial buildings; and
- procedures for activation/cancellation of warning.

In ensuring a successful evacuation, it is essential to have a strategic procedure and manned by pro-active administration. Therefore, this procedure must be approved by the relevant authority and governing body. To address the above issues a special workshop was held which was attended by the relevant emergency responders. Among the important outcomes of the discussion was the formulation of procedures based on the three types of tsunami warnings based on the Malaysian Meteorology Department (MMD) tsunami warning protocol.

A table top exercise was organized among the Langkawi District Disaster Management and Relief Committee (DDRC) members and key community leaders to formulate a Tsunami Emergency Response Plan. The outcomes of the table top exercise were:

- Roles and responsibilities of the main responding agencies (police, fire and rescue, health, information) and organizations (public works, marine, radio Langkawi,

district office, school, airport, wardens) during tsunami disaster were identified discussed and agreed.
- Response actions to be taken by various agencies during each of the three consecutive stages of tsunami disaster alert (tsunami advisory, tsunami watch and tsunami warning) were ascertained. An operational procedure was subsequently formulated.

Emergency exercise programs are a core part of readiness and assist in identifying gaps and issues on emergency preparedness. The lessons learned are integrated into updated plans and procedures that improve the ability to respond to and recover from an emergency. The Tsunami Evacuation Plan developed was tested through a drill carried out by the relevant emergency services and NGOs based on the guidelines stipulated in Directive 20. The drill was planned under condition of expected tsunami heights of 2 meters and the inundation area is the same as the inundated area of 2004. The simulated expected time of tsunami arrival was 1 hour and 20 minutes after the earthquake. It was observed and evaluated by a JICA tsunami disaster expert from the Asian Disaster Reduction Centre, Japan and by appointed local observers. An instrument was developed to assess the different aspects of emergency response to gauge the level of competency of the community in facing a tsunami emergency. The strength and weaknesses of the drill were noted during a post-mortem that was done after the exercise.

Conclusion

The project was able to accomplish all the set objectives as there was a generally satisfactory cooperation and participation from the various agencies and full corporation from the participating communities. The involvement of the local emergency responders, government agencies, NGO, hoteliers, local community consisting residents of the three villagers, community leaders, teachers and students in all the activities has enabled the researchers to implement all the proposed programs according to the set schedule. Sharing of experiences by various local and international experts has provided the researchers' valuable insights and support from MMD, MSC and ASM have facilitated in managing the project.

It is evident from the study that community based approach (where the local community is taken as the primary focus of attention in disaster reduction) to tsunami mitigation and preparedness is viable. This process has provided an opportunity for tapping traditional organizational structures and mechanisms (including formal and informal community leaders) and capability building activities with the community disaster committees and volunteers. As a result there is community ownership to the plans and this will facilitates review and updating of the emergency response plan.

The findings from the study indicate that that there are lessons learnt from the 2004 tsunami disaster and that the local communities are prepared to improve their capacity and capability. The initiative undertaken by the study to raise awareness and preparedness to tsunami disaster by adopting the community-based approach is found to be effective. This is evident from the participation, co-operation, team work that were demonstrated by all the stakeholders in all the activities organized. They were been able to produce their own tsunami emergency response plan that was successfully tested during the emergency exercise.

However, there were also weaknesses noted during the course of the study. A total of 34 recommendations were proposed to the Government and various agencies to consider and act upon them. The CBDP approach requires empowerment to be entrusted to the local community in decision making with regards to organizational arrangements and utilization of resources. Generally, empowerment is a social process that helps people be in charge and gain control of what they do (Robbins, 1997). In the context of developing community preparedness to disaster, it entails provision of capacity to implement strategies and programs that have been communally decided. The outcome of the study shows that the community is able to adopt CBDP approach. They had demonstrated the ability to decide and implement many components of their community preparedness to tsunami disaster such as evacuation routes, safe evacuation zones, warden system and emergency response plan. The centralized top-down management style that is presently being adopted need to be re-appraised so that it does not impede the implementation process and stifle local innovation and creative ideas. Successful management of the CBDP approach to disaster requires integrated coordination, cooperation and commitment from all members of the local community and a full support from the government.

The integrated tsunami emergency plan developed will ensure a systematic command, control, and coordination of all emergency response agencies and affected community in managing future tsunami events. This also constitutes a platform to institute a similar plan for other tsunami hazard prone areas in the country.

References

ADRC (2005), "Report of the survey on tsunami awareness in Sri Lanka: urgent study of the Great Sumatra earthquake and tsunami disaster", Asian Disaster Reduction Center, Japan, 4 April.

Aini, M.S., Fakhru'l-Razi, A., Ahmad Rodzi, M. and Fuad, A. (2008), "National preparedness to tsunami disaster", *Malaysian Social Matters*, Vol. 9, pp. 12–23.

ASM and MMD (2009), "Seismic and tsunami hazards and risk study in Malaysia: summary for policy makers", paper presented at Forum on Earthquake and Tsunami Risk in Malaysia, Putrajaya, 29 September.

Bogner, M.S. (2002), "Stretching the search for the 'why' of error: the systems approach", *Journal of Clinical Engineering*, Vol. 27 No. 2, pp. 110–16.

Collins, L. (2005), "Tsunami: a wake-up call for the US", *Part 1. Fire Engineering*, Vol. 1, pp. 63–74.

Godschalk, D.R. (1991), "Disaster mitigation and hazard management", in Drabek, T. and Hoetmer, G. (Eds), *Emergency Management: Principles and Practices for Local Government*, International City Management Association, Washington, DC, pp. 131–60.

Hammersley, M. (1996), "The relationship between qualitative and quantitative research: paradigm loyalty versus methodological eclecticism", in Richardson, J.T.E. (Ed.), *Handbook of Research Methods for Psychology and the Social Sciences*, BPS Blackwell, Leicester, pp. 89–107.

Kapucu, N. (2008), "Culture of preparedness: household disaster preparedness", *Disaster Prevention and Management*, Vol. 17 No. 4, pp. 526–35.

King, D. (2000), "You're on your own: community vulnerability and the need for awareness and education for predictable natural disasters", *Journal of Contingencies and Crisis Management*, Vol. 8 No. 4, pp. 223–8.

Lindell, M.K. and Whitney, D.J. (2000), "Correlates of household seismic hazard adjustment adoption", *Risk Analysis*, Vol. 20, pp. 13–25.

Malaysian Meteorological Department (MMD) (2008), "Initiatives on Sumatra 2004 tsunami, Putrajaya", paper presented at Kobe University, 23 June.

Mileti, D.M. (1999), *Disasters by Design: A Reassessment of Natural Hazards in the United States*, Joseph Henry Press, Washington, DC.

Nakamura, A. (2006), "Present status and recommendations on public awareness and education, emergency route planning for tsunami in Malaysia", report of JICA short-term expert from ADRC Japan, 29 December.

Paton, D. and Johnson, D. (2001), "Disasters and communities: vulnerability, resilience and preparedness", *Disaster Prevention and Management*, Vol. 10 No. 4, pp. 270–7.

Paton, D., Smith, L.M. and Johnson, D. (2000), "Volcanic hazards: risk perception and preparedness", *New Zealand Journal of Psychology*, Vol. 29, pp. 84–8.

Robbins, S.P. (1997), *Organizational Behavior. Concepts, Controversies & Application*, Prentice- Hall, Englewood Cliffs, NJ.

Simpson, D.M. (2001), "Community emergency response training (CERTs): a recent history and review", *Natural Hazards Review*, Vol. 2 No. 2, pp. 54–63.

Simpson, D.M. (2008), "Disaster preparedness measures: a test case development and application", *Disaster Prevention and Management*, Vol. 17 No. 5, pp. 645–61.

Turner, B.A. (1978), *Man-Made Disasters*, Wykeham Publications, London.

Further Reading

Irrigation and Drainage Department (IDD) (2005), *Post-Tsunami 26 December 2004 Investigation Report*, IDD, Kuala Lumpur.

Smith, K. (1993), *Environmental Hazards: Assessing Risk and Reducing Disaster*, Routledge, London.

Disaster Management in Cameroon: The Lake Nyos Disaster Experience

Henry Ngenyam Bang

Abstract

Purpose – The purpose of this paper is to review critically, how the Lake Nyos disaster (LND), which occurred in 1986, is being managed by examining the immediate post disaster management and long-term management. It reveals how the disaster management system in Cameroon influences the management style and process with regards to the technical and socio-economic management of LND.

Design/methodology/approach – Qualitative research methods for empirical and secondary data were adopted in the study, including interviews (with disaster managers and LND survivors) and reviews of policy documents and media reports. Triangulation of information sources in the analysis has been done to enhance credibility.

Findings – While significant progress has been made in technical management of LND, the socio-economic management has been poor. Although this can be partly attributed to the weak financial situation of Cameroon, the major problems seem to be related to human systems.

Practical implications – The disaster management has focused mainly on technical and structural mitigation measures with less consideration of non-structural measures. This has had dire consequences for the displaced disaster survivors. A major challenge still lies in tackling social vulnerability within the displaced disaster population.

Originality/value – This paper provides a comprehensive analysis of contemporary challenges facing the management of LND. This paper is important because published information on socio-economic aspects of LND is very scarce. This paper is part of a larger research that was conducted for a PhD in the UK.

Keywords: Lake Nyos disaster; Technical management; Social management; Disaster management; Disaster survivors; Disasters; Cameroon

Reprinted from *Disaster Prevention and Management*
Vol. 21 No. 4, pp. 489–506 (2012). doi:10.1108/09653561211256189

Introduction

This paper reviews the management of Lake Nyos disaster (LND) to learn how the disaster management process is impacting on the present risk and vulnerability in the disaster area and the affected population. This is done by analyzing the process of risk management and disaster preparedness in the Nyos area after the 1986 disasters which killed close to 2,000 people. To do this, the context of disaster management and disaster risk reduction is examined by looking back at how the disaster was and is still being managed. Although the disaster happened more than two decades ago, contemporary disaster management issues are examined in their long-term management context to expose the impact on the disaster area and affected populations. The perspectives of the survivors, affected populations and key stakeholders in the disaster management process provide rich empirical information, which is used to understand how the disasters are being managed. Therefore, the main aspects of LND management, including the main actors, the managerial and the procedural or government machinery employed are examined over short- and long-term time scales. Apart from providing an insight to disaster management in Cameroon, this paper identifies lessons, which can be learnt to improve on the current situation.

Method

A case study research strategy was chosen to analyze the management of LND using two study populations: the displaced victims of LND, presently living in resettlement camps and major stakeholders in disaster management in Cameroon. The research methodology adopted was both qualitative and quantitative, using empirical and secondary data obtained from fieldwork conducted between April and September 2007. Semi-structured interviews, questionnaire survey, direct and participant observation methods were used for primary data collection. Secondary data were generated through reviews of policy documents and literature concerning the issues under investigation from government ministries; research institutions; newspaper publishing houses in the country; internet sources and publications on the socio-cultural and economic aspects of LND.

In all, 180 survey questionnaires were administered to the displaced victims of LND living in three resettlement camps (Wum, Ukpwa and Buabua camps), and 25 semi-structured interviews were conducted at the Ukwa Resettlement camp using simple random sampling. About 20 interviews were conducted with key stakeholders in disaster management that were grouped into there main categories: one group worked with disaster survivors at the local level; the second group of key informants was the main policy makers in disaster management at the higher level of administration in the country and the third group was scientists and researchers, with some either involved in scientific research activities on Lake Nyos or act as advisers to the government.

The question schedules were structured to have both open-ended and closed questions. Questions for the disaster victims centered on strategies that have been adopted for the affected population to cope with and recover from LND. Themes for interview and survey questions focused on the impact or effect of displacement and relocating on the life of survivors. Interviews for disaster managers addressed the following issues: social and economic impact of the LND; assessment of Cameroon's natural hazard mitigation program; rating of risk to natural hazards in Cameron; Cameroon's vulnerability preparedness and resilience to natural hazards; natural hazard/disaster mitigation management plan for Nyos area; extend to which disaster management is incorporated into development policies; successes and failures in the management of LND and how the LND can be useful for future planning of similar disasters in the country. Direct and participant observation of social condition of survivors during the fieldwork; and participation in the 21st anniversary of LND (August 2007) also helped to enhance triangulation of data and strengthens the analysis presented in this paper.

Immediate Post-Disaster Management

It is difficult to get detailed and complete information on the management of LND partly because no detailed accounts and records were kept of the disaster management process. Few publications exist on the management of the crisis and immediate post-disaster phases and most government records on the event are not available or missing. Experience from fieldwork reveals this could be due to lack of a culture of record keeping or those involved in LND management removed the records for fear of being implicated in allegations of misappropriation of resources destined for victims. During the period after LND, *Cameroon Tribune* (the state-owned press) produced detailed coverage of the disaster with valuable information on some crucial aspects of the disaster management process. This, together with other accounts of the immediate aftermath of the disaster in foreign press reports, articles and government commissioned reports, provides a reasonable basis to reconstruct what transpired.

On the Night of the Apocalypse

The LND occurred at 9 p.m. on Thursday August 21, 1986 (see location of Lake Nyos on Figure 1). The disaster was highly unpredictable, sudden and unexpected to everyone in the country, including scientists, even though two years earlier a similar event at Lake Monoum had killed 37 people in Njindoum village. Smolowe and Philips (1986) describe the event:

> [...] a silent plume of colorless gas shot up from the turbulent depths of Lake Nyos [...] Villagers who had already bedded down for the night and others just finishing their evening meal quietly suffocated in their sleep.

Figure 1: Map of Cameroon showing Lake Nyos

The LND killed 1,746 people, and displaced 4,430 more (Freeth and Kay, 1987; Kling *et al.*, 1987). About 8,300 livestock died (Shanklin, 1988). In March 1987, the government organized an International Conference on LND in Yaoundé to seek the cause of the poisonous gas discharge. It was widely accepted by scientist that high concentration of carbon dioxide in lower part of Lake Nyos, released abruptly by overturning of bottom waters, was the mechanism responsible for the disaster (Sigvaldason, 1989).

The impact of LND in Cameroon, as reported by the government and many reports of the incident, concentrated mostly on the mortality and death of people and livestock. The effect on the local and regional economy has never been highlighted although it is well known that the death of almost all the cattle in Nyos affected the supply of beef in North West Region of Cameroon. The impact of each disaster affects the local economy and their cumulative effects on the country's economy can be tremendous. In Cameroon, just as in many developing countries, the economic impact of small-scale disasters on the lives and livelihoods of vulnerable communities, whose economy is largely in the informal sectors is rarely documented. This is an oversight because many of these vulnerable rural communities are the poorest, as is the case in Cameroon where the incidence of poverty in rural communities is 86.5 percent (Amin and Dubois, 2001).

Survivors experiences about the disaster's impact

Interviews with survivals show the death of relatives, livestock, the effect of some skin and respiratory diseases are the direct impacts from LND. Secondary effects due to the disaster were displacement of disaster survivors from their ancestral land and relocation in seven camps (Ukpwa, Buabua, Kimbi, Esu, Ipalim, KumFutu and Yemnge) scattered within the disaster area in Menchum Division. This has disrupted the social networks and community cohesion within the Nyos population, traditionally a very important survival strategy, as with most local communities in Cameroon. Loss of geographical identity, cultural identity and loss of economic livelihoods are other impacts of LND articulated by survivors.

Disaster manager's experiences in disaster impact

While disaster managers within the government sector focussed on the technical aspects of the disaster and its management, their peers in the non-government sector (opposition controlled Wum council) were more concerned with the socio-economic impact because they claimed to work with the affected disaster community and therefore, have a greater understanding of the problems faced by survivors. They said: disaster survivors are living in poorer conditions than in their original Nyos settlement; that many family structures and social ties that existed before the disaster have been destroyed; that the resettlement of survivors in camps far from their ancestral lands on smaller pieces of land has created tensions over farming space with their new hosts. Table I shows interview question themes, sub-themes and percentage of responses that focussed on technical or socio-economic factors.

Management of Relief Operations

The management of LND took place at national, regional and divisional levels. At the national level, a presidential decree created a National Committee for the Reception and Management of Relief Aid. Ministerial decree no. 86/1069 of August 27, 1986 created provincial committees, one to receive foreign aid coming into the country in Douala, while another in Bamenda received local aid coming

Table I: Recommendations on the management of the Lake Nyos disaster

Recommendations on the management of the Lake Nyos disaster	Implementation	Action taken
That a zoning map identifying known hazards, viable farming areas and areas of possible resettlement be produced	Poor	Hazard map produced is not comprehensive
That occupation patterns should be analyzed and plans for intensification of agricultural and stock-farming activities be implemented	Nil	No action
That access roads be constructed that will lead to Nyos and the resettlement camps	Poor	Contracts awarded but project yet to start
That other dangerous lake in the country be identified and a criteria for selecting lakes for further investigation be put in place	Nil	No action
That government should produce a long-term database for monitoring disasters	Nil	No action taken
That hazard information be integrated into regional development planning	Nil	No action taken
That emphasis be placed on local community-level disaster preparedness and planning	Poor	No concrete actions taken though mentioned
That the relevant information be sent to all social scientists who have worked in the NWP	Nil	No action
That emergency-preparedness training be initiated for all resident relief and mission personnel, for educational staff and for local community leaders	Poor	Most training are done at national level without local disaster managers
That a solutions be sought for the farmer-grazer difficulties, which have long preceded the current problem of displaced people	Partial	Insufficient effort made to resolve problem
That survivors be encouraged to farm to supplement their food and sell some for money	Poor	Farm to market roads remain very bad
That corn mills be provided for each resettlement center	Partial	Corn mills were given to survivors but no assistance provided for their repairs
That survivors be participants in the decision-making process concerning their future	Poor	Survivor are not consulted for DM actions
That traditional authority be incorporated into any emergency evacuation plans	Nil	No contingency planning has been done
That farm land and farming tools be allocated to survivors	Partial	Tools not given regularly and only few people get them

Sources: Tanjong (1986), Othman-Chande (1987), Shanklin (1988), Sigvaldason (1989)

into the region (Ngwa, 1992). UN agencies locally represented such as UNDP, World Food Program, international or local NGOs were not included in the committees (Othman-Chande, 1987).

The management of relief operations at the regional level was done by a committee of senior government officials under the auspices of the Governor of the North West Province (now North West Region). The committee had the responsibility to collect, transport and distribute all donations to the camps and hospitals in the disaster region (Ngwa, 1992). The third committee at the divisional level, established under the auspices of the senior divisional officer of Menchum, was responsible for the rescue and evacuation operations from the disaster zone; the temporal resettlement of the disaster survivors and for the reception and delivery of aid to the survivors (Fonte, 1986, p. 4; Nkemngu, 1986, p. 4). The authorities faced enormous challenges to give the required needs to the disaster victims because as explained later, a lot of unsolicited items were donated to the survivors, which did not meet their immediate needs.

Rescue Mission

The rescue mission from the disaster zone was conducted under the auspices of the governor of the North West Region and senior divisional officer of Menchum. Logistical problems and "fear of the unknown" hampered the rescue efforts in the immediate post-disaster period. Due to uncertainly in the cause of death during the disaster, many people, including government officials were afraid to enter the disaster zone and rescue survivors for fear their lives may be at risk (*Cameroon Tribune* of Wednesday August 27, 1986; Shanklin, 1988, p. 12). A Roman Catholic priest (Father Ten Horn), was the first non-native who entered the disaster zone and rescued many survivors. The priest gave orders that the dead be buried immediately in mass graves because no government officials were there (Shanklin, 1988). This single initiative saved some lives but the overall delay in evacuating the several sick survivors, placed more lives at risk.

A huge rescue operation, involving the police, went underway a few days later when authorities realized the area posed no immediate risks. The army later entered the affected zone and carried out the bulk of the rescue operation because they had the right vehicles for the poor condition of the road, which was a major handicap in the evacuation process (Othman-Chande, 1987; Krajick, 2003, p. 2). The poor road condition to Wum and the disaster region also prevented top government officials, including the president from visiting the disaster survivors (*Cameroon Tribune* of Wednesday August 27, 1986; *Cameroon Tribune* December 5, 1986, p. 1).

Due to lack of medical facilities (hospital, health center and medical staff) in Nyos and environs, the sick (survivors who had inhaled the toxic gas) were transported about 45 km to Wum (head quarters of Menchum Division) for treatment. Early reports also suggest that due to few medical staff in Wum government hospital, health practitioners were mobilized nationally and internationally to treat the sick survivors (Nkemngu, 1986; Shanklin, 1988).

Financial and Material Assistance

Much financial and material assistance was contributed after the LND by private and public companies, corporations, co-operatives, associations and people. Some of the material aids donated were 22,000 blankets, 1,430 tents, 5,000 gas masks,

1,000,000 kg of air-freighted food and 25 tons of vaccines. According to Othman-Chande (1987), some donated items were in excess and did not meet the immediate needs of the survivors. The Cameroon Government received cash donations amounting to more than 1.5 billion FCFA (about US$3,000,000) from both local and foreign donors (*Cameroon Tribune* of Wednesday September 12, 1986; Othman-Chande, 1987).

Though the negative consequences of inappropriate aid have long been recognized (Ghafory-Ashtiany, 1999; Bennett and Kottasz, 2000; Humanitarian Initiatives UK, Disaster Mitigation Institute, and Mango, 2001; Calvi-Parisetti, 2004), it remains a feature of many recent disaster responses such as a range of goods in the tsunami response (Telford *et al.*, 2006); culturally inappropriate hygiene kits in the Pakistan earthquake (Crawford *et al.*, 2006); expired medicines in Yogyakarta (IFRC, 2007) or unneeded high-energy biscuits in Pakistan (Reed *et al.*, 2007). Aid is proper only if it meets the needs of the affected population. Relief and recovery plans should be based on profound knowledge of the context of the community (ALNAP, 2008). Beneficiary surveys are now a feature of humanitarian, relief and reconstruction operations aimed at improving aid programs (IOM, 2005; Lindgren *et al.*, 2005; UNORC, 2006; Wilson *et al.*, 2007). Though there have been many complaints by survivors of the LND for more than two decades, empirical evidence suggests no formal means of complaint has been set up by the government or officials managing the disaster.

Management of Relief Aid

The LND had shortcomings in the overall management of the relief aid. Problems faced with the relief operation included uncoordinated aid donation and distribution, poor storage and transportation of aid materials, inconsistent local donor supply source and absence of some key relief organizations to coordinate relief operations (Ngwa, 1992; Othman-Chande, 1987). Non-cooperation among donor agencies and no assessment of the needs of disaster survivors was responsible for the donation of unsolicited materials and those that were in excess. This facilitated corruption since some goods destined for survivors ended up being sold in the streets and shops around the country (as reported in *Cameroon Post* of Tuesday August 30, 2005). The list below summarizes the main problems encountered with management of relief operations (Sources: Tanjong (1986), Othman-Chande (1987), Shanklin (1988), Sigvaldason (1989)):

- The headquarters of the National Relief Committee was located 500 kilometers away in Yaoundé, and the other distribution centers in Douala, Bamenda and Wum were located at considerable distances and travel time through a poor road network to and from the beneficiaries. This created problems with coordination of relief activities, personnel movements and storage especially of perishable items.

- Materials for burying the dead such as spades, gloves and boots arrived 11 days late, while other utensils in great need for carrying, treating and distributing water, as well as drugs to treat water-borne diseases fell short of demand. This highlights the patchy and uncoordinated aspect of aid distribution to the displaced persons.
- There was no permanent field staff from the Ministry of Health, Department of Nutrition and Social Welfare to advice on nutrition in the camps where there was communal food preparation during the first weeks.
- The Catholic Relief Services provided funds through the local archdioceses, but due to lack of staff, did not follow-up with the experience already acquired elsewhere in the field of relieving human suffering through supplies.
- The World Food Program authorized the purchase of assorted foodstuffs from its distant Yaoundé base but lacked staff to follow-up and check for a feedback on the food values derived from each foodstuff sent.
- Save the Children Fund sent help mostly to children but did not have any feedback from the field to correct any mistakes for future action.
- The UNHCR with headquarters in the capital Yaoundé, far away from the field had very few field staff to work with the displaced people.
- Problems in the camps included stress problems, which stemmed from poor centrally placed corn mills for many users, inadequate lighting in the camps and inadequate access to elementary medical care, overcrowding, and no permanent resident camp coordinator to assist and bring rapid solutions to such stress problems.

Promises and Pledges to Help Survivors

Government officials made several promises and pledges during the crises after the LND. The senior divisional officer of Menchum and Bui, the governor of the North West Region and the president all made promises to resettle the survivors of the disaster and build the road that goes to Nyos from Wum. Other development projects such as health centers and schools were also promised to the survivors (Othman-Chande, 1987; Shanklin, 1988, *Cameroon Tribune* (September 19, 1986).

The *Cameroon Tribune* (September 19, 1986, p. 4) published a letter sent by an elite from the disaster area to government officials managing the LND in which he makes suggestions that: a resettlement site 15-20 kilometers away from Nyos be chosen for resettlement; two-bedroom houses be built for each family that survived the disaster; primary schools, health centre, security post, market and water system be created for survivors; the road to Nyos be built; survivors be given an initial sum of money to start life, etc. Research evidence (Bang, 2009) suggests that if the government had followed the advice in this letter, the socio-economic problems of the Nyos survivors could have been greatly reduced. As will be seen in Table I and later in this paper, most of the promises and recommendations have not been applied 25 years after the disaster. This is because the problems of the LND survivors were either ignored or the government's priorities were diverted elsewhere (Bang *et al.*, 2009).

The Media

The LND caught the interest of media all over the world. During the early days of the disaster, there were many inconsistencies in both the local and international media reports of the incident. For example, a BBC report on August 21, 1986 entitled "hundreds gassed in Cameroon Lake disaster" claims 1,200 people were killed, when the actual number was 1,746. Though these reports were common, Othman-Chande (1987, pp. 98-9) claims the media failed to report on plans for the long-term rehabilitation of disaster survivors. After 25 years, this concern has turned out to be the greatest problem facing the management of the disaster.

Settlement of Survivors

Immediately after the disaster, some 1,979 survivors were evacuated and provided temporary accommodation in Wum, Kimbi, Nkambe, Kumfutu and Bafmen and later resettled in the seven camps mentioned earlier. About 40 percent of survivors went to live with relatives in Mmen (Othman-Chande, 1987; Shanklin, 1988; Ngwa, 1992).

Many recommendations (see Table I) were made by individuals, from the various post-disaster studies sponsored by Ministry of Higher Education and Scientific Research in 1986 and the International Conference on LND. The recommendations include both the social and technical aspects necessary to reduce the impact of the disaster for the survivors. But as will be seen later in this paper, the long-term management of the disaster was skewed toward technical management with most socio-economic and cultural problems ignored.

Opinion on the Management of the Crisis Period

Interview results show that disaster managers within the government sector felt the government managed the immediate post-disaster period properly although some acknowledged a few shortcomings during the management of the crisis period. On the contrary, their peers in academics like lecturers and researchers and those in the Wum council that manages the disaster survivors in the Ukpwa resettlement camp felt the delay in the supply of material and human resources was a main handicap during the crisis period. Even more important was allegations that government officials embezzled some material and financial aid provided by the international community. Mbuh (2005, p. 194) asset that over 80 percent of the aid destined to survivors was stolen by government officials managing the LND.

Research evidence suggests many LND survivors also felt the immediate aftermath of the disaster was well managed. The disaster survivors in the Ukwa

Resettlement Camp and others who had relocated to the disaster site were convinced the immediate relief and rescue efforts were properly handled. Their argument is based mainly on the goods and gifts given to them directly by representatives of donor groups and organizations, and those channeled through the government. Survivors' accounts show that material and financial help provided by the government dwindled rapidly after the disaster, due to corruption. Corruption allegations were also reported in newspapers and articles shortly after the disaster. According to David Alexander, reported in Mbuh (2005, p. 194) "[...] unnecessary aid seemed to have stimulated corruption[...]which retarded rehabilitation." A report in *Cameroon Post* (edition of Tuesday August 30, 2005) about the 19th anniversary of the LND also states that:

> [...] management of resources [...] was characterized by corruption and sheer dishonesty [...] frozen chicken destined for Nyos was being hawked in the streets of Yaounde [...]

Analysis of LND shows that distribution of goods and services fell prey to corruption networks and bureaucratic obstacles limited access to those in need. It was difficult to track the inflow of funds and to assess whether they reached their desired destination. Moreover, while public and international funds were more easily identifiable, private funds were difficult to track and monitor their expenditure. In the humanitarian operations after the LND, international aid entered into an already corruption-prone environment, exacerbating existing endemic corruption. In developing countries, humanitarian operations often take place in environments that are prone to corruption risks and the aid process itself can add to these risks (Walker and Maxwell, 2009).

Long-term Management

This section examines the disaster management processes that have been operational for a quarter century after the immediate post-disaster relief and temporary resettlement of LND survivors. Analysis of long-term management has been divided in this study into scientific or technical management, and social management.

Scientific / Technical Management of the LND

To mitigate the gas hazard in the lakes, in 2000 the Cameroon government initiated the Nyos and Monoum Degassing Project. The main objectives of the project was to: continuously monitor the physical, chemical and biological conditions in Lake Nyos and Lake Monoum; install carbon dioxide monitoring stations at both lakes to provide an audible and visual warning if a release of gas occurs and install permanent degassing pipes to remove the gas from both lakes. The government pledged to build roads and permanent buildings close to both lakes, educate the local people about the dangers of the lakes and makes sure Cameroonian scientists and technicians received proper training to manage the degassing equipments in the future. An international committee made up of eight members, known as the Nyos and Monoum Degassing Project Advisory Committee was established to provide guidance for the project (Kusakabe *et al.*, 2000; Kling *et al.*, 2006).

Prior to the start of the degassing project, scientific evidence showed that since the Lake Nyos and Lake Monoum disasters in the 1980s, both lakes had been experiencing carbon dioxide recharge at alarming rates resulting in gas saturation levels of up to 97 percent (Kling *et al.*, 2006). To reduce the build-up of these gases, controlled degassing started at Lake Nyos in 2001 and Lake Monoum in 2003. The current carbon-dioxide content in Lake Nyos is only slightly below the level estimated after the LND – amounts to 80 percent of the maximum level of 14.8 giga moles observed in January 2001 (Kusakabe *et al.*, 2008).

The main funding for the Nyos and Monoum Degassing Project has come from France, Japan and USA totalling about $680,000. The Cameroon Government had fulfilled one of her responsibilities, which was to build permanent storage buildings where scientific equipment for monitoring both Lakes is kept. However, the government has not fulfilled other project requirements such as support funding in the areas of road improvement.

Present risks in Lake Nyos

The two main risks identified in Lake Nyos are the risk of continuous gas recharge into the lake and the risk of flooding. Although the gas is being removed, Lake Nyos still has tremendous volumes of gas that pose grave danger to the local population (Krajick, 2003). According to US Geological Survey chemist Bill Evans, quoted in Krajick (2003), "at this rate, it could take 30 to 50 years to make Nyos safe – and in the meantime, there could be another eruption." Due to pipe design and implementation flaws, technical problems had developed with the degassing process in both Lakes, leading to only a very small quantity of the gas being removed. A rock fall or landslide from the cliffs around Lake Nyos could supply a tremendous amount of energy that could mix bottom waters up and trigger another gas burst (Kling *et al.*, 2006).

Scientific modeling has predicted that only about 25 percent of the gas in Lake Nyos will be removed by 2015 (Kling *et al.*, 2005). To further reduce this risk, the advisory Scientific Committee for the Nyos and Monoum Degassing Project recommended that more pipes be installed in both lakes to reduce the gas pressures at a much quicker rate (Kling *et al.*, 2006). Scientific studies carried out in 2005 on the structure of the dam that holds Lake Nyos's water in place have revealed that a breach of the dam would be imminent within the coming ten years. The most likely area where the dam could be breached easily is along a narrow spillway, which is the weakest part of the dam (UNEP/OCHA, 2005). Such a breach would lead to severe flooding in downstream Nyos valley, as far away as 108 km in Nigeria affecting an estimated 10,000 people in Cameroon and Nigeria (Lockwood *et al.*, 1988; Lockwood and Schuster, 1991). A breach of the dam could cause another carbon dioxide eruption.

An onsite physical assessment of the stability of the dam was carried out in this study based on the rock types and structures in the rocks found on the natural spillway of the dam in July 2007. A close onsite physical examination of the rocks on the natural spillway of the dam reveals that they are loosely consolidated pyroclastic rocks. Both lateral and horizontal cracks and zones of weaknesses were also very visible on the surface of the rocks, and more conspicuous on the upstream side. The layered pyroclastic rocks on the spillway show very visible signs of lateral erosion on the upstream side (see Plate 1). The rocks are becoming increasingly unstable due to weathering and erosion. Results from that assessment confirm fears that the dam could be breached if nothing is done.

Suggestions on how to prevent the flood hazard are that initially, the quantity of gas in the Lake should be lowered to safe levels, followed by a reduction of the water in the Lake after which the dam wall can then be removed. The full mitigation plan is a more complicated process involving scientific and engineering methods for depressurizing the gas in the lake and pumping the water out (Lockwood and Meyer, 1989; UNEP/OCHA, 2005; Kling *et al.*, 2006).

The present state of remediation in the Lake is at the stage where the gas is still being reduced and the level of the lake is held. The Scientific Advisory Committee for the Nyos and Monoum Degassing Project recommends that the flood mitigation

Source: Author

Plate 1: Fragile eroded inner surfaces of the spillway

process should be delayed until most of the gas in the lake has been removed. In the short term, the dam can be strengthened. Receipt of tenders to strengthen the dam was launched recently (Europe Aid, 2011). Experts believe the lake will be secure in two years time (ReliefWeb, 2011, p. 167). However, the risk of gas release later is still associated with the risk of flooding.

Opinion on the technical management of LND

Information from interview sources (government officials) reveals disaster managers believe enough attention has been given to the reduction of physical risks from Lake Nyos. Top government officials mention the Nyos and Monoum Degassing Project as a success in reducing the poisonous gases in Lake Nyos. Their peers at the local level argue that the Project could not be realized without foreign assistance. It is a widely held view that delay to build a good road to Nyos is a setback to the Project. Government officials are still uncertain as to when the Project will be completed.

Most survivors are also poorly informed about the risk mitigation process. There is no consistent information channel to update or give feedback on the progress of the degassing process. It is necessary to provide easily understandable information on disaster risks and protection options to citizens in high-risk areas to encourage them take actions to reduce risks and build resilience. Disasters can be substantially reduced if people are well informed and motivated toward a culture of disaster prevention and resilience, which in turn requires the collection, compilation and dissemination of relevant knowledge and information on hazards, vulnerabilities and capacities (WSSD, 2002; WCDR, 2005).

Social Management of Lake Nyos and Monoum Disasters

The social management of LND involves management of the socio-economic aspects of the disaster area, the resettlement camps and the displaced populations. As mentioned earlier, the government made promises to victims about their well-being and the development of the affected area with respect to both the technical and social aspects of the disaster (see Table I).

Recent social management plan for the Lake Nyos area

Within the last few years, the government seems to have taken the socio-economic aspects of disaster management more seriously. With the support of the UNDP and the European Union, in 2006, the government conceived a project on the rehabilitation of Lake Nyos and the psycho-social and economic resettlement of the local population. The objectives of the project are to: build the capacity of local structures dealing with disaster management; de-gas the Lake and secure the area; build rural infrastructure; develop land use planning and emergency preparedness plans; and constantly providing information and educating the population. The project proposal plan was estimated to cost about 7.4 billion FCFA, but with 6.6 billion planned for physical risk reduction measures (Oumarou and Ousman, 2006, p. 10; Loh, 2009). The very big proportion of the budget, planned for physical aspects again shows government's inclination more toward technical than social mitigation measures.

Awareness of disaster management/mitigation plan for the Nyos area
Interviews with disaster managers show that more than 95 percent hold the view that recently there has been more government interest in addressing the problems of LND survivors but only few respondents' had in-depth information about any current projects or plans for the survivors. The most widely held knowledge about the disaster mitigation plan relates to the Nyos and Monoum Degassing Project. Few disaster managers within the government departments are aware of the resettlement plans for the disaster victims. These top officials attributed the lateness in the start of the resettlement project to lack of funds that was diverted to the Nyos and Monoum Degassing Project. Research evidence also suggests administrators at the local level do not have detail information about the social resettlement project. They seem to get information about projects only during the period preceding commemorations of the LND when senior officials come to the area and engage them in preparations for the event. This shows that there is no steady stream of information from the higher to the lower levels of the administrative departments.

Government promises to disaster survivors
Most key personnel involved in LND management expressed concern that promises made to disaster victims were long overdue, and a social management plan had been in existence although not being implemented. They highlighted government failures in handling the social concerns of survivors over the years, despite continuous complaints by survivors and some local disaster manager. The awkward condition in which disaster survivors are living and their plea for attention for a quarter century have been making headline news in recent times, especially during commemorations of the LND. The *Cameroon Post* (a prominent newspaper in Cameroon) of August 30, 2005 discusses speeches made by survivors during the 19th anniversary of LND. Government neglect of survivors was the main theme of speeches delivered by survivors and local chiefs in the area (www.postnewsline.com/2005/08/lake_nyos_survi.html/). An article in the *Cameroon Tribune* (the state-owned newspaper) of August 30, 2007 also makes reference to the 21st anniversary of LND and discusses the dire socio-economic situation of the disaster survivors. While a significant amount of effort has been put into the physical risk reduction measures, much has yet to be done with regards to the social management of the disaster.

Reflecting on the Disaster Management

Main Constraints to the Management of LND

The research also examined disaster managers' perspectives on the main problems inhibiting the proper management of LND. Many top officials attributed the weak state of Cameroon's economy as the main limiting factor for the government to meet all promises made to disaster victims. These officials tended to blame the economic crisis Cameroon experienced shortly after LND and the devaluation of the CFA francs later in early 1990s as major factors that weakened government's financial ability to handle the long-term effects of LND.

Disaster managers at the local level, in the disaster affected region attributed improper planning and lack of follow-up of post-disaster projects as a major limitation in the long-term management. Some emphasized that concrete plans were not put in place for the survivor's resettlement and living conditions in the camps, and their eventual rehabilitation back to Nyos. The complexity of government's administrative mechanisms, the complicated process of approving decisions initiated at local levels and administrative bottlenecks were also identified as major constraints. Many local officials attributed poor governance as responsible for the poor management of social aspects of the disaster.

Lack of disaster management training is also a contributing factor. The disaster management process cannot function properly because many government administrators, and those involved in disaster management, are politicians who have been given such responsibilities based on political lineages rather than their knowledge, qualification or experience. General observation during the interview process suggests the trained administrators appointed to administer the regions and divisions always try to protect the interest of the government.

Another reason is that survivors are not fully involved in the decision-making process that affects their well-being. As such, social groups protesting the poor treatment of LND survivors have emerged from within the disaster-affected community. Civil society groups such as Mr Bamenda Organisation and the Buabua-Kimbi Lake Nyos Cultural and Development Association were formed to protest at the government's poor treatment of survivors and to mediate in solving the social problems in the disaster area. Disaster risk reduction should be underpinned by a more pro-active approach to informing, motivating and involving people in their own local communities (UNDP, 2004). Based on a review of post-disaster response in Indonesia, it has been noted that community-driven approach to post-disaster recovery, which builds on social capital, results in greater client satisfaction, more rapid disbursement and local empowerment (Leitmann, 2007).

Most local officials mentioned corruption as a major problem facing the management of LND. Due to political affiliations with the party in power, unscrupulous officials embezzled much of the money donated during the crisis period. This practice has continued since the LND. Interviews also reveal embezzlement; corruption and lack of accountability inhibit the management process and frustrate disaster management activities because financial and material resources do not reach their intended destinations.

How the Nyos Disaster Management Could have been Improved

Disaster managers expressed opinion that the management could have been improved if proper planning was done at the onset. The main thrust of the argument is that different committees with well-defined budgets could have been set-up to manage, monitor and report the progress of projects regularly to a central coordinating body. According to them, if this was done, the government could have realized the difficult situation of the disaster survivors.

Disaster officials at local levels said the situation could have been improved if they had a greater role in disaster management activities at all stages, including planning. Complicated administrative procedures to obtain requests and delivery of financial and material resources hamper the progress of management actions and swift realization of objectives. Failure to improve the road infrastructure to the various resettlement camps was another issue identified. It is believed this alone would have made a significant improvement to the entire management of the disaster, as many survivors would be able to transport agricultural produce for sale in Wum.

Usefulness of Lessons from the LND for Future Planning

Interview results suggests many disaster managers at the national level do not seem to recognize that lessons learned from the LND can be useful for further planning of disaster management and disaster risk reduction in the country (apart from the technical aspects). More than 95 percent acknowledged the LND offer a good platform for Cameroon to be ready for subsequent gas related hazards since the country has many crater lakes. Although these disaster managers think the degassing projects can be applied to other crater lakes in the country that might contain lethal amounts of poisonous gases, there was no evidence that plans exist to set this in motion.

The failures and challenges of management of social aspects of the LND have made many government officials wary of such discussion. However, it can be argued (as expressed by some local disaster managers) that the LND provides important lessons for the management of hazards that involve the displacement of large numbers of people. Lessons need to be learned in the areas of tackling social welfare and livelihoods of disaster survivors after resettlement. This highlights the need for proactive measures, since the phases of relief, rehabilitation and reconstructions following a disaster are windows of opportunity for rebuilding livelihoods and community resilience, and reconstruction of physical and socio-economic structures (WCDR, 2005). The results reinforce the necessity for skilled people in disaster management at all administrative levels. The Hyogo framework for action stresses the need to develop training and learning programs in disaster risk reduction targeted at specific sectors (e.g. development planners, emergency managers, local government officials).

Conclusion

A key feature of contemporary understandings of disaster risk reduction and disaster management are that they aim to avoid the potential losses from hazards, assure prompt and appropriate assistance to victims of disaster, achieve rapid and effective recovery, and reduce vulnerability. As has been shown in this paper, disaster occurrence and impacts do not only depend on exposure to extreme natural phenomena, but also to anthropogenic factors such as government policy, disaster management strategies and the effectiveness of the disaster management process. This paper has analyzed the management of LND over the short- and long term, based on secondary sources, personal observations and interviews with disaster managers and the affected populations. The overwhelming result is that while significant progress has been made in technical management (with some issues about its effectiveness), the socio-economic management of the disasters has not been well handled. Several governments' promised projects on the social and economic welfare of survivors and the disaster area has not been carried out for more than a quarter century. Recently, in 2007, the government conceived a program on the security and socio-economic re-integration of the Lake Nyos area that is yet to start. Although limitations to the socio-economic management are partly attributed to the poor financial situation of the country, the bulk of the problems seem to be related to human systems (e.g. lack of disaster management ability and skills, improper planning, negligence, corruption). These factors partly contribute to the ongoing vulnerability of survivors. According to respondents, the social management could have been improved if proper contingency plan was done at the onset, with local disaster officials incorporated into the process. Construction of the road to Nyos is another factor mentioned by disaster managers that would greatly ease the social problems of survivors. Although the management of LND, as analyzed in this paper reveals that adequate disaster management strategies in Cameroon are still lacking, the experience gained will certainly facilitate the management of subsequent hazards/disasters in the country that involves the displacement of people.

References

ALNAP (2008), "Responding to earthquakes 2008: learning from earthquake relief and recovery operations", available at: www.alnap.org/pool/files/ALNAPLessonsEarthquakes.pdf (accessed September 13, 2009).

Amin, A. and Dubois, L. (2001), *A 1999 Update of the Cameroon Poverty Profile*, World Bank, Washington, DC, available at: www4.worldbank.org/afr/poverty/pdf/internal/docnav/01794.pdf (accessed August 23, 2006).

Bang, H., Few, R. and Conway, D. (2009), "Present risks in lake Nyos: is Cameroon prepared for another great disaster?", *International Disaster and Risk Conference, IDRC*, Chengdu, available at: www.conftool.com/idrc2010/index.php?page=browseSessions&abstracts=show&print=yes&print=yes&form_session=115 (accessed January 17, 2011).

Bang, H.N. (2009), "'Natural' disaster risk, vulnerability and resettlement: relocation decisions following the Lake Nyos and Lake Monoum disasters in Cameroon", doctoral thesis, University of East Anglia, Norwich.

Bennett, R. and Kottasz, R. (2000), "Emergency fundraising for disaster relief", *Disaster Prevention and Management*, Vol. 9 No. 5, pp. 352–9.

Calvi-Parisetti, P. (2004), *Report: workshop of lessons learnt on the national and international response to the Bam earthquake: Kerman, Islamic Republic of Iran, 14-15 April 2004*, UN Office for the Coordination of Humanitarian Affairs, Geneva, available at: www.reliefweb.int/rw/RWFiles2004.nsf/FilesByRWDocUNIDFileName/SZIE-5Z3P85-ocha-irn-15apr.pdf/$File/ocha-irn-15apr.pdf (accessed June 8, 2008).

Crawford, P., Bysouth, K., Nichols, D. and Thompon, F. (2006), "CAER cluster evaluation: Pakistan earthquake", available at: www.ausaid.gov.au/publications/pdf/pakistan_eval.pdf (accessed June 10, 2008).

Europe Aid (2011), "Works to strengthen the Lake Nyos dam in Cameroon", Europe Aid Co-operation Office, available at: www.devex.com/en/projects/works-to-strengthen-the-lake-nyos-dam-in-cameroon (accessed September 15, 2011).

Fonte, P. (1986), "Divisional relief commission lends a helping hand", *Cameroon Tribune*, Vol. 19 (September), p. 8.

Freeth, J. and Kay, R. (1987), "The Lake Nyos gas disaster", *Nature*, Vol. 7000 No. 325, pp. 104–5.

Ghafory-Ashtiany, M. (1999), "Rescue operation and reconstruction of recent earthquakes in Iran", *Disaster Prevention and Management*, Vol. 8 No. 1, pp. 5–20, available at: www.emeraldinsight.com/Insight/viewContentItem.do?contentType=Article&contentId=870944 (accessed June 8, 2008).

Humanitarian Initiatives UK, Disaster Mitigation Institute, and Mango (2001), *Independent Evaluation: The DEC Response to the Earthquake in Gujarat: Sector Reports*, Disasters Emergency Committee, London, available at: www.actionaid.org.uk/content_document.asp?doc_id=349 (accessed June 8, 2008).

IFRC (2007), "Report of the Middle East forum on international disaster response laws, rules and principles", IFRC, Abu Dhabi, June 19-20, available at: www.ifrc.org/docs/pubs/idrl/me-forum-report.pdf (accessed June 25, 2009).

IOM (2005), "Settlement and livelihood needs and aspirations assessment of disaster-affected and host communities in Nanggroe Aceh Darussalam", available at: www.tsunamievaluation.org/NR/rdonlyres/BACEADC3-051A-44F9-B920 (accessed June 25, 2009).

Kling, G., Clark, M., Compton, R., Devine, D., Evans, W., Humphrey, A. and Tuttle., M. (1987), "The 1986 Lake Nyos gas disaster, Cameroon, West Africa", *Science*, Vol. 236 No. 4798, pp. 169–75.

Kling, G., Evans, W., Tanyileke, G., Kusakabe, M., Yoshida, Y., Satake, H. and Rouwet, D. (2006), "Technical report on the January 2006 field expedition to Lakes Nyos and Monoum, Cameroon", follow-up report of the US OFDA Technical Project, Cameroonian Nyos-Monoum Degassing Program, US/OFDA, Yaounde.

Kling, G.W., Evans, W.C., Tanykele, G., Kusakabe, M., Ohba, T., Yoshida, Y. and Hell, J. V. (2005), "Degassing Lake Nyos and Monoum: defusing certain disaster", *Proceedings of the National Academy of Science*, Vol. 102 No. 40, pp. 14185–90.

Krajick, K. (2003), "Efforts to tame second African 'killer lake'", *Science*, Vol. 299 No. 5608, pp. 805–7.

Kusakabe, M., Tanyileke, G., McCord, S. and Scladow, S. (2000), "Recent pH and CO2 profiles at Lakes Nyos and Monoum, Cameroon: implications for the degassing strategy and its numerical simulation", *Journal of Volcanology and Geothermal Research*, Vol. 97 Nos 1-4, pp. 241–60.

Kusakabe, M., Ohba, T., Issa, Yoshida, Y., Satake, H., Ohizumi, T., Evans, W.C., Tanyileke, G. and Kling, G.W. (2008), "Evolution of CO2 in Lakes Monoum and Nyos, Cameroon, before and during controlled degassing", *Geochemical Journal*, Vol. 42 No. 1, pp. 93–118.

Leitmann, J. (2007), "Cities and calamities: learning from post-disaster response in Indonesia", *Journal of Urban Health: bulletin of the New York Academy of Medicine*, Vol. 83 No. 1, pp. 144–53.

Lindgren, D., Matondang, M. and Putri, D. (2005), "Tsunami relief study: effectiveness of the tsunami relief effort", PowerPoint presentation prepared for UNICEF, TNS, Jakarta.

Lockwood, J. and Meyer, R. (1989), "Origin and age of the Lake Nyos maar, Cameroon", *Journal of Volcanology and Geothermal Research*, Vol. 39 No. 2, pp. 117–24.

Lockwood, J. and Schuster, R. (1991), "Geologic hazards at Lake Nyos, Cameroon, West Africa", *Association of Engineering Geologists' News*, Vol. 54 No. 2, pp. 28–9.

Lockwood, J., Costa, J., Tuttle, M., Nni, J. and Tebor, S. (1988), "The potential for catastrophic dam failure at Lake Nyos maar, Cameroon", *Bulletin of Volcanology*, Vol. 50 No. 5, pp. 340–9.

Loh, C. (2009), "Lake Nyos-survivors waiting for re-integration program", *Cameroon Tribune*, available at: http://allafrica.com/stories/200901300638.html (accessed September 15, 2011).

Mbuh, M. (2005), *Inside Contemporary Cameroun Politics*, AuthorHouse, London.

Ngwa, N.E. (1992), "Responding to unmet food needs of displaced persons or refugees: a case study for new approaches in Kousseri town and Nyos Area of the Republic of Cameroon", *GeoJournal*, Vol. 27 No. 4, pp. 323–30.

Nkemngu, M. (1986), "Menchum toxic gas explosion: death toll rises", *Cameroon Tribune*, Vol. 27 No. 2, p. 4.

Othman-Chande, M. (1987), "The Cameroon volcanic gas disaster: an analysis of a makeshift response", *Disasters*, Vol. 11 No. 2, pp. 96–101.

Oumarou, S. and Ousman, H. (2006), "Formulation d'un project de rehabilitation du Lac Nyos", UNDP, Yaounde.

Reed, S., Giossi, C.S. and Nuttal, P. (2007), "Evaluation of ICRC rapid deployment following the 8 October 2005 earthquake: executive summary", *Channel Research*, Geneva.

ReliefWeb (2011), "Briefing kit for Cameroon + news and press release", available at: http://reliefweb.int/sites/reliefweb.int/files/reliefweb_pdf/briefingkit-f7924646efcd16bae8cdb6b31cb21c34.pdf (accessed September 15, 2011).

Shanklin, E. (1988), "Beautiful deadly Lake Nyos: the explosion and its aftermath", *Anthropology Today*, Vol. 1 No. 4, pp. 12–4.

Sigvaldason, G.E. (1989), "International conference on Lake Nyos disaster, Yaounde, Cameroon 16-20 March, 1987: conclusions and recommendations", *Journal of Volcanology and Geothermal Research*, Vol. 39 Nos 2-3, pp. 97–109.

Smolowe, J. and Philips, B. (1986), "Cameroon the lake of death", *Time*, available at: www.time.com/time/magazine/article/0,9171,962228,00.html (accessed February 5, 2006).

Tanjong, L. (1986), "Survivals of the Lake Nyos tragedy speak out", *Cameroon Tribune*, Vol. 27 (August), p. 4.

Telford, J., Cosgrave, J. and Houghton, R. (2006), "Joint evaluation of the international response to the Indian Ocean tsunami", available at: www.tsunamievaluation.org/NR/rdonlyres/2E8A3262-0320-4656-BC81-EE0B46B54CAA/0/SynthRep.pdf (accessed June 15, 2008).

UNDP (2004), *Reducing Disaster Risk: A Challenge for Development, A Global Report*, UNDP, Geneva.

UNEP/OCHA (2005), *Lake Nyos Dam Assessment*, Joint UNEP-OCHA Environment Unit, Geneva.

UNORC (2006), "Sample survey on IDPs living with host communities: findings and analysis", Office of the United Nations Recovery Coordinator for Aceh and Nias, available at: www.reliefweb.int/library/documents/2006/unorc-idn-28mar.pdf (accessed April 2, 2008).

Walker, P. and Maxwell, D. (2009), *Shaping the Humanitarian World Abingdon*, Routledge, London.

WCDR (2005), "Hyogo framework for action 2005-2015: building the resilience of nations and communities to disasters", *International Strategy for Disaster Reduction*, available at: www.unisdr.org (accessed May 18, 2006).

Wilson, P., Reilly, D., Russell, R., Wright, M., Arini, A., Cempaka, D., Diastami, E., Narulita, L., Anindita, M., Bowo Santosa, Y., Handani, Y. and Wahyuningsih, Y. (2007), *Joint Evaluation of their Responses to the Yogyakarta Earthquake*, CARE, Catholic Relief Services, Save the Children and World Vision Indonesia, Jakarta, available at: http://crs.org/publications/pdf/M&E200707_e.pdf (accessed August 19, 2008).

WSSD (2002), "Report of the World Summit on Sustainable Development, Johannesburg, South Africa, 26 August-4 September, 2002", available at: http://daccessdds.un.org/doc/UNDOC/GEN/N02/636/93/PDF/N0263693.pdf?OpenElement (accessed April 12, 2009).

About the Author

Henry Ngenyam Bang is an interdisciplinary scientist with varied research interests. His core research interest is natural hazards/disasters and climate change, particularly their interactions with society, and the long-term trajectories of vulnerability and post-disaster recovery. He is also keen to understand how governance of disaster risks and disaster risk reduction can sustain the lives and livelihoods of people prone to disasters, with focus on developing countries. He has broad-base knowledge of geophysical hazards, disaster management, risk perception, environmental management, and policy and vulnerability issues related to disasters. He obtained a PhD in International Development (research on "natural" disasters) and second MSc in Environment and Development from the University of East Anglia, UK. His first MSc was in Applied Geology from the University of Buea, Cameroon, and BSc (Hons) Geology from Ahmadu Bello University, Zaria, Nigeria. Henry Ngenyam Bang can be contacted at: henrybang2001@yahoo.com

Emerald Gems: New Perspectives in Global Environmental Disasters

Impacts of Temporary Housing on Housing Reconstruction after the Bam Earthquake

Mojtaba Rafieian and Ali Asgary

Abstract

Purpose – This study aims to examine the impacts of temporary housing on housing reconstruction after disasters using data collected after the December 2003 Bam earthquake.

Design/methodology/approach – A questionnaire was developed and completed by 281 disaster-impacted households living in small and large campsites and on site of damaged properties provided by government and non-government agencies. Cross tabulation analyses were carried out to analyze the data.

Findings – Results of this study show that the type of temporary housing (campsite and on property site) that had been provided to the victims has impacted the speed, quality and the overall satisfaction of the housing reconstruction.

Practical implications – Provision of on-site temporary housing to disaster impacted population where possible could speed up a higher quality and more satisfactory housing reconstruction.

Originality/value – This paper provides original research evidences for the relationship between type of temporary housing and housing reconstruction.

Keywords: Housing reconstruction; Temporary housing; Transitional shelter; Bam Earthquake; Post disaster reconstruction; Disasters; Earthquakes

1. Introduction

Temporary housing (TH) is usually used for a few weeks or months following disasters in forms of tents, public mass shelters, rental accommodations, and prefabricated homes (Quarantelli, 1995). There are conflicting observations and conclusions regarding the provision of THs in post-disaster situations. Some studies have argued that TH provided by governmental and non-governmental agencies are unnecessary,

Reprinted from *Disaster Prevention and Management*
Vol. 22 No. 1, pp. 63–74 (2013). doi:10.1108/09653561311301989

expensive, late, long-lasting, and shift resources away from permanent reconstruction, and their sites can become a source for socio-environmental concerns (Davis, 1978; Office of the United Nations Disaster Relief Co-Ordinator (UNDRO), 1982; Bolin, 1990; Bolin and Stanford, 1991; Geipel, 2001; Shelter Project, 2004). On the other hand some other studies suggest that provision of TH can be essential for quick recovery and safe rebuilding (UNDP, 2006; Johnson, 2007).

There are different types and forms of post-disaster THs. In particular, families may be temporarily housed in campsites or housed near their damaged properties in units provided by disaster relief and governmental agencies. Previous studies show that TH in owners' places has more advantages as compared to campsites (Geipel, 1989; Barakat, 2003; Johnson *et al.*, 2005). However, there is a lack of research on the impacts that type of TH might have on the housing reconstruction process. This study aims to investigate the impacts that living in different THs have on the housing reconstruction process.

2. Post-disaster TH

Emergency shelter, temporary shelter, TH are the three common types of transitional shelter that disaster impacted population may or may not go through them. TH is provided to the disaster victims during the reconstruction period and allows returns to normal daily activities till permanent houses are built (Bolin, 1990; Johnson, 2007).

There are different types of TH in terms of their locations: on site and on campsites. On-site TH refers to the situation when affected families live on their land near their damaged properties. Campsites refer to TH on planned or unplanned campsites. Camps are usually in form of organized campsites using tents or prefabricated homes. Provision of TH in disaster-affected regions has been debated among the researchers and relief organizations in the past few years (Bektaş, 2005). TH is relatively expensive in relation to its intended life-span that is between several months to several years (UNDRO, 1982). TH is usually preferred in major disasters when the reconstruction takes longer period of time (Johnson, 2007). It has been said that in the developing country context, TH is often not necessary and should be skipped altogether in favor of accelerated permanent reconstruction (UNDRO, 1982). In contrast, some other studies suggest that judging by the frequency of use after recent large-scale disasters, the supply of TH units can be essential for quick recovery of the population and to allow time for safe rebuilding (Johnson, 2007; Duyne and Pittet, 2006).

3. TH after the Bam Earthquake

On December 26, 2003 at 1:56:57 (GMT) (5:26:57 a.m. local time) a magnitude Mw = 6.3 earthquake devastated the historical cities of Bam and Baravat in Kerman

Province of Iran. The official death toll was recorded as 26,271 and about 25,000 were injured (Asgary *et al.*, 2008). The quake destroyed more than 53,000 buildings, caused damage to infrastructure and lifelines and damaged the historical Bam Citadel (Havaii and Hosseini, 2004; Fallahi, 2008).

As a unique garden city, date production was the primary source of income before the earthquake. During the 1990s a major industrial complex residing various factories, including a Devo automobile assembly line was developed. The dominant culture of Bam is a tribal one, consisting of large "family" units with a very strong attachment to the land. There were 62,364 buildings in Bam prior to the earthquake, of which 34,531 were residential. Few homes were steel-framed or constructed of reinforced concrete; most were constructed of brick and steel (40.6 percent) or adobe (sun-dried brick and clay, 53.2 percent). About 84 percent of the buildings were built prior to the implementation of the 1991 seismic codes (Ghafory-Ashtiany and Hosseini, 2008).

A large number of stakeholders were involved in the recovery and the reconstruction process including community members and citizens' groups, government, civil society organizations, international organizations (UNDP, UNESCO), NGOs and voluntary associations, private sector companies, and professional groups (Asgary *et al.*, 2008). To facilitate and coordinate the reconstruction process, the "Bam Reconstruction Commission" was created. This commission appointed the Housing Foundation as the main executive organization for the reconstruction. Reconstruction of Bam started with some delays and about one year after the earthquake due to some complications created by land ownership, planning, and resources.

Reconstruction involved providing TH for disaster victims that took more time than anticipated (Tierney *et al.*, 2004; Ghafory-Ashtiany and Hosseini, 2008). Majority of the temporary houses were placed either on private damaged properties or located on streets adjacent to them (Plate 1). Others were settled in campsites

Plate 1: A sample of on-site TH after the Bam earthquake of December 2003

Plate 2: A sample of campsite TH after the Bam earthquake of December 2003

(Plate 2). Overall 35,905 TH units were built (26,900 units on sites and 9,005 in 23 congregated campsites). TH units were administered and built by the Housing Foundation, Iran's Defense Ministry (4,310), Government of Turkey (800), Islamic Relief of London (400), World relief (207), and others (2,100).

Government had trouble filling the TH units in the campsites and about 3,100 units remained vacant (Ghafory-Ashtiany, 2004) as people were reluctant to relocate to campsites that were too remote from the city center or their neighborhoods. The average TH units consisted of a single room of 16-20 square meters, costing about $2,500-$3,000. Because different materials suppliers and contractors were involved in the construction, there were some variations in the materials and design (Tierney *et al.*, 2004).

4. Methodology and Data

This research tries to find the impacts that different TH has on housing reconstruction. In particular we are interested in knowing if living in on-site temporary shelter or campsites has impact on the housing reconstruction process. Past anecdotal evidences suggest that people who are living on site of their damaged property during the reconstruction period may have better housing reconstruction experience. This happens because those who live on site can better control and monitor the reconstruction of their houses in a daily basis, and have better knowledge of and access to reconstruction and recovery resources. These people may receive a better quality product in a timely manner and earn higher satisfaction from the reconstruction.

In order to find if these claims are supported by facts, it was necessary to collect data from people who were living in both types of TH. We were interested in understanding if there is any association between living in different TH and the following aspects: perceived length of the reconstruction period, ability to access reconstruction staff and administrators, ability to monitor the housing reconstruction, housing reconstruction progress, quality of the reconstructed houses, overall satisfaction of the reconstruction, and impacts of settlement type on reconstruction. Figure 1 shows the conceptual model used in this study.

A questionnaire was designed in Persian language and distributed among a sample of residents in campsites and people living in their property sites selected through a multi-stage sampling process. For the campsites samples questionnaires were distributed among a random sample of residents in five major campsites and a number of smaller campsites scattered around the city.

For the on-site residents, the city was divided into five districts and from each district eight streets were randomly chosen and five houses from each street were systematically selected using the first odd numbers. When no one was in the house the next house was chosen. Survey was conducted in 2006. Questionnaires were delivered to the respondents and collected one or two days after.

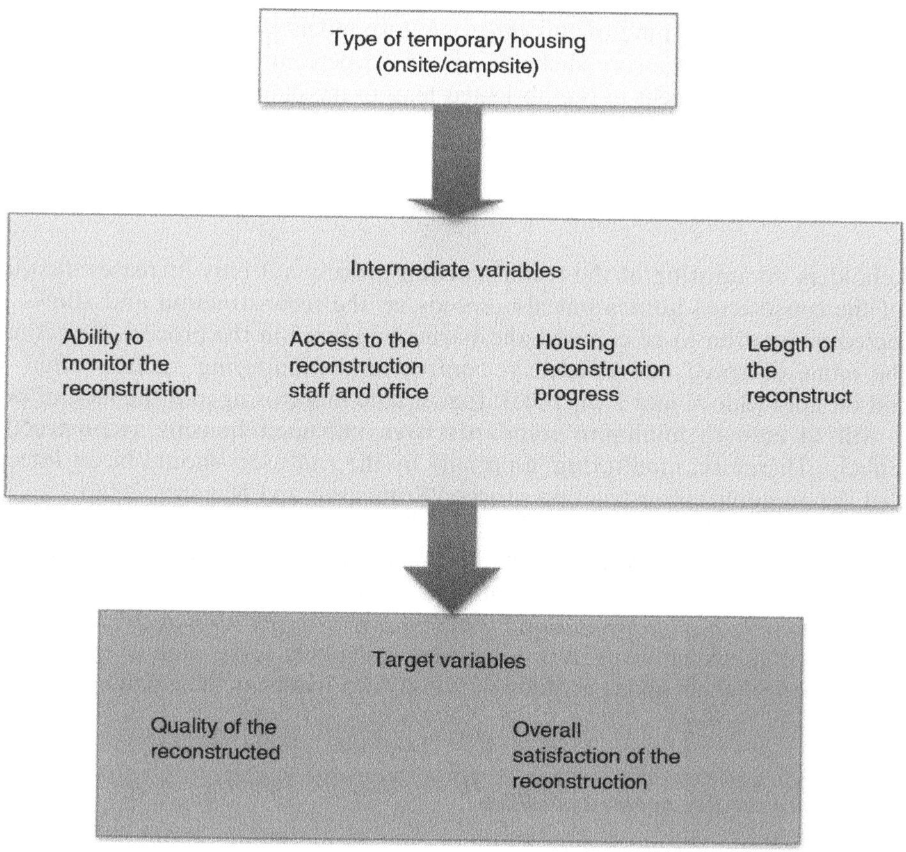

Figure 1: Conceptual relationships between the type of TH and selected variables

Considering 35,000 temporary shelters as our study population, using the Cochran formula, 285 participants were required. We distributed 200 questionnaires in the campsites and 200 in property sites.

5. Findings

Overall 150 completed questionnaires from the campsites and 131 questionnaires from the property sites were collected. They were mainly from families with three to six members. About 28 percent of the respondents were employed in the government and public sector, 16.7 percent were doing daily labor jobs, and 43 percent were employed in the private sector mostly in retail and general services before the earthquake. The rest were either unemployed or retired. Average age of the respondents was 41 years and majority of the respondents (250 or 89 percent) were male. About 13 percent of the respondents were illiterate, 37.4 percent had less than high school diploma, 31 percent had high school diploma, and 17.8 percent had post-secondary education. About 61.2 percent of the respondents had one or more fatalities during the earthquake. At the time of this interview respondents had spent an average of 19.8 months in the temporary shelters. About 2.5 percent of the respondents were living in tents, 76.9 percent in prefabricated temporary shelters, and 15.3 were using both tents and prefabricated shelters.

5.1 Monitoring of the Housing Reconstruction

Stakeholders' monitoring of the reconstruction process not only increases the quality of the constructed houses but also speeds up the reconstruction and allows the impacted population to be exposed and participate more in the process. Sometimes, in the name of speed and efficiency, controls and monitoring systems often are placed on hold (Silove and Zwi, 2005). Inadequate monitoring and the lack of political will to enforce minimum standards have impacted housing reconstruction negatively. Therefore, monitoring, especially by the end users should be an integral part of the on-going reconstruction process (Srinivasan and Nagaraj, 2006).

Respondents in this study were asked about how much they monitor the reconstruction of their house. Majority of the households were closely monitoring the reconstruction of their house. χ^2-test of data (23.771 significant at 00.00) for those who live temporarily in campsites and those who live on site of their property shows that respondents who lived in campsites were less likely to be able to monitor the reconstruction of their house as good as those who live near their damaged houses (Figure 2).

5.2 Access to the Reconstruction Office

During the reconstruction process people need to make frequent visits to the government's reconstruction office in Bam to meet and talk with the staff and managers

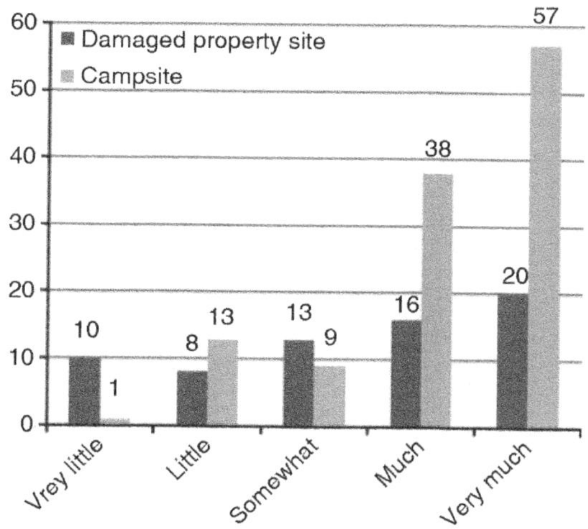

Figure 2: Cross-tabulation graph between "type of TH" and "perceived monitoring of the reconstruction processes"

for various needs, issues, and obstacles. About 51 percent of the respondents mentioned that they were able to meet with the head of the reconstruction office to discuss issues and seek help and assistance. We were interested in understanding whether there was any association between accesses to the reconstruction office and the type of TH (Figure 3).

Based on χ^2-value (0.127) we did not find any significant relationship between these two variables. In other words living in different types of temporary settlement does not seem to increase or decrease the need to meet the head of the reconstruction office.

5.3 *Housing Reconstruction Progress*

We asked a series of questions to evaluate the status of housing reconstruction. Particularly we asked respondents to indicate the percentage of progress that they have made with their housing reconstruction. Majority of the respondents stated that they have had <50 percent progress and the rest were equally divided between around 50, more than 50 and 100 percent. We could not find statistically significant relationship between the reconstruction progress level and the type of TH ($\chi^2 = 3.041$). These findings suggest that living in the previous house place does not necessarily increase the housing reconstruction progress level (Figure 4).

5.4 *Perceived Length of the Reconstruction*

Reconstruction period can last several years but its actual length depends on a number of factors including the resources of the affected community and the level and

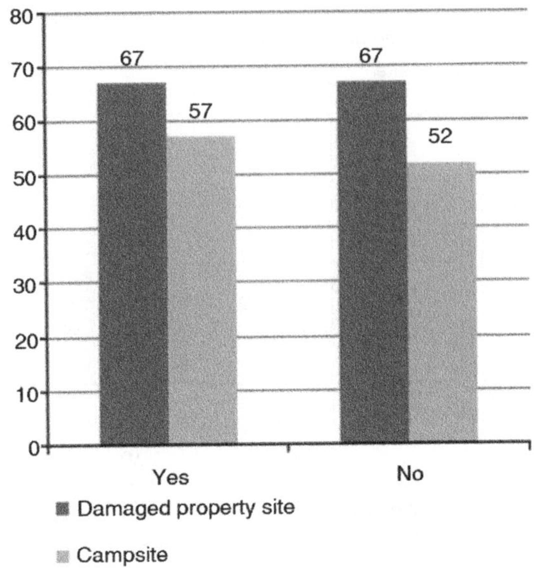

Figure 3: Cross-tabulation graph between "type of TH" and "access to reconstruction administration office"

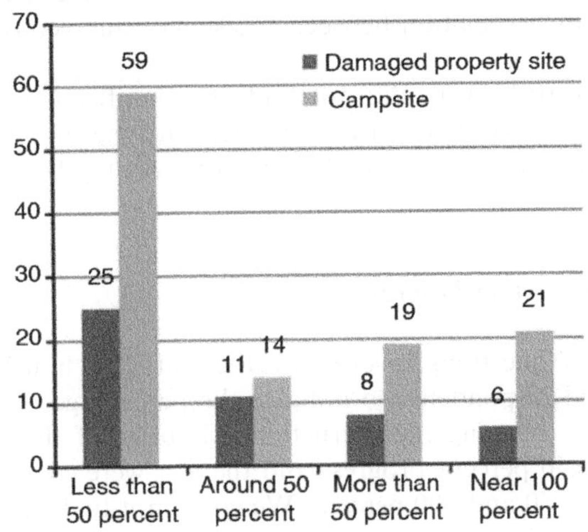

Figure 4: Cross-tabulation graph between "type of TH" and "housing reconstruction progress"

the extent of participation and monitoring by the impacted families (UNDRO, 1982; Barakat, 2003). Many other factors such as suspension of normal regulations, special design procedures and building permit processes, inclusion of participatory processes and gender sensitivity, and management of the reconstruction process can speed up the reconstruction process (Byrne and Baden, 1995; Schwab *et al.*, 1998). One argument made against the speed of the recovery and reconstruction is "the quality" issue. During the reconstruction period, getting people out of TH becomes the most pressing issue for politicians, donors, and disaster-affected people. However, it is argued that pushing for speedy reconstruction might reduce the quality of the reconstructed buildings and further increase the future vulnerability of the impacted population. Bam reconstruction was delayed in the first six months due to a number of socio-economic problems, but speeded up after that. Delay in preparation of the physical plan, problem with registration of beneficiaries, debris removal contributed to the delays.

Respondents were asked about their perceptions of the length of the reconstruction process. Overall, only 10.2 percent of them believed that the Bam reconstruction was a very lengthy process. We found χ^2-value (2.937 significant at 0.087) suggests that there is a relatively significant association between the respondents' perceptions of the length of the reconstruction process and type of temporary shelter. These findings are theoretically reasonable, as displaced people psychologically would like to go back to their previous neighborhood and house sooner than those who are near their previous house (Figure 5).

5.5 *Quality of Reconstructed Houses*

Quality of the housing reconstruction could be impacted by the type of TH and where impacted populations live during the reconstruction period. It was expected

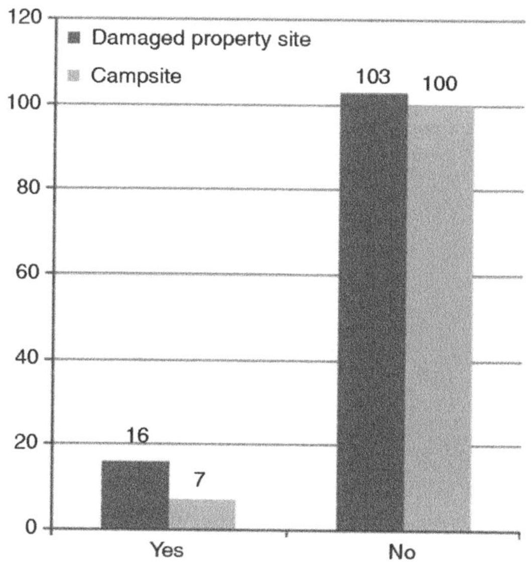

Figure 5: Cross-tabulation graph between "type of temporary shelter" and "perceived length of the reconstruction processes"

that people who are living on site of their properties have more control and monitoring capabilities over the rebuilding process and thus will obtain better quality products. We asked two questions to measure the respondents' opinions about the architectural and earthquake resistance qualities of their under the reconstruction houses. The first question asked how much earthquake resistant is their current house as compared to the previous house. Out of those who responded to this question (187 out of 279) considerable number of them believed that their houses are much or very much earthquake resistant as compared to their previous house. Only 8.6 percent of them believed that their new house is not much or not very much earthquake resistant. In response to the architectural and design quality of the new houses, again more respondents believed that their new house is better than their pervious damaged house.

Cross-tabulation analysis of data revealed that there is a statistically significant difference between the two groups in their opinions about the earthquake resistance of their new houses. People who are living in their old house are more likely to believe that their new house is being built much or very much earthquake resistant. Similar pattern was observed for architectural quality of houses (Figure 6). More people who were living on site believed that the architectural design of their new house is much or much better than their previous house ($\chi^2 = 13.622$ with significant level of 0.009).

5.6 *Overall Satisfaction with the Reconstruction and Type of TH*

Reconstruction process, especially in the very beginning had many social, economic, cultural, and technical problems. The protest in Bam in March of 2004 was an

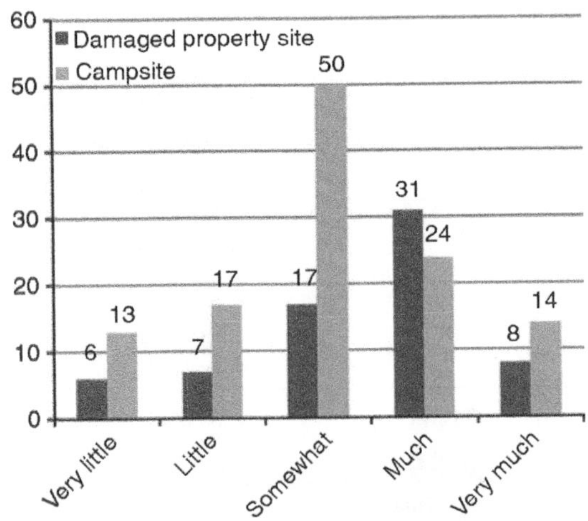

Figure 6: Cross-tabulation graph between "type of TH" and "architectural quality of the reconstructed houses"

expression of public frustration with the reconstruction and recovery process and with unmet promises of aid and of the public's need for a more direct voice in the recovery process (Tierney *et al.*, 2004). Despite these, two years after the disaster, the reconstruction was well undergoing and significant number of damaged houses had been either rebuilt or repaired. Both campsite and on-site sample residents were asked about their satisfactions with the reconstruction progress. Majority of respondents were very much (25 percent), much (19.0 percent), or somewhat (44.4 percent) satisfied with the reconstruction process. Only 11.5 percent of the respondents were either little or very little satisfied. According to the cross-tabulation results (χ^2 value of 7.239 with significant level = 0.124), type of TH was not found to have any significant impact on respondents' overall satisfaction with the reconstruction process (Figure 7).

5.7. *Impacts of TH Type on the Reconstruction*

Does living in campsites or on site of damaged property have impacts on the housing reconstruction? Considerable percent of the respondents who were living in the campsites believed that their TH had negative impacts on their housing reconstruction (Figure 8). Cross-tabulation and χ^2-test show a significant difference between the two groups (χ^2 = 9.602 with significant level of 0.048). More people who were living on the site of damaged properties perceived very little or little negative

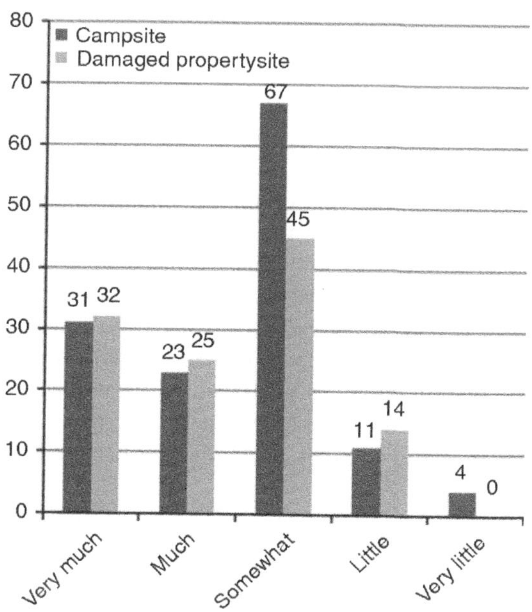

Figure 7: Cross-tabulation graph between "types of TH" and "overall satisfaction from the reconstruction processes"

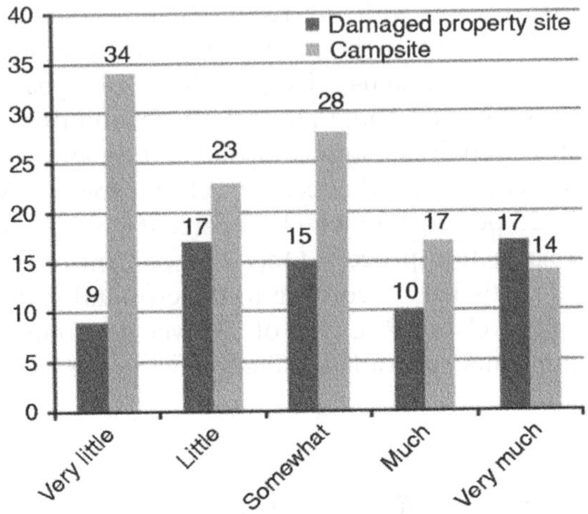

Figure 8: Cross-tabulation graph between "perceived impacts of TH" on "housing reconstruction"

impacts on the reconstruction of their house as compared to those living in campsites.

Studies conducted after the end of the housing reconstruction further highlight our findings. For example, Omidvar *et al.* (2011) reported that the pace of reconstruction was one of the survivors' major concerns. This was more of a concern for those who were living in campsites than those were in their own property. Lack of financial sources and building materials also caused some delays in the reconstruction that were common among both groups of impacted households. In particular they found that 80 percent of the people who have found the reconstruction progress enough speedy were among those who had sustainable participation during there construction period. In part this could be explained by the type of TH that people had during the reconstruction among other factors.

Although this approach provides some insight into our understanding of the type of TH on post-disaster housing reconstruction, one needs to consider a couple of limitations. First, there are many social, political, environmental, and economical factors that influence the quality and speed of reconstruction that need to be considered as well. Second, respondents' subjective and psychological perceived assessments of the quality, speed, and effectiveness of the reconstruction process may not be sufficient for policy making. Further research needs to be carried out using more objective measures.

6. Conclusion

This study showed that type of TH did not have any influence on the impacted households' overall satisfaction with the reconstruction process and access to the reconstruction administrators. These can be explained by the facts that there are many other factors that contribute to people's satisfaction from the reconstruction process such as funding sources, technical support, availability of skilled workers, coordination among the stakeholders. Living on campsites or on site of properties did not limit people's access to the reconstruction administrators. This study found that perceived length of the reconstruction period was longer for those who lived in camps. It explains the socio-psychological aspects of living in campsites as temporary locations and the need to move onto the permanent housing. Overall housing reconstruction progress has been better for those who lived on their property sites. Our results also showed that living on property sites increases the seismic design and construction quality of the houses as judged by the sample population. Impacted population living on campsite has less monitoring opportunities, which by itself can impact the quality of the reconstructed houses.

Therefore, these findings not only support the previous research that TH in form of campsites are not suitable from socio-economic and cultural perspectives, but also show that TH in form of campsites can have some negative impacts on housing reconstruction.

References

Asgary, A., Badri, A., Rafieian, M. and Hajinejad, A. (2008), "Utilizing post-disaster development opportunities after bam earthquake and the role of stakeholders", *International Journal of Humanities*, Vol. 15 No. 2, pp. 33–52.

Barakat, S. (2003), "Housing reconstruction after conflict and disaster", Network paper, No. 43, Humanitarian Practice Network, ODI, London, pp. 1–35.

Bektaş, E. (2005), *A Post-Disaster Dilemma: Temporary Settlements in Duzce City-Turkey*, Erasmus University Rotterdam, HIS, Rotterdam.

Bolin, R. (1990), "The loma prieta earthquake: studies of the short-term impacts", University of Colorado, Boulder, CO.

Bolin, R. and Stanford, L. (1991), "Shelter, housing and recovery: a comparison of US disasters", *Disasters*, Vol. 15 No. 1, pp. 24–34.

Byrne, B. and Baden, S. (1995), "Gender, emergencies, and humanitarian assistance", Briefings on Development and Gender (BRIDGE) Report, Brussels, November.

Davis, I. (1978), *Shelter After Disaster*, Polytechnic Press, Oxford.

Duyne, B.J. and Pittet, D. (2006), *Towards Sustainable Post-Disaster Housing Reconstruction; an Empirical Assessment of a Housing Reconstruction Project in Tsunami-hit Coastal Tamil Nadu*, ISAAC, Lugano.

Fallahi, A. (2008), "Bam earthquake reconstruction assessment: an interdisciplinary analytical study on the risk preparedness of Bam and its cultural landscape: a world heritage property in danger", *Structural Survey*, Vol. 26 No. 5, pp. 387–99.

Ghafory-Ashtiany, M. (2004), "Bam Earthquake of 05:26:26 of 26 December 2003", Ms6.5. *J Scismol Earthq Eng*, Vol. 5, pp. 1–3.

Ghafory-Ashtiany, M. and Hosseini, M. (2008), "Post-Bam earthquake: recovery and reconstruction", *Natural Hazards*, Vol. 44 No. 2, pp. 229–41.

Geipel, R. (1989), *Long-Term Consequences of Disasters; the Reconstruction of Friuli, Italy in Its International Context, 1976-1988*, Springer-Verlag, New York, NY.

Geipel, R. (2001), "Doing more for those made homeless by natural disasters", Working Paper Series No. 1, Disaster Management Facility, World Bank, Washington, DC.

Havaii, M.H. and Hosseini, M. (2004), "Bam earthquake from emergency response to reconstruction", *Journal of Seismology and Earthquake Engineering*, Vol. 5 No. 4, pp. 229–37.

Johnson, C. (2007), "Strategic planning for post-disaster TH", *Disasters*, Vol. 31 No. 4, pp. 435–58.

Johnson, C., Lizarralde, G. and Davidson, C.H. (2005), "A systems view of TH projects in post disaster reconstruction", *Construction Management and Economics*, Vol. 24 No. 4, pp. 367–78.

Omidvar, B., Zafari, H. and Khakpour, M. (2011), "Evaluation of public participation in reconstruction of Bam, Iran, after the 2003 earthquake", *Natural Hazards*, Vol. 59 No. 3, pp. 1397–412.

Quarantelli, E.L. (1995), "Patterns of sheltering and housing in US disasters", *Disaster Prevention and Management*, Vol. 4 No. 3, pp. 43–53.

Schwab, J., Topping, K.C., Eadie, C.C., Deyle, R.E. and Smith, R.A. (1998), "Planning for post-disaster recovery and reconstruction", Report No. 483/484, FEMA, American Planning Association, Chicago, IL.

Shelter Project (2004), "Transitional settlement, displaced populations", the Martin Centre for Architectural and Urban Studies department of Architecture, University of Cambridge, Cambridge, available at: www.shelterproject.org (accessed 25 November 2011).

Silove, D. and Zwi, A.B. (2005), "Translating compassion into psychosocial aid after the tsunami", *The LANCET*, Vol. 365 No. 9456, pp. 269–71.

Srinivasan, K. and Nagaraj, V.K. (2006), "The state and civil society in disaster response: post-tsunami experiences in Tamil Nadu", *Journal of Social Work in Disability & Rehabilitation*, Vol. 5 Nos 3-4, pp. 57–80.

Tierney, K.T., Khazaei, B., Krmigold, F. and Parsizade, F. (2004), "Reconnaissance report on BAM earthquake social and public policy issues", *Journal of Seismology and Earthquake Engineering*, Vols 5-6 No. 4, Special Issue on Bam Earthquake, pp. 209–15.

UNDP (2006), "Progress Report: UNDP sustainable housing reconstruction program in bam through community mobilization and participation", UNDP, available at: www.undp.org.ir/reports/shelterreport.doc (accessed 16 September 2011)

Office of the United Nations Disaster Relief Co-Ordinator (UNDRO) (1982), *Shelter After Disaster: Guidelines for Assistance*, United Nations, New York, NY.

About the Authors

Mojtaba Rafieian, PhD, is an Associate Professor of Urban and Regional Planning at Faculty of Art and Architecture at Tarbiat Modares University. His research and teaching interests include housing planning and policy, urban regeneration and management, and urban planning theories and technique. He has published several books and articles in these areas.

Ali Asgary, PhD, is an Associate Professor and Graduate Program Director of Disaster and Emergency Management Program at the School of Administrative Studies at York University. His research and teaching interests cover disaster recovery and reconstruction, business continuity, disaster and emergency economics, GIS and virtual technology applications in disaster and emergency management. Ali Asgary is the corresponding author and can be contacted at: Asgary@yorku.ca

In Pursuit of Ideal Emergency Planning in Korea

Kyoo-Man Ha

Abstract

Purpose – This paper aims to document the present situation of emergency planning in Korea, and subsequently to provide related alternatives by comparing the reality of "mere awareness approach" and the appropriate strategies to "sincere accommodation approach."

Design/methodology/approach – With the inferences of other countries, mere awareness approach and sincere accommodation approach have been systematically analyzed via the same four components: government employees, traditional minority; foreign-born population; and animals.

Findings – The major tenet of this paper is that Korea has to change its mere awareness approach to sincere accommodation approach to sincerely facilitate ideal emergency planning.

Originality/value – It is certain that no distinctive research, such as the issue of diverse professionals in emergency planning process, has ever been conducted on the ideal emergency planning in Korea. Thus, conducting a research on how Korea will substantially improve the level of emergency planning in the field of emergency management seems appropriate. Further, the research may let international scholars in the field of emergency management know what has happened or what will be needed in the area of Korean emergency planning.

Keywords: Diverse workforces; Mere awareness; Sincere accommodation; Korea; Emergency measures; Contingency planning; Disasters

Introduction

In Korea, many stakeholders have pointed out the poor conditions of emergency planning around government employees, traditional minority, foreign-born population, and animals, to name a few. However, they have formally mentioned the necessity of ideal emergency planning, without seriously attempting to correct those poor conditions. To make matters worse, it is certain that no distinctive research,

Reprinted from *Disaster Prevention and Management*
Vol. 21 No. 5, pp. 624–633 (2012). doi:10.1108/09653561211278743

such as the issue of diverse professionals in emergency planning process, has ever been conducted on the ideal emergency planning in Korea. Thus, conducting a research on how Korea will substantially improve the level of emergency planning in the field of emergency management seems appropriate. Further, the research may let international scholars in the field of emergency management know what has happened or what will be needed in the area of Korean emergency planning.

This paper aims to describe how Korea has been doing on its current emergency planning in the field of Korean emergency management and then recommends measures that could improve emergency planning by analyzing both, barriers to "mere awareness approach," and alternatives to "sincere accommodation approach." Throughout the paper, these two approaches will be deliberately compared, especially with inferences of other foreign cases. For a systematic study, these two approaches will be analyzed via the same four players:

(1) government employees;
(2) traditional minority;
(3) foreign-born population; and
(4) animals.

This paper will maintain that Korea has to change its mere awareness approach to sincere accommodation approach as the next key step.

The Importance of Ideal Emergency Planning in Korea

The manner of planning for various emergencies plays a critical role in managing emergency, because the very purpose of emergency planning is to make a difference in managing emergency. Ideal emergency planning is not a temporary event but a continuous process (Palm, 1987, pp. 95-7 and 101-2). The purpose of ideal emergency planning is to develop and maintain emergency operations plan. In the Korean context, ideal emergency planning means inclusiveness, public-private partnership in emergency management, and consultation in decision making.

When considering that emergency management requires coordination among many individuals and organizations, ideal emergency planning should be a team effort again terrible emergency. Also, different emergencies require different response capabilities and expertise. Hence, one of the most important issues in ideal emergency planning is to identify all stakeholders who have to be involved to include animals alongside all humans.

Emergency management is a new field in Korea. As evidence, no major research has ever been done on the matter of ideal emergency planning in the Korea, such as the support for diverse professionals in the field of emergency planning. However, there is a clear research trend on the issue in the international field of emergency management. Especially, many scholars have shown their interests in studying the issue in advanced nations (Britton, 2001-2002, pp. 47-50).

Emergency planning may cause the biggest failure in the field of emergency management, particularly when it combines with political, economic, and social elements in the society. In other words, because those elements play a role in determining vulnerability during emergency planning process, related emergency planning will be a main cause of catastrophe.

When ideal emergency planning including diverse workforces is included into the field of emergency management, there are many benefits. Such as, ideal emergency planning produces different viewpoints on emergency and its management, while it allows diverse experiences to solve the difficult problems faster and more efficiently (FEMA, 2010, pp. 7-9). With the above reason, it can be summarized that the biggest benefit of ideal emergency planning is to either dramatically or incrementally increase the efficiency of emergency management.

At first glance, many Koreans have recognized the importance of ideal emergency planning, but its real measure has been superficial. That is why the current way of embodying emergency planning in Korea will be called "mere awareness approach." On the other hand, it is inevitable for Korea to overcome the aspect of mere awareness approach in emergency management in the near future. Emergency planning should be fully based on every stakeholder's sincerity, without which the approach will be merely self-congratulatory again. That is why the future approach will be called "sincere accommodation."

As shown in Figure 1, the ideal emergency planning will be one big circle, after four small gears arbitrate their locations through changing from mere awareness approach to sincere accommodation approach. These two approaches will consist of four important players:

(1) government employees;
(2) traditional minority;
(3) foreign-born population; and
(4) animals.

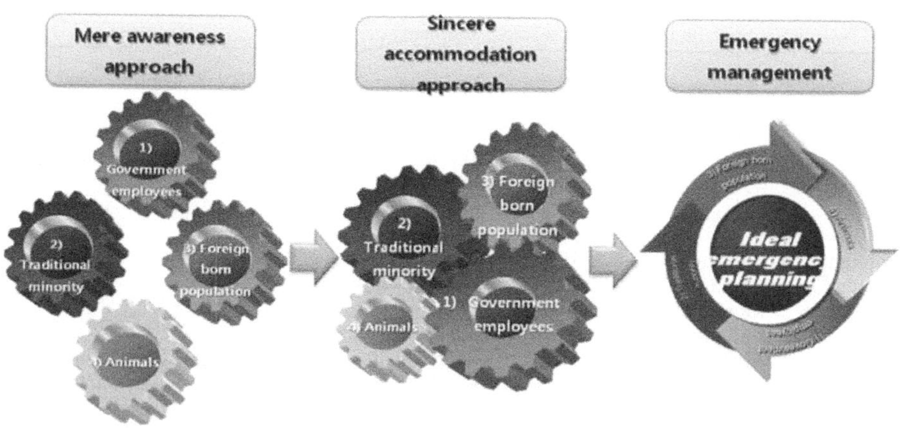

Figure 1: A model illustrating the transition from mere awareness approach to sincere accommodation approach

Four players have been chosen because they have played many important roles in shaping the current emergency management system, which lacks ideal emergency planning.

Barriers to Mere Awareness Approach in Korea

(1) Government Employees

The National Emergency Management Agency (NEMA), as a central government body, has comprehensively managed all kinds of emergency in Korea. As local government bodies, 17 fire departments and 186 fires stations are nationally located to fight against fire, whereas the section of emergency management in each local government is tasked to deal with other non-fire-related emergencies (NEMA, 2012).

In both central and local governments, two major professionals have substantially worked for emergency management. One is firefighters, whereas the other is civil engineers. In almost every aspect of the government's emergency planning, the viewpoint of these two professionals has been exclusively reflected.

The other professionals have failed to participate in emergency planning in the NEMA and local governments. In other words, the viewpoint of the other professionals, such as emergency psychologists, meteorologists, and culture experts, has been seriously neglected during the process of decision making on emergency management in Korea.

The NEMA has officially proclaimed that the institution is trying to manage every emergency in Korea with the support of local governments. However, by employing mainly firefighters and civil engineers, comprising 86 percent of 350 employees as shown in Table I, the institution has attempted to manage fires, flood,

Table I: Important statistic numbers on four players

Unit	Specific items	Numbers	%
1. Government employees in the NEMA	Firefighters and civil engineers	Approximately 300/350 NEMA employees	Approximately 86
	Others	The rest	Approximately 14
2. Traditional minority in Korea	Women	Approximately 24 million/50 million people	Approximately 48
	Persons with disabilities	Approximately 2 million/50 million people	Approximately 4
3. Foreign-born population in Korea	Registered foreign-born industrial workers, immigrants, and illegal immigrants	Approximately 1 million/50 million people	Approximately 2
4. Animals in Korea	Pets	Approximately 10 million pets/50 million people	Approximately 20
	Service animals	Approximately 100 service dogs/70,000 blind people, etc.	Approximately 0.14

Sources: MW (2012); NEMA (2010, pp. 257-8); NEMA (2012)

and typhoon (NEMA, 2010, pp. 257-8). Thus, it is true that this has shown many aspects of mere awareness approach.

Though it has been well known that diverse professionals have participated in the emergency planning process in the US governments, elected officials have shown no genuine support for emergency planning in general. Many politicians have preferred their own political agenda to promoting emergency planning; the only goal being re-election, which has caused a perennial problem in the USA.

(2) Traditional Minority

In Korea, traditional minority includes women and persons with disabilities in the field of emergency management. Women have been portrayed as a vulnerable group during emergency, whereas persons with disabilities, approximately 4 percent of the total population as shown in Table I, have been described as those who have difficulty in evacuating during emergency (Ministry of Health and Welfare (MW), 2012).

Women's roles have recently been improved through the activity of voluntary organizations and community-based organizations. Also, the status of persons with disabilities has greatly improved, thanks to the Article 6 of Act on Persons with Disabilities' Social Welfare (MW, 2012).

However, this does not mean that traditional minority has come to play equal roles in managing emergency. As such, both women and persons with disabilities have been almost excluded from emergency preparedness planning. No emergency program has attempted to specify what to do with traditional minority, nor how to approach the task.

Korea has recently tried to do many things for the traditional minority – by indirectly supporting the activity of women's voluntary organization, or by helping persons with disabilities via 911 mobile phones (NEMA, 2010, p. 96). However, the nation still has excluded the traditional minority during the process of important decision making. Therefore, Korea's efforts for traditional minority have surely been mere awareness approach.

The UN Population Fund (UNFPA) integrated reproductive health into emergency planning for displaced population in West Africa in 2003. However, mainly because of funding scarcity, the program was not fully implemented (Delargy and Alakbarov, 2004, pp. 345-8). In short, despite the UNFPA's proclamation, West Africa failed to reflect the importance of traditional minority to the department of emergency planning.

(3) Foreign-born Population

As shown in Table I, the number of foreign-born population in Korea is approximately one million, including about 760,000 registered foreign-born industrial workers, 200,000 immigrants mostly via international marriage, and 40,000 illegal immigrants. Of the total population, 2 percent are foreign born (NEMA, 2012).

Many Korean business owners have made their profits by employing foreign-born population (Davis and Bali, 2008, pp. 1177-8). Many foreign-born workers are more vulnerable to emergency than the majority of Koreans because of their minimal knowledge of Korean language and other cultural differences. As a result, their possibility of being hit by an emergency was much higher than that of Korean workers.

Although many, including public and private institutions, have openly maintained via web sites that they have employed foreign-born population taking into account its cultural adaptation, including emergency planning, related emergency victims have not decreased considerably. It also is true that language barrier has been the biggest cause of diverse emergencies to foreign-born population.

Some aspects of emergency planning in the UK have also disregarded the significance of foreign-born population in its decision-making process. Such as, to fight against the 1996 Manchester bombing, the nation developed an emergency plan. Yet, the planning failed to appropriately collaborate with key stakeholders, including foreign-born population (Batho *et al.*, 1999, pp. 226-31).

(4) Animals

Many farm animals have been hot issues during emergency. This paper includes two more categories of animals – pets and service animals. Earlier, the Koreans had very restrictive views on the use of animals, mainly because almost all animals were used as food and an aid in rice farming.

Since the end of 1990s, an increasing number of Koreans have started living with their pets in their home. Approximately one of five Koreans, which is about 20 percent of its population, has currently lived with a pet, as shown in Table I. The number of service animals is still small, but has steadily increased in the complicated society.

However, almost no emergency planning department has ever allocated time or space to explain what to do with animals during emergency. The Basic Act on Emergency and Safety Management has not specified anything about pets and service animals (NEMA, 2012). The Act has emphasized only on human beings in the field of emergency management.

Unexpectedly, many Koreans have recently shown their love toward pets and service animals and even agreed to regulate the Act of Animal Protection. At first glance, they have shown humanity toward animals, yet they have not been seriously involved in dealing with them in the field of emergency planning. Therefore, mere awareness approach is still applicable to the case of animals.

Santorini, Greece has always faced a potential hazard of volcano eruption. However, Santorini has not developed any formal emergency plan for animals, because of functional confusion among emergency planners. It means that when the volcano erupts, all animals may surely face related catastrophe (Dominey-Howesa and Minos-Minopoulos, 2004, pp. 298-303).

Alternatives to Sincere Accommodation Approach in Korea

(1) Government Employees

Since experiencing a series of terrible emergencies such as Ruapehu volcano eruption in 1995, governments in New Zealand have realized the importance of all stakeholders for emergency planning. Especially, governments have supported it by way of coordination, communication, and training (Paton *et al.*, 1998, pp. 6-11). Further, the nation has practiced an educational program for the purpose (Finnis *et al.*, 2010, pp. 180-1).

To modify mere awareness approach on government employees in Korea, it is necessary for NEMA and local governments to sincerely accommodate the other professionals into the field of emergency. Rather than allowing firefighters and civil engineers to fiercely compete for own benefits, NEMA has to open doors to the other professionals.

Since analysis reveals that the definition of emergency management includes those efforts which the governments have made with the support of close partners, the emergency planning among government employees should be urgently facilitated. Without initiating ideal emergency planning among government employees, the extent of emergency planning in the field of emergency management in Korea would not be effectively improved. Thus, the heads of NEMA must show their leadership.

This does not mean that firefighters and civil engineers have to stop their influence over the public policy on emergency management in public organizations, only because emergency planning among government employees is evolving. There is a need to share work experiences with the other professionals at the government level by the practical approach of relying on coordination, communication, training and exercise, and education, akin to the case of New Zealand.

Like emergency threats, the works on emergency planning are constantly changing, considering that emergency happens everywhere. The works include numerous disciplines, as a result diverse jobs are created. Adequate job opportunity should be fairly provided to the other professionals with different skills, values, backgrounds, and interest (Jones, 2006, pp. 4-8).

(2) Traditional Minority

Israel has recently supported the participation of traditional minority in the field of emergency planning, because the nation has proven that traditional minority perceives the threat of emergency more than the majority (Soffer *et al.*, 2011, pp. 37-40). In Malaysia, the government has made efforts to train traditional minority in emergency management via ideal emergency planning. Particularly, Malaysia has continued to review and revise emergency planning for the purpose (Shaluf and Ahamadun, 2008, pp. 86-92).

In Korea, an attempt to raise the status of women and improve the conditions around persons with disabilities in the field of emergency planning has not been practically accomplished yet (Kim and Won, 2008, pp. 7-21), unlike Israel and Malaysia. Hence, it is necessary for stakeholders to sincerely improve their roles, on the basis of sincere accommodation approach.

The fact that women have distributed emergency food, hygiene towels, and rendered similar humanitarian services does not only have negative connotations. As long as women take a specializing role in providing humanitarian aid to similar emergency sites, their role would still be effective for those who handle emergency situations. However, women's role should be much more expanded into the decision-making process, mainly because women also are stakeholders regarding ideal emergency planning (Fulu, 2007, pp. 856-8).

More alternatives have to be provided for persons with disabilities. In particular, persons with disabilities should be included in the list of stakeholders who set up emergency plans, and thus participate in significant decision making. If difficult, at least a point man must be nominated for persons with disabilities (Fire Engineering, 2009, p. 38).

Based on above facts, one of the most important policy alternatives for the traditional minority is to allow women and persons with disabilities to take part in decision-making process in the field of emergency planning. To do so, it is necessary to amend some articles in the Basic Act on Emergency and Safety Management (NEMA, 2012). Such as, the definitions in Article 3 should stipulate the term "every stakeholder" including women and persons with disabilities. The Article should continue to mention that "every stakeholder shall participate in decision making."

(3) Foreign-born Population

In Italy, many scholars strongly expressed their interests in developing robust methods for foreign-born population in emergency planning. As a result, Italy has desperately tried to make quick decision on foreign-born population via ideal emergency planning (Baxter *et al.*, 2008, pp. 455-8).

On the other hand, Korea has generally neglected the importance of emergency preparedness for foreign-born population. Like Italy, Korea should take care of foreign-born population's emergency planning more seriously via sincere accommodation approach because many foreigners and immigrants have lost their lives resulting from emergency in Korea.

Social integration should be considered to solve the isolation problem of foreign-born population through the major processes (Schipper and Pelling, 2006, pp. 31-4). In so doing, it is necessary for those who are married to immigrants or those who have kept a close relationship with foreign workers in the industry to initiate sincerely inviting foreign personnel into the field of ideal emergency planning.

It has been pointed out that because foreign-born population does not have abundant resources to deal with catastrophe, related vulnerability and resiliency have deteriorated. In this context, foreign-born population should utilize their informal network, which is based on trust, among themselves, so they can acquire what they want more reliably. One of the most important alternatives is to effectively teach Korean emergency management terms to foreign-born population. At the same time, the foreign-born population has to make a self-interest group to get practically involved in emergency planning, in particular by utilizing their informal network.

(4) Animals

The USA has tried to include animals such as household pets, service animals, and livestock into emergency planning. However, it is true that animals may be restricted to human shelters under the name of public health, allergies, or hygiene (Sherman-Morris *et al.*, 2010, pp. 352-63).

Many pets and service animals are living with human beings in the same space in Korea, but nothing has been substantially done regarding emergency planning toward those animals. Hence, Korea has to directly deal with the matter of animals during emergency, as done in USA. Or, Korea sincerely should accommodate appropriate measures for animals via sincere accommodation approach.

The term "zoonosis" is a disease, which may be transmitted to human beings from animals or vice versa. Zoonosis may occur in some areas in Korea, so related risks may be reintroduced to those areas. Because of zoonosis, many are afraid of staying with animals in the same shelter during emergency.

In addition, it is true that owners must stay with their animals in the same shelter during emergency to take care of them. Despite zoonosis, Korea has to sincerely consider the matter of public health with the mix of dogs, cats, horses, and other animals in the same shelter during emergency.

For the purpose, Korea must amend the Basic Act on Emergency and Safety Management by stipulating that "both pets and service animals shall be allowed to stay with their owners in predesignated shelters during emergency." In addition, animal lovers may improve related awareness by posting information about Korea's lack of emergency planning for animals on the web, in an effort to initiate implementation of related policy alternatives. At any rate, the admission of animals to authorized emergency shelters with their owners should be focussed on sincere accommodation approach. Those who are afraid of animals or zoonosis may evacuate to regular shelters.

Conclusion

This paper has tried to investigate both, the present situation of Korean emergency planning and future-oriented alternatives, by supporting for ideal emergency planning, especially with the references of other foreign cases. For the purpose, this paper has tried to compare the barriers to "mere awareness approach" and the alternatives to "sincere accommodation approach."

This paper asserts that Korea should change from mere awareness approach to sincere accommodation approach for the ideal emergency planning. To implement related policy alternatives practically, this paper has supported four strategies, such as governments' innovative leadership for government employees, amendment of the Basic Act on Emergency and Safety Management for traditional minority, making interests group for foreign-born population, and amendment of the Basic Act on Emergency and Safety Management with posting related contents on web site for animals.

This paper has initiated to study the ideal emergency planning in Korea, and, specifically, it aims to contribute to its development in the domain of emergency management. Accordingly, international scholars may have a good chance to know the level of emergency planning in Korea, especially thanks to the result of this paper.

It will be necessary for other scholars to examine the key players, which have not been analyzed in this paper. By further exploring those players, the scholars will increase the level of ideal emergency planning in the field of emergency management in Korea. At the same time, they will ultimately contribute to development of international emergency management.

References

Batho, S., Williams, G. and Russell, L. (1999), "Crisis management to controlled recovery: the emergency planning response to the bombing of Manchester city centre", *Disasters*, Vol. 23 No. 3, pp. 217–33.

Baxter, P.J., Aspinall, W.P., Neri, A., Zuccaro, G., Spence, R.J.S., Cioni, R. and Woog, G. (2008), "Emergency planning and mitigation at Vesuvius: a new evidence-based approach", *Journal of Volcanology and Geothermal Research*, Vol. 178 No. 3, pp. 454–73.

Britton, N.R. (2001-2002), "A new emergency management for the new millennium?", *Australian Journal of Emergency Management*, Vol. 16 No. 4, pp. 44–54.

Davis, B.C. and Bali, V.A. (2008), "Examining the role of race, NIMBY, and local politics in FEMA trailer park placement", *Social Science Quarterly*, Vol. 89 No. 5, pp. 1175–94.

Delargy, P. and Alakbarov, R. (2004), "Thinking ahead about reproductive health: contingency planning and emergency preparedness in crisis situations (Iraq and West Africa)", *Disasters*, Vol. 28 No. 3, pp. 340–50.

Dominey-Howesa, D. and Minos-Minopoulos, D. (2004), "Perceptions of hazard and risk on Santorini", *Journal of Volcanology and Geothermal Research*, Vol. 137 No. 4, pp. 285–310.

Federal Emergency Management Agency (FEMA) (2010), *Diversity Awareness Course*, FEMA, Washington, DC.

Finnis, K.K., Johnston, D.M., Ronan, K.R. and White, J.D. (2010), "Hazard perceptions and preparedness of Taranaki youth", *Disaster Prevention and Management*, Vol. 19 No. 2, pp. 175–84.

Fire Engineering (2009), "Disaster plans do not address needs of those with disabilities", *Fire Engineering*, Vol. 162 No. 11, p. 38.

Fulu, E. (2007), "Gender, vulnerability, and the experts: responding to the Maldives Tsunami", *Development & Change*, Vol. 38 No. 5, pp. 843–64.

Jones, E. (2006), "Careers in homeland security: many jobs, one mission", *Occupational Outlook Quarterly*, Vol. 50 No. 2, pp. 2–15.

Kim, Y.J. and Won, J.S. (2008), *SDI Policy Report: Disaster Prevention Strategies for Seoul*, SDI Publishing Group, Seoul.

Ministry of Health and Welfare (MW) (2012), "Act on persons with disabilities' social welfare", available at: www.mw.go.kr/front/sch/search.jsp (accessed April 19, 2012).

National Emergency Management Agency (NEMA) (2010), *Statistical Data on Emergency Management*, Gunwoo System, Seoul (in Korean).

NEMA (2012), "Homepage of NEMA", available at: www.nema.go.kr/nema_cms_iba/main/ (accessed June 18, 2012) (in Korean).

Palm, R. (1987), "Pre-disaster planning: the response of residential real estate developers to special studies zones", *International Journal of Mass Emergencies and Disasters*, Vol. 5 No. 1, pp. 95–102.

Paton, D., Johnston, D. and Houghton, B.F. (1998), "Organisational response to a volcanic eruption", *Disaster Prevention and Management*, Vol. 7 No. 1, pp. 5–13.

Schipper, L. and Pelling, M. (2006), "Disaster risk, climate change and international development: scope for, and challenges to, integration", *Disasters*, Vol. 30 No. 1, pp. 19–38.

Shaluf, I.M. and Ahamadun, F.R. (2008), "An overview on the offshore emergency response planning in Malaysia", *Disaster Prevention and Management*, Vol. 17 No. 1, pp. 83–93.

Sherman-Morris, K., Schumacher, A., Drobot, S. and Mcneal, K.S. (2010), "Hurricane preparedness and response among pet care providers along the gulf coast: an investigation of hurricanes Gustav and Ike", *International Journal of Mass Emergencies and Disasters*, Vol. 28 No. 3, pp. 345–67.

Soffer, Y., Goldberg, A., Adini, B., Cohen, R., Ben-Ezra, M., Palgi, Y., Essar, N. and Bar-Dayan, Y. (2011), "The relationship between demographic/educational parameters and perceptions, knowledge and earthquake mitigation in Israel", *Disasters*, Vol. 35 No. 1, pp. 36–44.

About the Author

Kyoo-Man Ha is an Adjunct Professor in the Department of Emergency Management at Inje University, Republic of Korea. Kyoo-Man Ha can be contacted at: ha1999@hotmail.com

Innovations and Lessons Learned from the Canterbury Earthquakes: Emergency Department Staff Narratives

Sandra Richardson and Michael Ardagh

Abstract

Purpose – The purpose of this paper is to identify innovations and lessons learned from interviews with members of the multidisciplinary healthcare team who participated in the response to the 22 February earthquake, affecting the Canterbury region of New Zealand's South Island.

Design/methodology/approach – Narratives from individual staff members who were associated with the Christchurch Hospital Emergency Department response were recorded and analysed. This data, together with other contextual documents have been used to identify the responses of healthcare workers to an unexpected natural disaster. Perspectives were sought from a range of individuals, including allied health professionals, social workers, Maori health workers, orderlies, medical and nursing staff.

Findings – The individual as well as the organisational responses to the earthquake events are significant, and need to be considered in relation to future planning and responses. In particular, the importance of encouraging and supporting a culture which values innovation and responsiveness was identified. While specific, practical responses to the earthquake disaster are noted, it is also important to acknowledge the implication for individuals of an acute, unanticipated event.

Research limitations/implications – The findings from this study have the potential to illuminate possible responses in other crisis situations, and to guide the development of targeted support measures in response to disaster events.

Originality/value – Little documentation has occurred to date relating the experiences of health care responders who are not only reacting to a natural disaster, but are also part of it. This is a unique and valuable perspective that has relevance within a number of settings.

Keywords: Disasters; Emergency response; Thematic analysis; Nursing; Allied health

Reprinted from *Disaster Prevention and Management*
Vol. 22 No. 5, pp. 405–414 (2013). doi:10.1108/DPM-09-2013-0167

Introduction

In September 2010, a 7.1 magnitude earthquake occurred in the Canterbury region of the South Island of New Zealand (NZ). As part of the subsequent aftershock sequence, a 6.3 quake followed on 22 February 2011 (Stevenson *et al.*, 2011). While the September event presented a higher rating on the Richter scale, it was the February occurrence that caused major loss of life, and compounded the structural damage that had already occurred. This represented a significant event in a country that has a history of seismic episodes, and where considerable effort has been made to ensure that damage is limited through strict building codes and public education. Prior to this, the Canterbury region was not considered an area of high risk (Canterbury Earthquakes Royal Commission, 2012).

This research focuses on the experiences of those working in the Emergency Department (ED) of Christchurch's only tertiary-level hospital during the February earthquake. It highlights the experiences, perceptions and reality of individuals who were part of, and responding to, a major disaster.

Background

The September 2010 earthquake caused significant damage to infrastructure, buildings and roads, yet there was a surprisingly light injury burden, and no direct fatalities from this event (Ardagh *et al.*, 2012). This was viewed by many as a fortunate escape, particularly in comparison to the Haiti earthquake of the same magnitude which occurred shortly afterwards (Ardagh *et al.*, 2012; Lee and Tenny, 2010). In Canterbury, the September event was seen as a "learning" experience which had limited consequences in terms of injury; however, it was also perceived that the "worst" had now happened, that nothing could be this bad again (Canterbury Initiative, 2011).

The Canterbury region hosts NZ's second largest city, Christchurch, located on the edge of the Canterbury plains, bordered by the Port Hills and the Pacific Ocean (Christchurch City Council, 2013). The city had a population of approximately 400,000 in 2010, and in addition, experienced a high level of national and international tourism. While there are seven hospitals within the city, only one of these is a tertiary-level, acute-admitting facility with ED services. The other hospitals are specialised for rehabilitation, mental health, non-acute medical and surgical services, and include two private surgical facilities.

The central facts of the February earthquake have been well reported, occurring mid-week, at 12.51 p.m., a time when the central business district and associated cafes, bars and shops were particularly busy. The epicentre was located on the Port Hills approximately 10 km from the city centre, and was shallow, at only 5 km deep. These factors, in association with the highest-ever recorded peak ground acceleration contributed to a death toll of 185 and over 6,000 reported injuries within the first 24 hrs (Ardagh *et al.*, 2012; Canterbury Earthquakes Royal Commission, 2012; Reyners, 2011; Richardson *et al.*, 2013).

The initial management of the injured and the hospital response have been reported by Ardagh *et al.* (2012), but there is little known about the individual experiences of those staff and volunteers involved in the initial phase of care (Richardson *et al.*, 2013). The ED has an annual throughput of approximately 85,000 patients. In addition to medical and nursing staff there are radiographers, social and allied health workers based in the ED and on-call specialty staff including Maori Health workers. At the time of the earthquake there were ten medical staff (four Consultants, three Registrars and three House Officers) together with 22 nursing staff (including three orientating to the department, and one "casual" from elsewhere in the hospital) working. Within minutes, additional staff arrived in the ED, offering to help.

The use of narrative or story telling is not uncommon in disaster literature, often presented as viewpoint, case study or the personal experiences of individuals involved in the disaster, its response, recovery and rehabilitation phases (Chiarella, 2011; Decklebaum, 2010; Shagets, 2013). The stories of victims and the eye-witness accounts of rescuers and responders are reported; however, there has been little systematic exploration of the experiences of those who are part of, and responders to, a disaster event. Where individual experiences are reported in the wake of a disaster, these are often those of "outsiders" – international health or rescue workers who have responded to a disaster event, but are not part of the affected community (Lau, 2010; Hughes and Trantham, 2011; Wells, 2011). The voices of individuals who are carrying out "usual" activities (even if in unusual circumstances) are seldom heard, and the extremes of response are more likely than these to be acknowledged, particularly in the popular media. When healthcare staff are recognised, it is typically those in unusual circumstances, or called on to act outside their usual roles (Bayer, 2012; Health, Quality & Safety Commission New Zealand, 2011; Johnston, 2011). Of equal significance, however, is the contribution of those individuals and groups called on to continue to provide care in situations that are far beyond the normal.

In the Christchurch experience, staff working in the ED were part of the disaster itself, experiencing the same physical reactions, fear and uncertainty as those who were designated as "victims" of the incident. They were working in a multi-storey building that had suffered physical damage, yet unlike other workers in similar circumstances, were unable to evacuate the area, continuing to work and to provide care for unknown numbers of patients. Like others in the central city, they were isolated from information and unaware of the extent of the disaster or potential implications. Rather than people leaving the workplace, more staff came to offer their assistance (Ardagh *et al.*, 2012; Canterbury Initiative, 2011; Corin, 2011; de Ryke, 2012; Richardson *et al.*, 2013).

The experiences of these individuals need to be acknowledged and remembered; the ability to contribute in a meaningful way provided an opportunity for some to make sense of the situation, to feel that they were still in control of their environment. For others the experience was less positive, but still one that will remain part of their identity, as both professionals and as members of a community that experienced an unanticipated crisis event. Inevitably, such experiences have provided greater understanding of the range of responses that can be anticipated. It is appropriate to learn from the event itself, but also to learn from these individual reactions – to avoid the tendency to mythologise or understate the impact and contribution of "ordinary" people, working in extraordinary circumstances (West, 2000).

Design

This study developed from the experiences of the authors, who were present and worked in the ED during the February earthquake. The significance of the event and of the individuals who were part of this was recognised, and the decision made to capture the experience. A phenomenological approach seeking to expose the lived experience of individuals was identified as the most appropriate design. In order to facilitate this, individual, open-ended interviews were undertaken, commencing two weeks after the event and carrying on intermittently over the following eight months. Narratives from individuals who were associated with the Christchurch Hospital ED response were recorded and analysed. Ethical approval to conduct the study was granted from the Multi-Region Ethics Committee.

Perspectives were sought from a range of individuals, including allied health professionals, social workers, Maori Health Workers, Orderlies, Medical and Nursing staff. Staff were recruited by word of mouth, through internal notices placed in the hospital's on-line CEO Letter and Nursing Newsletter. E-mail invitations were sent to line managers of staff not based in ED, for example to the Head Orderly, Chaplain's office, Security office and to the Maori Health Workers. Over 90 interviews were completed, and excerpts from some of these are used to illustrate this discussion.

All interviews were audiotaped or digitally recorded, then transcribed verbatim. Analysis involved identification of core themes, recognition of sub-themes and acknowledgment of conflicting viewpoints. Examples of participants' stories were also matched against the timeline of events, and used to create a more rounded view of the experiences and activities within the ED.

Findings and Discussion

The depth of information gathered is more than can be encompassed in a single paper and for this reason only a selection of the findings is able to be presented. The aims of the study included identifying and acknowledging the feelings and responses of individuals. The focus was on those who were part of the initial response within the ED, whether this was their usual place of work or not. Many of the staff had been at work at the time of the earthquake, while others came in from home or elsewhere in the hospital.

Experiences at the Time of the Quake

The moment of the event proved one of the strongest memories, with people recalling their physical and emotional reactions. For some, their response was not what they expected, and many of their actions were automatic rather than planned:

> I was having my lunch [...] and I jumped under the table [...] and while it was still shaking I phoned my daughter [...] and I knew to call quick because the networks would be down. So I saw nothing except the phone that I was phoning on while it was still shaking. And I didn't think it was that bad [...] (ED Nurse).

> I was in the Allied Health office [...] and there was [sic] two of us there, the physio and I and it just started and I was standing up and it was going shake shake shake shake shake. And I was standing there and she was going, "Get under the table" and then the lights went out. And then I banged my head trying to get under the table, but you could hear things falling [...] (Maori Health Worker).

One doctor, working in the Women's Hospital, described the initial impact:

> The building shook like nothing I've ever felt. I had to grab hold of the bump rail on the hallway to stay upright on my feet [...] (Doctor).

He checked on his patients, then made his way towards the ED:

> I got within about three metres of the join between the two hospital buildings and the first aftershock hit. And I can still see the buildings move [...] one and a half feet apart. And it took me about three months before I could walk over that gap without fearing it, being scared of it. I mean, I saw some of the wooden framing shoot across in front of me down the side of the corridor, and the corridor's about 10 feet wide at that point [...] (Doctor).

One of the Orderlies working that day had been at lunch, noted the impact of the quake, realised it was more than just another aftershock:

> I was up in the cafe. A guy that I was having dinner with [...] I just said, 'Mate, that just left the September one behind. That was massive.' You could tell, it was just so much more violent (Orderly).

His first thoughts were to contact family, and then to move down to the ED, but he recalled the effect of the quake on other staff and members of the public also in the cafeteria:

> The lady beside us, she fainted. Just unconscious on the floor. And there were asthma attacks. One of the first things I wanted to do was just get hold of my daughter. That's all I wanted to do, initially. And I remember coming down the stairs [...] and I think I only stood on about four stairs on the way down [...] at the bottom, there was a lady there. She was having an asthma attack as well. It was just pandemonium. It was terrible [...] (Orderly).

It being lunch time, some staff were outside the hospital during their break:

> I had just come alongside the nurses' hostel when the ground shook. There were three of us. Out there we had to grab a post, because literally we couldn't stand up. And then the windows started falling out of the building, the nurses' hostel. We heard the glass, and we thought, "This is pretty serious" (ED Radiologist).

Other staff were out of the hospital, but made efforts to come in:

> I was walking to work, and it was probably [...] I don't know [...] half an hour after the earthquake, and everybody was pouring out of the CBD. And I was walking along the path, and the river was full of liquefaction and boiling and the footpaths were damaged, trees were down, but it felt quite surreal. I was walking against the crowd. And everybody was pouring out of town, and you were sort of weaving. It was like watching a movie in slow motion. The statue had fallen down outside Christ's college. The head was buried in the footpath [...] (ED Clerical Worker).

Reassurance, Contact and Communication

A key aspect that most participants commented on was the need to contact family and friends, to let people know they were safe and to confirm the status of those they were trying to contact. Many staff members had children in school, elderly parents, siblings or partners potentially at risk. Because there was little initial flow of information, it was difficult to identify the severity and range of the event, or to judge the likelihood of widespread injury and mortality. Individuals struggled to contact each other, with damage to the cellular network, power and infrastructure making this a difficult, and for some, impossible, task:

> Even though we had patients here, people here, all you could think about was your family. Like making sure that your family is ok, that's

> the first thing. I guess it could be selfish in some ways, not thinking about patients first. But it was [...] I thought we were going to die, because of the way the building shook. Plus, we are on the ground floor and you know, if things happen, we'll be the ones to die first. And I didn't know whether to save myself or the patients or what to do (ED Nurse).

A benefit of the high number of people assisting in the ED was that some staff were able to leave, check on family, and then return to assist at a later point:

> So for some reason I had my mobile with me that day, thank God, and I phoned up my partner [...] and his first words were, "Ooh, that was a big one" [...] my daughter was in preschool, so I was like, "Get her now, it's a big one. Get her" because I knew she'd be terrified, because my daughter's had a lot of problems since the first earthquake. And she'd just come right [...] (Hospital Nurse).

The need to contact loved ones was universal, with acknowledgment that this may be difficult:

> [...] we were all concerned about the family issues, but we realised quite quickly we couldn't get any communication through at all. So we sort of had to realise that we'd try on the journey to contact family. We left messages but we were aware that it may take some time to come through (Hospital Chaplain).

> A lot of senior, I think, nursing staff were saying [...] that we should try and contact family to make sure that they were safe. And for me that was the hardest bit because I couldn't make contact with anyone [...] (ED Doctor).

Often communication was interrupted, or some calls would go through and others would not. This left people waiting for replies, uncertain whether there were problems with the phone system, or problems for the person they were trying to contact:

> It was just my son. So I was texting him, because he could have been up some scaffolding on the day or anything. And they hang off some pretty weird places. So I texted him, and no replies. Getting texts from all over New Zealand by now. But there was only one text that I wanted [...] Those texts: he replied to every one of my texts, but they didn't come in until three or four in the morning (Hospital Radiographer).

Making Sense of the Unreality

It was difficult for people to know what was happening during the initial phase of the earthquake and a sense of unreality was experienced by many. The perceptions of normality, of the nature of the world in which we live had altered. An unspoken assumption of safety was lost (Huggard, 2011):

> I think it was quite quick that I kind of realised that it was going to be pretty horrendous, because the first patient [...] the first child was being rushed in [...] and when she came in, crushed, asphyxiated and looked dreadful – and she's done really well – but at the time it just looked like an absolute no-go. I think then it dawned that actually we're required here. This is the job that I do and kind of all, "just keep on trying" (ED Doctor).

> It felt really foreign. It felt like I was in a different place. And I think [...] largely because it's just such a different – not environment, it's the same environment – it's just such a different feeling, because you don't know how many people are trapped. You don't know what's coming in (ED Nurse).

> "[...] and I also heard a rumour that was going round that a few people said to me that the hospital was sinking and that we should all evacuate ED. And for about a couple of minutes I really thought that was true [...]" (Social Worker AW) then later, going home: "And it was just pouring, pitch black and these massive cracks in the path. And it was just so surreal and crazy, quite like being in a movie" (Social Worker).

> [...] seeing people coming up the one-way street like tooting their horns and people in the back of Utes, we were then kind of like, "Oh crap." And then someone had said, "The town's a mess. Stuff's collapsed." And we were like, "Oh God." And the hordes of people coming in, it was just so unreal. People like, "Get out the way." And then you're clearing for someone to come on the roof of a car or doors open with their legs hanging out [...] (Radiologist).

> So it was like I remember seeing an episode of House where he had to crawl into a building and amputate a woman's foot. And I thought, "It's not TV." I was trying to remind myself that this was actually really happening. But it was really quite surreal [...] (ED Doctor).

Recognising Vulnerability

There is often a presumption, both by the public but also within professional groups, that those working in front line and emergency roles are somehow immune to the effects of repeated exposure to trauma and distress. Many ED doctors and nurses are reluctant to acknowledge this vulnerability, and there can be a culture of mental and physical toughness within the workplace, where working long hours, missing meal breaks and using black humour to normalise situations is common. For other health professionals and those volunteers who came into ED there is even less distance from emotions, with many experiencing things outside their comfort zone, facing sights, sounds and smells that remain linked to this moment in time. In addition to the direct exposure to the consequences of the quake, for many there was a reliving of others' experiences, listening to the stories shared by patients, relatives and colleagues. Recognition has occurred of the risks for health workers resulting from repeated exposure to traumatic incidents (Hodgkinson and Stewart, 1991; Huggard, 2011; Kawamura *et al.*, 2006; Sullivan and Wong, 2011):

> And you don't think that things like this will affect you as much as they do, but they do. Like you don't expect it to, but it does. And you always think working in ED you're so tough because you see all this stuff and you become so immune to it. But not when you're personally involved (ED Nurse BB).

> Just the surreal craziness of ED. Like I remember bloody footprints around ED. I just happened to look down and see these footprints in blood and it was just crazy [...] (Social Worker AW).

> And it was kind of like, "What can I do to help?" But there was nothing I personally could have done at the time. Like I don't really know any first aid, to any degree or anything. I only do x-rays. And our machines – we don't have power down here anyway. So there's physically nothing that I believe I could have done at that time (Radiographer LR).

> But yes, we all got affected. Some of the people; one of the ones who was on the ground, she was fine at the time until about three hours later. And then she was away for two weeks. So you know [...] and even now, there's one girl who's away now, a different one. One of the ones who was fantastic in the thing, she's away now for two weeks [...] (Blood Bank staff DW).

> So I do try to compartmentalise things. And so I think that's probably why I've coped. Because if I try to think, "Ok, this person's dead, I can't do anything for them, I'm going to forget about them

> […] well, not forget about them, but I'm not going to get too emotionally tied up with them." So I think that's probably how I've coped, is by trying not to be emotional about it. And whether that's a good thing or a bad thing I don't know (ED Doctor DR).

Research Limitations

This study presents a range of perceptions and experiences, and while commonalities are apparent within these, it must be remembered that these are also unique and individual. As such, generalisation cannot be assumed, but a clearer understanding of the nature of such experiences is possible. The circumstances surrounding the interviews were traumatic for many, and these occurred across an extended time period after the initial event. It is likely that objectivity and accuracy of recall were affected, but the intention is not to identify a strict hierarchy of events, but rather to explore the subjective and contextual responses that occurred.

Implications

The findings from this study have the potential to inform other crisis situations, and to guide the development of targeted support measures in response to such events. The impact of disaster experiences on individuals and groups such as those working in the Christchurch event need to be captured.

Several issues have been highlighted as a result of this study which have wider application than the specific context of the Canterbury earthquakes. These points have the potential to inform future planning and policy, and have particular relevance to workforce development and the importance of establishing a culture of resilience and responsiveness:

- Recognition that disaster and crisis events have individual, as well as institutional and professional, significance. As such, intervention and support needs to be targeted not only at group and professional levels, but also at that of the individual.
- Assumptions are often made about the resilience and robustness of frontline carers and emergency staff. It is important to recognise that the need for support may not be recognised or easily articulated.
- Direct experience of trauma is not necessary for an individual to be impacted by disaster. Be aware of the potential for secondary or vicarious trauma to occur.
- Individuals responding to crisis events are part of family and social groupings as well as holding occupational roles. There need to be measures in place that acknowledge the effect of these competing roles, and to manage the needs of individuals to contact family and friends.
- Initial responses to a disaster event may involve a sense of confusion, be overwhelming and lead to reactions that were not anticipated. Providing clear

processes and rehearsal of roles can help structure automatic responses when the unexpected occurs.

- Individuals may experience role confusion, the need to adapt to changing expectations, and be exposed to unfamiliar and disturbing experiences. Education and awareness of potential experiences may assist with individual adaptation in times of crisis. Development of a culture that fosters resilience will support workforce adaptability and innovation.

Conclusion

The individual, as well as the organisational responses to the earthquake events are significant, and need to be considered in relation to future planning and responses. In particular, the importance of encouraging and supporting a culture which values individuals and encourages responsiveness was identified. While the specific, practical responses to the earthquake disaster have previously been identified, there is also a need to acknowledge the experiences of individuals. By understanding the range of responses, perceptions and interpretation of crisis events, it is possible to develop systems that will support a resilient workforce culture.

References

Ardagh, M.W., Richardson, S.K., Robinson, V., Than, M., Gee, P., Henderson, S., Khodaverdi, L., McKie, J., Robertson, G., Schroeder, P.P. and Deely, J.M. (2012), "The initial health-system response to the earthquake in Christchurch, New Zealand, in February, 2011", *Lancet*, Vol. 379 No. 9831, pp. 2109–2115.

Bayer, K. (2012), "CTV site was 'chaos' after collapse, inquest told", *The New Zealand Herald*, 2 November, available at: www.nzherald.co.nz/nz/news/article.cfm?c_id=1&objectid=10844602 (accessed 27 April 2013).

Canterbury Earthquakes Royal Commission (2012), "Final report", available at: http://canterbury.royalcommission.govt.nz/ (accessed 27 April 2013).

Canterbury Initiative (2011), *Canterbury Earthquake Interviews*, Canterbury Initiative, Christchurch.

Chiarella, M. (2011), "Nurses in the park: a personal account of the Christchurch earthquake", *Australian Nursing Journal*, Vol. 18 No. 9, pp. 20–21.

Christchurch City Council (2013), "Christchurch. The garden city", available at: www.christchurch.org.nz/ (accessed 27 April 2013).

Corin, C. (2011), "The Christchurch hospital social work service response in the first hours after the Christchurch earthquake of 22nd February 2011", *Aotearoa New Zealand Social Work*, Vol. 23 No. 2, pp. 58–62.

Decklebaum, D.L. (2010), "The Haiti earthquake: a personal perspective", *Canadian Medical Association Journal*, Vol. 182 No. 5, pp. E241-E242.

de Ryke, R. (2012), "The Christchurch earthquake: ultrasound in a mass trauma event", *Australasian Journal of Ultrasound in Medicine*, Vol. 15 No. 3, pp. 78–81.

Health Quality & Safety Commission New Zealand (2011), "Christchurch earthquake – healthcare workers show skill and professionalism", available at: www.hqsc.govt.nz/our-programmes/reportable-events/news-and-events/news/241/ (accessed 30 April 2013).

Hodgkinson, P. and Stewart, M. (1991), *Coping with Catastrophe: A Handbook of Disaster Management*, Routledge, London.

Huggard, P. (2011), "Caring for the carers: the emotional effects of disasters on health care professionals", *Australasian Journal of Disaster and Trauma Studies*, Vol. 2, pp. 60–62, available at: http://trauma.massey.ac.nz/issues/2011-2/AJDTS_2011-2_Huggard.pdf (accessed 28 April 2013).

Hughes, R.T. and Trantham, P. (2011), "When disaster strikes, humanity becomes our patient", *The Permanente Journal*, Vol. 15 No. 3, pp. 118–122.

Johnston, M. (2011), "Christchurch earthquake: doctor uses hacksaw in amputation", *The New Zealand Herald*, 25 February, available at: www.heraldsun.com.au/news/special-reports/christchurch-earthquake-melbourne-medical-specialist-used-hacksaw-to-amputate-mans-legs/story-fn7z04co-1226011642235 (accessed 28 April 2013).

Kawamura, T., Goto, T., Matsuda, N., Niike, K., Kato, H. and Osawa, T. (2006), "Psychological influence of the Kobe earthquake on nurses after 10 years", *Journal of Japan Municipal Hospital Association*, Vol. 45 No. 6, pp. 851–853.

Lau, D. (2010), "Disaster relief: helping the survivors of the Haiti earthquake", *Emergency Nurse*, Vol. 17 No. 10, pp. 18–21.

Lee, S. and Tenny, M. (2010), "The Haiti earthquake: disaster lessons and response from an emergency medicine perspective", *Western Journal of Emergency Medicine*, Vol. 11 No. 1, pp. 5–6.

Reyners, M. (2011), "Lessons from the Destructive Mw 6.3 Christchurch, New Zealand, Earthquake", *Seismological Research Letters*, Vol. 82 No. 3, pp. 371–372.

Richardson, S., Ardagh, M., Grainger, P. and Robinson, V. (2013), "A moment in time: emergency nurses and the Canterbury earthquakes", *International Nursing Review*, Vol. 60 No. 2, pp. 188–195.

Shagets, F.W. (2013), "Thoughts on the May 2011 Joplin, Missouri Tornado", *Southern Medical Journal*, Vol. 106 No. 1, pp. 113–114.

Stevenson, J., Kachali, H., Whitman, Z., Seville, E., Vargo, J. and Wilson, T. (2011), "Preliminary observations of the impacts the 22 February Christchurch earthquake had on organisations and the economy: a report from the field", *Bull N Z S Earthquake Eng*, Vol. 44 No. 2, pp. 65–76.

Sullivan, S. and Wong, S. (2011), "An enhanced primary health care role following psychological trauma: the Christchurch earthquakes", *Journal of Primary Health Care*, Vol. 3 No. 3, pp. 248–251.

Wells, E. (2011), "Transformation in Haiti: finding purpose while responding to disaster", *Plastic Surgery Nursing*, Vol. 31 No. 2, pp. 60–64.

West, B. (2000), "Mythologising a natural disaster in post-Industrial Australia: the incorporation of cyclone Tracey within Australian national identity", *Journal of Australian Studies*, Vol. 24 No. 66, pp. 198–205.

About the Authors

Dr Sandra Richardson is a Senior Lecturer in the Centre for Postgraduate Nursing Study at the University of Otago, Christchurch and Nurse Researcher in the Emergency Department, Canterbury District Health Board. Sandra's research interests include Emergency Department crowding, advanced nursing practice and the impact and experience of the Canterbury earthquake events. Sandra worked in the Emergency Department during the February quake and over the period of the Canterbury earthquake events. Dr Sandra Richardson is the corresponding author and can be contacted at: sandra.richardson@otago.ac.nz

Michael Ardagh is a Professor of Emergency Medicine, Emergency Department, Christchurch Hospital. Mike's interests include bioethics, Emergency Department crowding and processes and earthquake injuries and the health system response. He is also Chairman of the RHISE group (Research into the health impact of Seismic events). He worked in the Emergency Department during the February quake and over the period of the Canterbury earthquake events.

Multi-agency Community Engagement During Disaster Recovery: Lessons from Two New Zealand Earthquake Events ☆

David Johnston, Julia Becker and Douglas Paton

Abstract

Purpose – The purpose of this paper is to look at the role of community participation in reducing anxiety and trauma in communities during two New Zealand earthquakes: the 1987 Edgecumbe and 2003 Te Anau events and explore the effectiveness of various approaches in providing information, reducing stress, and facilitating a recovery process.

Design/methodology/approach – The principle methods of data collection were semi-structured interviews were undertaken between October 2006 and March 2007 with key agencies and individuals involved in the response and comprehensive analysis of papers, reports and articles in newspapers. The research was undertaken prior to the 4 September 2010 and 2011 earthquakes in^emr_print-file= Canterbury, New Zealand, and therefore community recovery from these events are not discussed in this paper.

Findings – Effective survival and recovery from disasters depends not just on people's abilities to cope with the physical impacts of the event, but also on how the societal environment complements and supports the complex and protracted processes of community recovery. Central to recovery is how society organises, mobilises and coordinates the diverse range of organizational and professional resources that can be called upon to assist recovery.

Originality/value – The paper offers insight into the effectiveness and benefit of incorporating of community participation in reducing anxiety and trauma in communities during earthquakes.

Keywords: Earthquakes; Disasters; Anxiety; Trauma; Community recovery; New Zealand

☆The authors would like to acknowledge the support of the Earthquake Commission and the New Zealand Foundation for Research Science and Technology in undertaking this research.

Reprinted from *Disaster Prevention and Management*
Vol. 21 No. 2, pp. 252–268 (2012). doi:10.1108/09653561211220034

Introduction

Effective survival and recovery from disasters depends not just on the physical impacts of the event but also on how the societal environment supports the complex and protracted processes of recovery (Gordon, 2004). Societal resources (e.g. emergency management, protective services) and organisational capabilities (e.g. to coordinate response activities on a large scale) are crucial in determining how well people adapt to stress, change and emergencies (Coles and Buckle, 2004). The coordination of diverse professional resources is required to deal with the physical consequences of disaster (e.g. emergency management, search and rescue, rebuilding), the societal consequences (e.g. ensuring continuity of essential physical infrastructure and services) and the personal consequences (e.g. managing the traumatic stress experienced by survivors, managing relocation and so on). Effective recovery is a function of the how well such resources can be mobilised and their actions coordinated to facilitate societal recovery.

Although New Zealand has been subject to significant natural hazard events in the past, there has been a relatively calm period over the past 70 plus years. In fact there have been no major urban disasters in recent times in New Zealand, with the last significant fatalities in the 1931 Hawkes Bay earthquake (Dowrick and Rhoades, 2005). This relatively quiet period has led to a degree of complacency and limited understanding of disaster risk. This is further compounded by the relatively frequent exposure of New Zealanders to relative minor events (e.g. floods, snow storms, earthquakes), increasing the likelihood that people normalise to this level of experience rather than anticipating what could occur in the future from larger events.

Currently, only limited research has been conducted in New Zealand to identify how communities and individuals respond to disaster events. An important issue here is accommodating community diversity. Paton *et al.* (2001) showed the heterogeneity of even small communities in a case study of the impacts of the 1995-1996 Ruapehu eruptions, and highlighted the need to manage the community recovery process in a contingent rather than a prescriptive manner. That is, community diversity (e.g. demographics, experience, community characteristics) has a significant influence on how communities confront recovery issues, their ability to use resources to meet their own needs and their ability to use their experience to develop future resilience (Paton, 2006).

Ward *et al.* (2008) described the community recovery process following the Ohura floods in 1998. Despite the multi-agency community consultation that took place and the development of a future mitigation plan for Ohura, the agreed recovery actions within the plan did not progress due to a number of interrelated factors, such as the election of a new local council and evolving community attitudes to the proposed mitigation options as the recovery progressed. Their research highlights some of the inherent problems of getting communities to participate in complex decision making in times of stress immediately after the disaster event. These findings reiterate those of Gordon (2008) and Spee (2008) who investigated the social response to the 2005 Matata debris flow and outlined the problems of community participation in complex decision making after the debris flow event.

International research on recovery highlights the importance of not only strong local government capacity, but also of a cohesive system of public, private and volunteer groups integrated into the community (Mileti, 1999; Rubin, 2000, 2009; Norman and Coles, 2002; Dynes, 2003; Coles and Buckle, 2004; Gordon, 2004; Smith and Wenger, 2006; Hayashi, 2007; Johnson, 2009; Siembieda, 2010). This research has also highlighted that effective recovery planning must consider in advance issues around community involvement, the provision of information and procedures for making recovery decisions. Mileti (1999) describes the shift in conceptualising disaster recovery from a linear phenomenon to a more interactive process between decision makers and a variety of groups and institutions, including households, businesses and the broader community.

Adaptive Capacity

When confronted with demands that differ from or exceed normal circumstances individuals and communities are compelled to adapt to this new environment to survive. This process of adaption has been conceptualised by and expanded as a multi-level resilience model (Paton, 2009) (Figure 1). The model explores a number of indicators of resilience, and the interaction (pathways) between personal factors (self-efficacy, outcome expectancy and action coping); community factors (community participation and problem articulation); and institutional factors

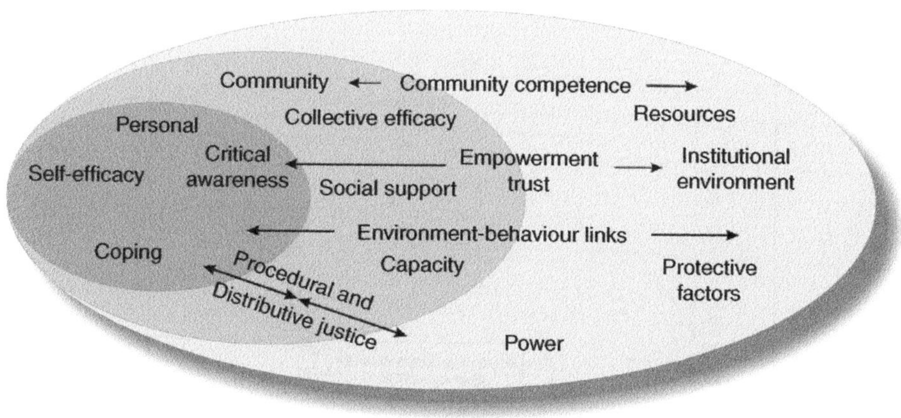

Note: Presented in Daly *et al.* (2009)
Source: Adapted from paton (2006)

Figure 1: A model of community resilience, showing selected indicators at each level (personal, community and institutional) and relationships between them (empowerment and trust). Understanding their contribution and relationship to each other is essential to improve conceptualisation of the recovery process. A key interaction identified in the process is the role of community participation in reducing anxiety and trauma in communities (Landau *et al.*, 2008; Walsh, 2007). De Terte *et al.* (2009) highlight the importance of integrating individual psychological resilience with the wider context of family, community and societal resilience. They also note the importance of community participation both before an event and afterwards (during recovery) in reducing anxiety and trauma.

This paper discusses the results of an exploratory study investigating the role of community participation in reducing anxiety and trauma in communities following two New Zealand earthquakes: the 1987 Edgecumbe and 2003 Te Anau events (Figure 2) – the two most significant earthquakes in New Zealand in 30 years prior to the data collection (in 2006 and 2007). The lack of significant events makes it important to capitalise on past events to identify lessons that can be used to

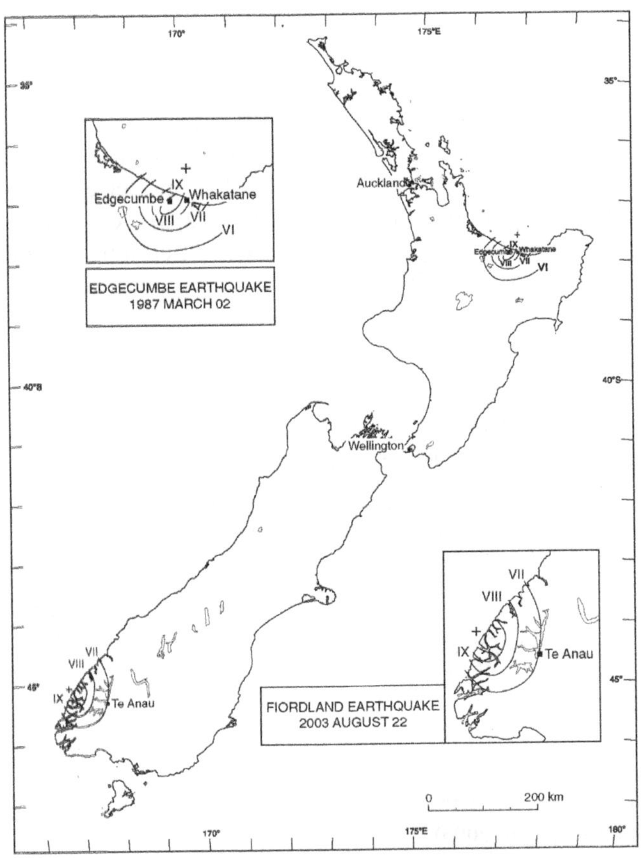

Figure 2: Location map of the 1987 Edgecumbe and 2003 Fiordland earthquakes, with modified Mercalli isoseismals

facilitate future response capability. By drawing on past events, this paper explores the effectiveness of various approaches in providing information, reducing stress and facilitating a recovery process.

Method

The principle methods of data collection for this study were semi-structured interviews were undertaken between October 2006 and March 2007 with key agencies and individuals involved in the response to the two events; and comprehensive analysis of papers, reports and articles in newspapers in print across New Zealand following both events. A systematic content analysis of the themes arising from this material was undertaken. The analysis of the response to the 2003 earthquake also draws on the results of a community survey undertaken by the research group (Leonard *et al.*, 2004). The 4 September 2010 and 22 February 2011 Canterbury earthquakes had not occurred at the time of this study, and therefore were not included in the research.

1987 Edgecumbe Earthquake

The 2 March 1987 M_L 6.1 Bay of Plenty earthquake (commonly known as the "Edgecumbe earthquake") occurred at shallow depth beneath the Rangitaiki Plains in the Bay of Plenty (Nairn and Beanland, 1989; Anderson and Webb, 1989). The main shock followed a large M_L 5.2 foreshock seven minutes previously. The earthquake caused heavy damage in Edgecumbe, Te Teko, Kawerau and Matata to both residential properties and industry. Luckily there was only one indirectly associated death and a small number of injuries. Total losses were estimated at around NZ $374 million (in 1987 dollars) making this event the most costly natural disaster in New Zealand in the last 50 years (as of 2007).

Department of Scientific and Industrial Research (DSIR) Meetings

In the weeks following the earthquake, the DSIR was approached by one of the impacted industries – the Caxton Pulp and Paper Mill to brief staff on issues related to the earthquake (New Zealand Geological Survey, 1987). From this meeting and other feedback from the community it was identified that there was considerable misinformation relating to the earthquake. Consequently, a number of public meetings were organised by the DSIR, involving staff from three divisions (New Zealand Geological Survey, Geophysics Division and Physics and Engineering Laboratory). Public meetings were held on the evenings of 14 and 15 April 1987, in Edgecumbe and Kawerau, respectively. About 450-550 people attended the Edgecumbe meeting and around 250-300 the Kawerau meeting.

The Edgecumbe meeting was held in the Edgecumbe College Hall and was chaired by the Mayor of Whakatane (Bob Byrne) with introductions by the chairman of the Edgecumbe Community Council and by the disaster relief coordinator, Muir Coup. The Kawerau meeting was held in the Kawerau Intermediate Hall and was chaired by the Mayor of Kawerau, Lynne Hartley (New Zealand Geological Survey, 1987).

The meeting held in Edgecumbe started with a civil defence (CD)-compiled video of the earthquake's effects and continued with presentations from experts. At both the Edgecumbe and Kawerau meetings, the expert presentations included information on the earthquakes themselves; regional geology, faulting and deformation; regional volcanism and relationship to the Edgecumbe earthquake; strong ground motions and structural damage; and ground damage (New Zealand Geological Survey, 1987). The nature of the information presented varied a little depending on the inferred technical understanding of the audience. Maps, diagrams and posters were also displayed during the presentations and used for post-meeting discussions. After the presentations the audience were able to ask formal questions of the presenters, with more informal questioning continuing afterwards. The main issues raised in both meetings are summarised in Table I.

In addition to the public meetings, two presentations were made by DSIR to senior pupils of Edgecumbe College on 15 April. These pupils had already had some exposure to the subject matter having experienced the earthquake themselves and being involved in prior talks and a DSIR-run field trip to the Edgecumbe Fault the week before.

A number of smaller meetings discussing aspects of the earthquake were also held between DSIR and various organisations (e.g. Caxton, a meeting in Hamilton with Ministry of Works and Development, Electricorp, Petrocorp and Tonkin and Taylor Consultancy) and other individuals. A 20-minute radio interview was undertaken with Dr Euan Smith on the local radio station Radio 1XX. Subsequent DSIR meetings were also held at later dates (e.g. in Whakatane Beacon, 1987c, d).

In an "immediate report" (New Zealand Geological Survey, 1987) produced following public meetings, Wood and Smith concluded that there was need for factual information about the earthquake, its aftershocks and related effects; and information was needed in various forms – talks, radio interviews, and news and magazine articles. Wood and Smith found that there was an overwhelming need by residents and agencies for factual information about the earthquake and its effects. This was backed up by anecdotal evidence in newspapers at the time, with one article suggesting that people left the meetings "[...] feeling better; they seemed reassured" (Whakatane Beacon, 1987b). In addition, a number of people interviewed as part of this research felt that the DSIR meetings were helpful as they were also attended by elected representatives and experts (e.g. engineers) who could provided useful information and advice for individuals which could be used to help them to solve their immediate problems and gain control back of their lives (Byrne, 2006).

Both the DSIR and anecdotal evidence back up the concept that multi-agency consultation and engagement with the community is a vital part of the recovery

Table I: Principal issues raised at three of the public meetings after the 1987 Edgecume earthquake and the 2003 Fiordland earthquake (14 April 1987 Edgecumbe College Hall; 15 April 1987, Kawerau Intermediate Hall; 28 August 2003, Te Anau)

Principal issues raised at public meetings		
14 April 1987 – Edgecumbe College Hall	15 April 1987 – Kawerau Intermediate Hall	28 August 2003 – Te Anau Holiday Inn
White Island activity[a] Earthquake and volcanic eruption predication[b] Aftershocks Ground-level changes – flooding[c] Matahina Dam performance[d] Affects on properties Advice and assistance for practical recovery tasks	White Island activity[a] Aftershocks Nature of earthquakes (including ground motions, wave directions and sounds) Unmapped faults[e] Science response limited by funds[f]	Nature of earthquakes (including ground motions, wave directions and sounds) Damage – including reasons for distribution of damage and potential future damage to buildings Aftershocks Nature of rock/ground conditions Insurance, EQC and private Counselling to address concern and stress Advice about appropriate care of children and the elderly following an earthquake Current CD and volunteering arrangements

Notes: [a]People were worried that White Island was going to become active as a consequence of the earthquake, and produce a tsunami; [b]people were concerned about the link with the earthquake and activity from the Okataina Volcanic Centre; [c]people were concerned about flooding on the Rangitaiki River due to the subsidence following the earthquake; [d]there was concern about the long-term integrity of the Matahina Dam and the potential for a dam-break flood which would affect towns downstream; [e]the Edgecumbe Fault (source of the earthquake) was unmapped, and therefore unidentified before the earthquake occurred. People were concerned about movement from other unmapped faults on the Rangitaiki Plains; [f]the Edgecumbe earthquake occurred at a time of government science funding restructuring. People were concerned about funding for on-going and future science research and response
Sources: Modified from New Zealand Geological Survey (1987); Southland District Council (2003)

process. Such consultation helps communities understand the impacts of disaster events and assists in taking steps to move towards an effective recovery.

Psychologists' Meetings

After the Edgecumbe earthquake, a number of psychology-based meetings were organised by Chris Sides, a clinical psychologist from the Eastern Bay of Plenty. These meetings were held in March almost immediately after the earthquake (from 11 to 13 March), and in the locations of Edgecumbe, Kawerau, Whakatane and Otakiri. Psychologist Tony Taylor from Victoria University, Wellington, and Lewis

Rivers from Timaru addressed the meetings (Sides, 1989). Rivers had the personal background of being impacted by severe flooding in Timaru in 1986.

The meetings were originally organised for the benefit of teachers working in the area affected by the earthquake, but were also often attended by schoolchildren and their parents (Sides, 2006). In total, five meetings were held with respect to schools, with approximately a 30-35 per cent teacher turnout in Whakatane, 70 per cent in Kawerau and 100 per cent from Edgecumbe/Te Teko (Sides, 1989). Other interested parties were also involved in speaking with the psychologists at separately requested gatherings (e.g. social welfare agencies, clergy, etc.) (Sides, 2006). Over 500 people were spoken to during the course of the meetings including 220 teachers and 70 Department of Social Welfare (DWS) workers (c. Taylor, 1987).

The purpose of the meetings was:

(1) to get (peoples') own experiences in perspective;
(2) to talk over techniques for helping others; and
(3) to enquire about the kind of personal reactions – that might arise among survivors in the near future for which they might have to prepare themselves.
    - as teachers;
    - as parents; and
    - as CD, DWS, insurance (c. Taylor, 1987; Sides, 2006).

The meetings were not lectures or presentations, but open-ended question and answer sessions where people could ask anything they liked. Questions tended to be similar from meeting to meeting and included recurring themes such as evacuation, financial issues, children's reactions, the ability of children to resume learning, teachers' ability to cope and the impact on class programmes (c. Taylor, 1987). The meetings were found to be most useful immediately after the event itself, when people had the most unanswered questions (Sides, 2006). Later on, other avenues for communication were set up (e.g. the welfare and information centre at Edgecumbe squash rooms) where people could also go and ask specific questions.

Six weeks after the Edgecumbe earthquake, two surveys were undertaken to assess the psychological status of survivors. The first survey was directed at students in Form 1 (equivalent to Year 7) and above. It sought information on students' fears, and the effect of their fears on behaviour. Understandably, those who had experienced greater impacts from the earthquake said that they were more frequently afraid of earthquakes, although not a single respondent reported that it was affecting their behaviour (Sides, 1989).

However, when interpreting this finding, it is important to draw a distinction between current and future behaviour. The significance of clarification stems from the relationship between levels of earthquake fear and anxiety and a reduction in the likelihood that people will prepare for future earthquakes (Paton *et al.*, 2005). Thus, the impact of fear may be less on immediate day-to-day behaviours, and more on preparatory behaviours, with the change in the latter significantly increasing future risk status. For example, high levels of anxiety typically reduce the likelihood that people will actively prepare (Paton *et al.*, 2005). Furthermore, because changes in people's emotional response influence how people perceive the effectiveness of hazard mitigation, it can reduce the likelihood of their willingness to engage with others to discuss hazard mitigation (Paton *et al.*, 2008a, b). Working with community members to resolve and manage anxiety is thus crucial. While normally seen as the province of clinical psychologists, the effective management of anxiety calls for a multi-agency response that also promotes community recovery and rebuilding to facilitate community self-help and build resilience for future events (Paton, in press). For example, anxiety is reduced when people develop their understanding of the relationship between hazard activity and hazard consequences and how mitigation measures can effectively reduce loss and increase personal safety (Paton *et al.*, 2006). A key issue here concerns the perceived credibility of experts to provide relevant information. This means that the effectiveness of this facet of response will be a function of the integrated action of psychologists, emergency managers and, in the case of children, teachers.

The second survey was sent to teachers who were working in areas that had experienced range of earthquake damage, from light to severe, and included the locations of Whakatane, Kawerau, Edgecumbe and the Rangitaiki Plains. As well as asking about damage, administration issues and social impact, the survey also asked specific questions relating to the effectiveness of the meetings held by the visiting psychologists. It queried the ability of those psychological services to meet peoples' emotional needs and enhance those peoples' ability to cope with the stresses and challenges of the disaster (Sides, 1989).

Teachers were allowed to discuss the survey, and work in groups or syndicates to fill out the forms together. In total, the views of 162 primary and secondary school teachers were reported on 88 survey forms (approximately a 50 per cent return rate) (Sides, 1989).

Table II replicates the findings of the teacher survey with respect to the evaluation of talks by visiting experts. In general there was a high level of agreement by teachers that the talks from visiting experts provided realistic and relevant information (87 per cent); helped get their experiences in perspective (74 per cent); helped them understand children's needs (75 per cent); and provided useful information in the handouts (97 per cent). A high percentage of respondents (88 per cent) were also glad that the meetings were arranged (Sides, 1989). However, there was a notable difference between the more impacted areas of Kawerau and Edgecumbe, and the less-affected area of Whakatane, where approximately a third of Whakatane respondents did not think that information presented was realistic and relevant.

The more impacted the teachers the more likely they were to agree that the meetings were useful. Individual comments from the samples reflect those figures with respondents from the less-impacted town of Whakatane providing more comments on the fact that the meetings were "irrelevant" or "too late", and Edgecumbe/Kawerau respondents being very pleased to have an opportunity to participate in the meetings. From participating in the meetings Edgecumbe/Kawerau respondents knew that they were not alone, that people cared, that they were normal, that they could confirm their efforts and that mutual support and reassurance was available (Sides, 1989).

Table II: Teacher evaluation of the talks by visiting experts (i.e. psychologists)

	Strongly agree (%)	Agree (%)	Disagree (%)	Strongly disagree (%)	Whole area agreeing (%)
(i) *The information presented was realistic and relevant*					
Whakatane	0	66	0	33	87
Kawerau and Edgecumbe	14	77	8	0	
(ii) *The meeting helped me get my experiences in perspective*					
Whakatane	5	15	40	45	74
Kawerau and Edgecumbe	18	72	10	0	
(iii) *The meeting helped me understand children's needs and how to meet them*					
Whakatane	0	50	0	50	75
Kawerau and Edgecumbe	21	61	14	4	
(iv) *The handouts were useful*					
Whakatane	5	80	10	5	97
Kawerau and Edgecumbe	23	77	0	0	
(v) *I'm glad these meetings were arranged*					
Whakatane	5	58	0	37	88
Kawerau and Edgecumbe	24	70	4	1	
Totals					
Whakatane	3	54	11	33	57
Kawerau and Edgecumbe	20	72	7	1	92
Overall	16	68	8	8	84

Source: Sides (1989)

Suggested improvements for the meetings included more participation by the audience to re-work their own experiences together using the local context (i.e. focusing on the context and experiences for their local situation). In addition, follow-up meetings or the formation of smaller self-supporting groups were also suggested as being beneficial (Sides, 1989).

The data from the survey undertaken by Sides (1989) provides firm evidence that undertaking communication and engagement with communities post-disaster provides a significant benefit to people in high-impact disaster areas. This is reflected in the survey of teachers who in general agreed that the meetings held by psychologists were useful, and who were interested in continuing engagement over a longer time frame into the recovery phase.

Other Methods of Engagement

In order to determine the other methods of engagement that occurred within the community after the Edgecumbe earthquake, we conducted informal interviews with ten people to ask what they remembered with respect to recovery after the earthquake and the community involvement in the process. Those interviewed were either people who were in employed positions at the time of the earthquake and were involved in the recovery process or community members themselves. The interviews were semi-structured around a series of pre-prepared questions.

As could be expected, people's memories about the earthquake had deteriorated somewhat in the 20 years since the event, but we were still able to identify some important comments about the community involvement in recovery. All comments have been verified as much as possible by comparing with written records from immediately after the earthquake. In general, the interviewees remembered a number of types of engagement that took place after the earthquake that were useful to them and that assisted with their recovery – as shown in the list below:

(1) Meetings convened by the DSIR to outline the reasons for and nature of the Edgecumbe earthquake and likelihood of any future events. These meetings occurred immediately after the earthquake as well as many months later.
(2) Meetings held by psychologists, which focused on teachers in particular. These meetings were held to outline the expected psychological impacts of the earthquake and to discuss coping mechanisms.
(3) Informal meetings held by more "grass-roots" community groups (e.g. the weekly women's support group held at the Presbyterian church in Edgecumbe).
(4) Meetings held at the welfare/information and recovery centres involving people from the CD unit, disaster welfare committee, other welfare agencies, housing committee, engineering committee, Maori affairs and education sector. Many of these meetings were internal rather than "public meeting" based. However, there was also some interaction between the different recovery committees and other external organisations. For example, on request, a team from the recovery centre at Edgecumbe went across to talk to a meeting of workers at the Edgecumbe dairy factory (Bay Milk Products) in a question and answer/ discussion-type forum (Lorraine, 2006). People were also able to come into the welfare/information and recovery centres to talk with people and organisations stationed there about welfare and recovery issues.
(5) Federated Farmers initiated some meetings for their members. For example, a Federated Farmers public panel discussion was held towards the end of March 1987 which was attended by representatives from the Department of Social Welfare, the Bay of Plenty Catchment Commission, Rangitaiki Drainage Board, Bay of Plenty Electric Power Board, Bay Milk Products, Whakatane District Council and Farmers Mutual Insurance (Whakatane Beacon, 1987a) as well as the public.
(6) Some meetings were held with respect to restoration work (e.g. community meetings which discussed the rebuilding of the Edgecumbe community hall).
(7) After the earthquake many residents from Te Teko were evacuated to Onepu Marae where they stayed there for several days. Many found the environment a supportive and comforting place, and found it difficult to return home to their damaged homes. As well as the support and engagement which existed within the

Marae environment, there was also external engagement with other agencies (e.g. the Mayor of Whakatane, Bob Byrne, came and spoke to people staying on the Marae with respect to returning home and beginning the recovery process).

2003 Te Anau Earthquake

The 21 August 2003 M_w 7.2 Fiordland earthquake was centred ~10 km northwest of Secretary Island at a depth of ~20 km (Reyners *et al.*, 2003). It was New Zealand's largest shallow earthquake in the last 35 years and was felt strongly over much of Otago and Southland. Damage was relatively minor although spectacular, with items thrown from shelves in Te Anau and the cracking of many concrete structures (Hancox *et al.*, 2003; Forsyth and Johnston, 2005). Damage to residential properties in Te Anau is reported by Leonard *et al.* (2004), based on responses from a community survey.

Following the earthquake, the Southland District Council held a public meeting on the evening of 28 August 2003 in the Te Anau community hall (Southland District Council, 2003). The public response to the meeting exceeded the initial expectations of the organisers with in excess of 300 people attending. Presenters from several agencies (The Earthquake Commission (EQC), GNS Science, Department of Conservation (DoC) and Civil Defence Emergency Management) discussed issues around the earthquake, including the cause, impacts and aspects of the local and central government responses (Table II). The mayor at the time, Frana Cardno, chaired the meeting.

Many of people's concerns were primarily addressed during the talks themselves, as a variety of topics were touched upon by the speakers including:

- the nature of plate tectonics around the world and within New Zealand;
- an explanation of earthquake magnitude and intensity;
- the origin of the Fiordland earthquake and its relationship to subduction zone earthquakes and the Alpine Fault;
- comparisons of the Fiordland earthquake with past earthquakes in the same area;
- earthquake risk in Fiordland compared with other areas of New Zealand (for context);
- insurance, including the role of EQC and private insurance companies, who and what is covered by insurance, excess issues and the claim process; and
- what people can do to reduce their risk and increase their preparedness for future earthquakes at an individual and business level.

Following each of the talks, audience members were able to ask questions of the speakers. The public asked the GNS Science speaker a number of questions about the nature of earthquakes including what kind of ground motions an earthquake produces, how earthquake waves worked and what influence earthquakes had on different ground conditions. They were also interested in finding out what potential future earthquake damage might occur for buildings (both inside and out). Aftershocks were asked about several times, as was a question about whether residents would experience any bigger earthquakes.

A few questions were asked of the EQC representative about insurance issues including the role of the EQC and its relationship to private insurance, what items the EQC cover and the length of the claim period. The representative from the Ministry for Civil Defence and Emergency Management fielded questions about current CD/volunteering arrangements, issues relating to the care of children and the elderly after an earthquake, and counselling opportunities.

Agencies were able to use the public meeting as an opportunity to present initial information and then direct the audience to areas where they could find further details. For example, EQC were able to give advice on what number to call to make contact, and advised the public that they would also be receiving more information about the claims process in the mail and through the assessors. The Ministry for Civil Defence and Emergency Management alerted the audience to the fact that brochures on how to prepare for disasters were available, and that they could collect these from the Te Anau public library or from their CD representative. GNS Science also handed out earthquake "felt reports" that people could take home, fill out (describing the effects of the earthquake at their location), and send back to GNS Science.

At the end of the meeting the mayor summed up the feelings of many attending the event by stating "I guess we all need to talk about it [the Fiordland earthquake] and it's important that we can get together and hear people such as yourselves. I know personally after hearing what you have to say, Dr Warwick Smith [from GNS Science], that I can relax a little, because when you read the conflicting newspaper reports, and some warning us that any day we are going to get the big one, we were sort of starting to get a bit nervous. So it was really good to hear your explanation" (Southland District Council, 2003).

In addition to anecdotal evidence, Leonard *et al.* (2004) notes the importance of the Te Anau public meeting in their community survey, with 33 per cent of residents surveyed reporting they attended the meeting (see list on p. 260). The survey also found that around 70 per cent of those who did not attend knew someone who attended. Overall, the community rated the meeting as "very useful" (Table III).

Table III: Attendance at the public meeting, held by Southland District Council (2003) with speakers from EQC, GNS, DoC and CD , one week after the earthquake (on Thursday, 28 August)

% (*n* = 156)	All
Yes I attended the meeting	32.7
I didn't attend but yes I know someone who did attend the meeting	46.2
No, I don't know anyone who attended	21.2

Source: Data from Leonard *et al.* (2004)

The study found that public meetings are clearly an effective and well received a way of communicating information to those both with and without damage or loss.

Discussion

The lack of empirical data and theoretically based research on disaster recovery in New Zealand is due to both the lack of research endeavour and the absence of significant disasters in the recent times. Much of the material that is available is in the form of reports describing and/or reviewing the recovery aspects of specific New Zealand events have been published (e.g. Baines, 1984 – Southland floods (1984); Bell, 1986 – Aorangi floods (1986); Davy, 1992 – Edgecumbe earthquake (1987); Luketina, 1986 – Southland floods (1984); Forsyth *et al.*, 2004 and Becker and Richardson, 2000 – Queenstown floods (1999); and Walton *et al.*, 2004 – Weather Bomb floods (2002)). However, as has been shown in this paper, material such as this can contribute to an improved understanding of disaster recovery and input into the development of a more informed and evidence-based disaster recovery policy and practice in New Zealand.

The disaster recovery environment presents many challenges for government and non-government agencies, businesses, community groups and individuals. As has been shown in the literature and described in this paper there are many competing demands, not only for physical resources but also for information, support and participation in the recovery process and usually an unprecedented requirement for interagency collaboration with each other and with affected communities. The need for effective community participation and consultation in recovery is now widely acknowledged in current New Zealand recovery planning (Ministry of Civil Defence and Emergency Management (MCDEM), 2005; Norman, 2006). The importance of participation and consultation relates to both its role in helping people understand and make meaning of a recent experience and providing a collective forum for developing future community resilience. Experiences documented in both the Edgecumbe and Te Anau examples illustrate how community participation can assist in recovery. Communication and information provision can assist with helping people understand what has happened, how the recovery process works and what actions people need to take to recover. Community participation allows an outlet for people to articulate and solve problems, empowers them to take action, and as a result assists in reducing anxiety and trauma and helps build resilience to cope with future events.

However, there are still significant gaps in our current arrangements. Due to the need for multiple agencies to be involved, and the varying needs of the affected community during recovery, there is a strong case for the integration, where possible, of the efforts of a diverse range of agencies. Many agencies may have had only limited interaction with one another prior to the event. The multi-agency public meeting following 2003 Te Anau earthquake illustrated usefulness of a coordinated public meeting to support the community in a number of ways. Provision of scientific information about the event was identified as important by many attendees at both 1987 and 2003 meetings to help them understand what had happened and what to expect in the future. The public meetings also allowed the emergency management and other welfare agencies an opportunity to inform the public on welfare arrangements, on other support available and importantly, to seek feedback from the affected population. The EQC used the meeting at Te Anau to explain and answer questions related to issues on insurance and the claims process (Table IV).

Despite the effectiveness of the meetings none of the agencies involved had any formal connections prior to the event and arrangements were made in an ad hoc manner. Lack of prior planning for multidisciplinary and multi-agency interactions can limit the effectiveness of the response and recovery. In the early stages of the 1995 Ruapehu eruptions in New Zealand, the lack of prior arrangements was seen as a significant issue (Paton *et al.*, 1998a, b, 1999; Johnston *et al.*, 2000).

The benefit of prior communication and planning amongst agencies that must cooperate in an emergency has been commonly seen in relation to the effectiveness of hazard warnings (e.g. summarised in Leonard *et al.*, 2008). This was recently highlighted during the response to a dam-break flood at Mt Adams, West Coast, New Zealand in 1999 when communication difficulties and misunderstanding between the science advisors and the emergency managers led to delays in warning at-risk communities (Becker *et al.*, 2007). In contrast, the benefits of prior planning for multidisciplinary and multi-agency warning response were seen during the 18 March 2007 Ruapehu lahar. More than a dozen agencies were required to work together in response to an impending lahar, many with their own internal multiple boundaries of authority (Galley *et al.*, 2004; Keys and Green, 2008). An effective and coordinated response to the event was observed by our research team (Becker *et al.*, 2008). This was achieved through clearly documented, shared and agreed planning; cooperation and communication at regular planning meetings and especially during exercises; and education through the meetings, exercises, documentation and media coverage. A key element was a concerted and sustained team approach across a wide range of agencies. This was aided by political, media and

Table IV: Usefulness of the public meeting (from 1 = very useful to 5 = not at all useful)

%	All	Of those answering the following to "any damage/loss at all" in question 1 Yes (%)	No (%)
Very useful	33.3	30.3	39.4
	33.3	33.3	33.3
	23.2	25.8	18.2
	7.1	7.6	6.1
Not at all useful	3.0	3.0	3.0
N	99	66	33

Source: Data from Leonard *et al.* (2004)

public interest in averting a disaster, and the relative ease of forecasting the timing of occurrence of the event as the lake filled.

Although public meetings provide an effective vehicle for engaging the community in a post-disaster situation it must also be remembered that there are several limitations to the process and other approaches need to be considered. The work undertaken by Sides (1989) and colleagues after the Edgecumbe earthquake highlights this fact, with teachers in the high-impact areas finding the initial meetings held very useful, but having a desire to continue with the psychological support in a more participatory and engaging fashion.

The work by Ward *et al.* (2008), Gordon (2008) and Spee (2008) highlights caution in making recovery decisions when a community is under stress. There are problems of getting communities to participate in complex decision making in times of stress immediately after a disaster event. This may be alleviated by ensuring that communities are participating in similar participatory decision-making processes prior to an event, so that the process and structure is familiar to them, thus putting them in a more recognisable and less stressful environment after a disaster.

In summary, due to our location on an active tectonic plate boundary and the associated high seismic risk it is only a matter of time before New Zealanders are again impacted by a major damaging earthquake. The relatively calm period over the past 70 plus years (prior to September 2010), with no major urban earthquakes in recent times had led to a degree of complacency and limited understanding of earthquake risk in many sectors on our society. This was further compounded by the relatively frequent exposure to relative minor earthquakes, increasing the likelihood that people normalise to this level of experience. New Zealand would benefit from strengthening the capability and capacity to effectively recover from such events by improved models of the recovery process and enhanced arrangements to facilitate multi-agency coordination. Future research will follow community recovery following the 2010 and 2011 Canterbury earthquakes to further investigate the presence and benefits of community meetings and effectiveness of community participation in the recovery process.

References

Anderson, H. and Webb, T. (1989), "The rupture of the Edgecumbe earthquake", *New Zealand Journal of Geology and Geophysics*, Vol. 32 No. 1, pp. 43–52.

Baines, R.T. (1984), "Southland floods – January 1984", Disaster recovery final report, New Zealand Police Library, Wellington.

Becker, J., Johnston, D., Paton, D., Hancox, G., Davies, T., McSaveney, T. and Manville, V. (2007), "Response to landslide dam failure emergencies: issues resulting from the October 1999 Mount Adams landslide and dam-break flood in the Poerua River", Westland, New Zealand", *Natural Hazards Review*, Vol. 8 No. 2, pp. 35–42.

Becker, J., Manville, V., Leonard, G. and Saunders, W. (2008), "Managing lahars the New Zealand way: a case study from Mount Ruapehu volcano", *Natural Hazards Observer*, Vol. XXXII No. 5, pp. 4–6.

Becker, J. and Richardson, V. (2000), "The November 1999 Queenstown floods and Frankton landslide", Science Report No. 2000/12, Institute of Geological and Nuclear Sciences, Lower Hutt, p. 24.

Bell, J. (1986), "Aorangi disaster recovery coordination report", unpublished report, New Zealand Police Library, Wellington.

Byrne, B. (2006), Former Mayor of Whakatane at the time of the Edgecumbe Earthquake, personal communication, 8 December.

Coles, E. and Buckle, P. (2004), "Developing community resilience as a foundation for effective disaster recovery", *The Australian Journal of Emergency Management*, Vol. 19 No. 4, pp. 6–15.

Daly, M., Becker, J., Parkes, B., Johnston, D. and Paton, D. (2009), "Defining and measuring community resilience to natural disasters: a case study", *Tephra*, Vol. 22 (July), pp. 15–20.

Davy, J.L. (1992), "The Edgecumbe earthquake: impacts, responses, lessons learnt", unpublished report, New Zealand Police Library, Wellington.

de Terte, I., Becker, J. and Stephens, C. (2009), "An integrated model for understanding and developing resilience in face of adverse events", *Journal of Pacific Rim Psychology*, Vol. 3 No. 1, pp. 20–6.

Dowrick, D.J. and Rhoades, D.A. (2005), "Risk of casualties in New Zealand earthquakes", *Bulletin of the New Zealand Society for Earthquake Engineering*, Vol. 38 No. 4, pp. 185–214.

Dynes, R. (2003), "Finding order in disorder: continuities in the 9-11 response", *International Journal of Mass Emergencies and Disaster*, Vol. 21 No. 3, pp. 9–23.

Forsyth, J., Clark, E., Becker, J. and Kerr, J. (2004), "Queenstown floods revisited: the planning response to the 1999 Queenstown floods: changes made to planning for natural hazards in Queenstown", Science Report No. 2004/07, Institute of Geological and Nuclear Sciences, Lower Hutt, p. 30.

Forsyth, J. and Johnston, D. (2005), "Survey of Te Anau and Manapouri businesses following the 2003 Fiordland earthquake", Science Report No. 2005/13, Institute of Geological and Nuclear Sciences, Lower Hutt, p. 17.

Galley, I., Leonard, G., Johnston, D., Balm, R. and Paton, D. (2004), "The Ruapehu lahar emergency response plan development process: an analysis", *Australasian Journal of Disaster and Trauma Studies*, Vol. 2004-1, pp. 1–33.

Gordon, R. (2004), "The social system as site of disaster impact and resource for recovery", *Australian Journal of Emergency Management*, Vol. 19 No. 4, pp. 16–22.

Gordon, R. (2008), "A 'Social Biopsy' of social process and personal responses in recovery from natural disaster", Report No. 2008/09, GNS Science, Lower Hutt, p. 14.

Hancox, G., Cox, S., Turnbull, I.M. and Crozier, M.J. (2003), "Reconnaissance studies of landslides and other ground damage caused by the MW7.2 Fiordland earthquake of 22 August 2003", Science Report No. 2003/30, Institute of Geological and Nuclear Sciences, Lower Hutt, p. 32.

Hayashi, H. (2007), "Long-term recovery from recent disasters in Japan and the United States", *Journal of Disaster Research*, Vol. 2 No. 6, pp. 413–18.

Johnston, D.M., Houghton, B.F., Neall, V.E., Ronan, K.R. and Paton, D. (2000), "Impacts of the 1945 and 1995-1996 Ruapehu eruptions, New Zealand: an example of increasing societal vulnerability", *Geological Society of America Bulletin*, Vol. 112, pp. 720–9.

Johnson, L. (2009), "Developing a management framework for local disaster recovery: a study of the US disaster recovery management system and the management processes and outcomes of disaster recovery in 3 US cities", PhD dissertation, Department of Informatics, Kyoto University, Kyoto.

Keys, H.J.R. and Green, P.M. (2008), "Ruapehu lahar New Zealand 18 March 2007: lessons for hazard assessment and risk mitigation 1995-2007", *Journal of Disaster Research*, Vol. 3, pp. 284–96.

Landau, J., Mittal, M. and Wieling, E. (2008), "Linking human systems: strengthening individuals, families and communities in the wake of mass trauma", *Journal of Marital and Family Therapy*, Vol. 34 No. 2, pp. 193–209.

Leonard, G.S., Johnston, D.M. and Paton, D. (2004), "Analysis of Te Anau residents' impacts, awareness and preparedness following the 2003 Fiordland earthquake", Science Report No. 2004/37, Institute of Geological and Nuclear Sciences Limited, Lower Hutt, p. 57.

Leonard, G.S., Johnston, D.M., Paton, D., Christianson, A., Becker, J. and Keys, H.J.R. (2008), "Developing effective warning systems: ongoing research at Ruapehu volcano, New Zealand", *Journal of Volcanology and Geothermal Research*, Vol. 172 Nos 3-4, pp. 199–215.

Lorraine, B. (2006), Former Recovery Coordinator for the Edgecumbe Earthquake, personal communication, 8 December.

Luketina, F. (1986), "The 1984 Southland floods", Research Report Series No. 4, Research Section, Department of Social Welfare, Wellington.

Mileti, D. (1999), *Disasters by Design: A Reassessment of Natural Hazards in the United States*, Joseph Henry Press, Washington, DC, 351pp.

Ministry of Civil Defence and Emergency Management (MCDEM) (2005), *Focus on Recovery: A Holistic Framework for Recovery in New Zealand (IS5/05)*, MCDEM.

Nairn, I.A. and Beanland, S. (1989), "Geological setting of the 1987 Edgecumbe earthquake, New Zealand", *New Zealand Journal of Geology and Geophysics*, Vol. 32 No. 1, pp. 1–14.

New Zealand Geological Survey (1987), "Immediate report: Edgecumbe earthquake – DSIR presentations", EDS IR 87/06, File 843/14, New Zealand Geological Survey, Lower Hutt.

Norman, S. (2006), "New Zealand's holistic framework for disaster recovery", *The Australian Journal of Emergency Management*, Vol. 21 No. 4, pp. 16–9.

Norman, S. and Coles, E. (2002), "Order out of chaos? A critical review of the role of central regional and local government in London", *International Journal of Mass Emergencies and Disaster*, Vol. 20 No. 3, pp. 347–67.

Paton, D. (2006), "Disaster resilience: integrating individual, community, institutional and environmental perspectives", in Paton, D. and Johnston, D. (Eds), *Disaster Resilience: An Integrated Approach*, Charles C. Thomas, Springfield, IL, pp. 306–19.

Paton, D. (2009), "Community sustainability and natural hazard resilience: all-hazard and cross-cultural issues in disaster resilience", *The International Journal of Environmental, Cultural, Economic & Social Sustainability*, Vol. 5 No. 1, pp. 345–56.

Paton, D. (in press), "Psychological rehabilitation plans for disaster survivors", *Kaohsiung Journal of Medical Sciences*, Vol. 27.

Paton, D., Bürgelt, P.T. and Prior, T. (2008a), "Living with bushfire risk: social and environmental influences on preparedness", *Australian Journal of Emergency Management*, Vol. 23 No. 3, pp. 41–8.

Paton, D., Johnston, D. and Houghton, B. (1998a), "Organisational response to a volcanic eruption", *Disaster Prevention & Management*, Vol. 7 No. 1, pp. 5–13.

Paton, D., Johnston, D., Houghton, B., Flin, R., Ronan, K. and Scott, B. (1999), "Managing natural hazard consequences: planning for information management and decision making", *Journal of the American Society of Professional Emergency Planners*, Vol. 6 pp. 37–48.

Paton, D., Johnston, D., Houghton, B. and Smith, L. (1998b), "Managing the effects of a volcanic eruption: psychological perspectives on integrated emergency management", *Journal of the American Society of Professional Emergency Planners*, Vol. 5, pp. 59–69.

Paton, D., McClure, J. and Bürgelt, P.T. (2006), "Natural hazard resilience: the role of individual and household preparedness", in Paton, D. and Johnston, D. (Eds), *Disaster Resilience: An Integrated Approach*, Charles C. Thomas, Springfield, IL, pp. 105–27.

Paton, D., Millar, M. and Johnston, D. (2001), "Community resilience to volcanic hazard consequences", *Natural Hazards*, Vol. 24 No. 2, pp. 157–69.

Paton, D., Smith, L.M., Daly, M. and Johnston, D.M. (2008b), "Risk perception and volcanic hazard mitigation: individual and social perspectives", *Journal of Volcanology and Geothermal Research*, Vol. 172 Nos 3-4, pp. 179–88.

Paton, D., Smith, L.M. and Johnston, D. (2005), "When good intentions turn bad: promoting natural hazard preparedness", *Australian Journal of Emergency Management*, Vol. 20 No. 1, pp. 25–30.

Reyners, M., McGinty, P., Cox, S., Turnbull, I., O'Neill, T., Gledhill, K., Hancox, G., Beavan, J., Matheson, D., McVerry, G., Cousins, J., Zhao, J., Cowan, H., Caldwell, G. and Bennie, S. and the GeoNet Team (2003), "The Mw7 Fiordland earthquake of August 2003: background and preliminary results", *Bulletin of the New Zealand Society for Earthquake Engineering*, Vol. 36, pp. 233–48.

Rubin, C. (2000), "Emergency management in the 21st century: coping with Bill Gates, Osama bin-Laden and Hurricane Mitch", Working Paper No. 99, Natural Hazards Research Centre, University of Colorado, Boulder, CO.

Rubin, C.B. (2009), "Long-term recovery from disasters: the neglected component of emergency management", *Journal of Homeland Security and Emergency Management*, Vol. 6 No. 1, doi: 10.2202/1547-7355.1616

Sides, C. (1989), "The impact of the Edgecumbe earthquake on children and their teachers", paper presented at the 1989 World Congress of the World Federation for Mental Health, Auckland, 21-25 August.

Sides, C. (2006), Clinical Psychologist, personal communication, 24 December.

Siembieda, W. (2010), "Special issue on 'Building Local Capacity for Long-term Disaster Resilience' part 2 toward an enhanced concept of disaster resilience: a commentary on behalf of the editorial committee", *Journal of Disaster Research*, Vol. 5 No. 5, pp. 487–93.

Smith, G.P. and Wenger, D. (2006), "Sustainable disaster recovery: operationalizing an existing agenda", in Rodriguez, H., Quarentelli, E.L. and Dynes, R. (Eds), *Handbook of Disaster Research*, Springer, New York, NY, pp. 234–57.

Southland District Council (2003), "Earthquakes and aftershocks, the Fiordland earthquake", video of public meeting, The holiday Inn, Te Anau, 28 August released by Southland District Council, Invercargill, September.

Spee, K. (2008), "Community recovery after the 2005 Matata disaster: long-term psychological and social impacts", Report No. 2008/12, GNS Science, Lower Hutt, p. 40.

Taylor, T. (1987), *The Edgecumbe Earthquake*, unpublished, Taylor T. Report p.1.

Walsh, F. (2007), "Traumatic loss and major disasters: strengthening family and community resilience family process", Vol. 46 No. 2, pp. 207–27.

Walton, M., Johnston, D., Leonard, G., Gray, W., Bell, R. and Paton, D. (2004), "The Waikato Weather Bomb: understanding the impact", Economic research report, New Zealand Institute, Wellington, p. 137.

Ward, J., Becker, J. and Johnston, D. (2008), "Community participation in recovery planning – a case study from the 1998 Ohura flood", Report No. 2008/22, GNS Science, Lower Hutt, p. 23.

Whakatane Beacon (1987a), "Guidance for residents", Whakatane Beacon, 20 March.
Whakatane Beacon (1987b), "Earthquake discussions reassuring", Whakatane Beacon, 22 April.
Whakatane Beacon (1987c), "Finding out about the quakes", Whakatane Beacon, 12 May.
Whakatane Beacon (1987d), "Meeting had to move", Whakatane Beacon, 26 May.

Further Reading

Saunders, W., Becker, J. and Johnston, D. (2005), "Civil defence emergency management after the February 2004 Manawatu-Wanganui flood event: a focus on recovery", Science Report No. 2005, Institute of Geological and Nuclear Sciences, Lower Hutt, p. 15.

Operationalizing "Resilience" for Disaster Risk Reduction in Mountainous Nepal ☆

Karen I. Sudmeier, Michel Jaboyedoff and Stephanie Jaquet

Abstract

Purpose – The purpose of this paper is to describe empirical research intended to fill the perceived gap in practical guidance methodologies for assessing resilience.

Design/methodology/approach – To do so, an interdisciplinary team of researchers studied landslide risk in four different communities of Central and Eastern Nepal using a case study approach. Two case studies on flood-affected communities were developed for comparison sake in more urban areas. Methods combined qualitative participatory approaches to develop indicators of resilience as well as a household survey and focus group discussions for collecting data on the indicators.

Findings – What the research results demonstrate is a relatively straightforward and simple means for obtaining data on the state of a community's resilience as a relatively simple "snapshot" of resilience at one period in time, assuming that resilience is an outcome that can be improved over time with the "right" set of interventions.

Research limitations/implications – The main limitation of this research is that it focussed mainly on outcome indicators; although some process indicators of resilience were identified (i.e. grazing management practices, skills training, organizational skills and learning through education), these need to be more comprehensive and validated through community consultations.

☆This research was entirely support by a grant from the Swiss National Science Foundation (grant no. 26083591) during the period 2009-2011, for which we are extremely grateful. Many thanks to Dr J.C. Gaillard and Ms. Sushma Shrestha University of Auckland, New Zealand for valuable inputs during the research period. Dr Ilan Kelman (CICERO, Norway), Christopher Belperron (Mission East, Nepal) Manuela Fernandez (University of Lausanne) and Dr Carolina Garcia, Disaster Risk Management Specialist, Colombia who provided very useful comments to a previous draft of this manuscript. Many thanks also to colleagues Jerome Dubois, Alain Breguet, University of Lausanne, Gopi Krishna Basyal, National Society for Earthquake Technology, Nepal, Sanjaya Devkota, FEED International Ltd, Nepal, Sundar Sharma, Department of Water Induced Disaster Prevention, Nepal.

Reprinted from *Disaster Prevention and Management*
Vol. 22 No. 4, pp. 366–377 (2013). doi:10.1108/DPM-02-2013-0028

Originality/value – The paper provided data and a straightforward methodology for measuring resilience and has thus contributed to the literature on this topic, while providing practical ideas for future research on resilience building measures and indicators.

Keywords: Resilience; Disasters; Nepal; Landslides

1. Introduction: Addressing an Acute Policy-research Gap

This paper is the result of five years of assessing and measuring resilience, vulnerability and risk in six communities of various sizes and ethnic compositions affected by landslides and flooding throughout Central and Eastern Nepal. The concept of resilience is at the heart of a debate on the next generation of international development policies and the extent to which disaster risk reduction (DRR), humanitarian aid and poverty alleviation are converging toward a more integrated and systematic approach (Grünewald and Warner, 2012). Proponents believe that resilience can be a binding force, while critics point out the dangers of resilience as a magic bullet that detracts donors and government attention away from addressing root causes of risk, or prevention, and rather focusses on more effective recovery (Grünewald and Warner, 2012; Cannon and Müller-Mahn, 2010; Lewis and Kelman, 2010; Reghezza-Zitt *et al.*, 2012; Gaillard *et al.*, 2010). As a result, there is a growing trend for resilience to be considered as "bouncing forward" (Manyena *et al.*, 2011), which postulates that resilience can only take place if vulnerabilities are addressed and people are better off after a shock than before one. Consequently, this paper considers resilience to be: the ability of a system, organization, community, household or individual to change in a positive manner, when faced with adversity.

This paper takes a pragmatic approach to resilience, as a concept that is being mainstreamed – for better or for worse – into international development, DRR and humanitarian discourses and one that can be potentially useful if it is conceived as a systems approach to DRR. Resilience also represents one of the largest policy-research gaps with millions of dollars in public funding currently spent on resilience building, without the means to adequately evaluate or monitor what resilience means in practice. The purpose of this paper is therefore to contribute to the debate on resilience by proposing an operational framework at the community scale, for which very little empirical research exists, developed for landslide-affected communities in mountain areas of Nepal, but which could be used in other geographic contexts as well.

2. Toward an Operational Framework for Assessing Resilience

While recognizing the pitfalls in measuring qualitative and dynamic processes and outcomes, this paper focusses on an operational approach to resilience to address the large research gap on this topic. According to Cutter *et al.* (2008), "While there is some consensus in the literature regarding the factors that produce hazards vulnerability and those that enhance community resilience to disasters, there is less agreement on how to measure them. While we conceptually or sometimes intuitively understand vulnerability and resilience, the devil is always in the details, and in this instance, the devil is measurement" (Cutter *et al.*, 2008, p. 7). If we are to believe that resilience is a useful concept for which millions of dollars are being invested, then we should also be able to work out the details.

Based on a literature review, a measure of resilience can be useful to NGOs and policy makers if it responds to a number of defined criteria:

- establish clear boundaries for what resilience means and if possible, defined by the target population;
- analyze underlying risk factors and how resilience building measures reduce risks;
- consider that resilience is context specific to ensure that any measures are relevant to the target audience;
- consider that resilience is threat specific as a population might be resilient to one threat but not another; and
- consider both outcome and process indicators for resilience.

Beyond engineering (Bruneau *et al.*, 2003; Tierney and Bruneau, 2007), economic (Rose, 2007) and organizational metrics of resilience (Kendra and Wachetendorf, 2003; Robert *et al.*, 2010), there are few attempts at quantifying resilience and vulnerability, although research is rapidly expanding in this field. Most of the above measures of resilience indicate some type of efficiency in anticipating and responding effectively, efficiently and equitably to disturbance.

The most well-known metrics of social vulnerability developed at the county level for all 50 US states is the Social Vulnerability Index (SoVI) 2006-2010 (Cutter *et al.*, 2003; Cutter and Finch, 2008), based on "a broad set of indicators to explore differences in social vulnerability among places using census geography (counties, census tracts, census block groups)" (Cutter *et al.*, 2008, p. 10). SoVI provides a useful visual illustration of differences between the states and counties for preparedness and response and highlights areas where differences in underlying social vulnerabilities are the greatest. Seven indicators explain 72 percent of the variance in the data: race and class; wealth; elderly residents; Hispanic ethnicity; special needs individuals; Native American ethnicity; and service industry employment (Cutter *et al.*, 2008). Although a very useful index, one criticism of SOVI is that it focusses on vulnerability indicators, not capacities, thus assuming that vulnerability is the flipside of resilience, which is not necessarily the case. Another set of indicators of community resilience, "The top twenty" attributes of disaster resilient communities were developed by Twigg (2009) and tested by NGOs. One of the few community-based empirical assessments of resilience, Kafle (2011) proposes a useful system for measuring both outcome and process indicators. Others that influenced this work included the "Community based disaster risk index" (Bollin and Hidajat, 2006), "Quantifying Resilience and

Vulnerability" (The Risk to Resilience Team, 2009) and the Sustainable Livelihoods Framework (DFID, 1997; Mayunga, 2007) upon which the conceptual framework of this work is based.

The following section describes field work conducted in Nepal in 2008-2010 that attempted to unpack resilience as well as develop a monitoring and evaluation framework for operationalizing the concept.

3. Assessing Resilience – Case Studies from Nepal

3.1 Nepal Context

Nepal is considered a hotspot for disasters and poverty and a natural place for studying landslides (Harmeling, 2010; MoHA, 2009). With a population of 23 million, it is also one of the world's poorest countries, ranking 138th out of 169 countries in the UNDP, 2009 Human Development Index (UNDP, 2009). According to recent data, the country has however made recent strides in poverty alleviation, an astonishing drop by 18 points from 31 to 13 percent under the poverty limit, largely due to the high amounts of remittances, now received by 55.8 percent of all households (CBS, 2011; Khanal, 2011). Another important point marking Nepalese society is its caste system, which was officially abolished in 1962 but continues to reinforce inequalities in access to resources, land tenure and education (Bista, 2004). Over 80 percent of Nepal can be considered mountainous or hilly while the remaining 20 percent lies in the northern Ganga Basin plains, or the Terai (Figure 1). The bulk of the population in 2008 (83 percent) was considered rural and 48.7 percent of

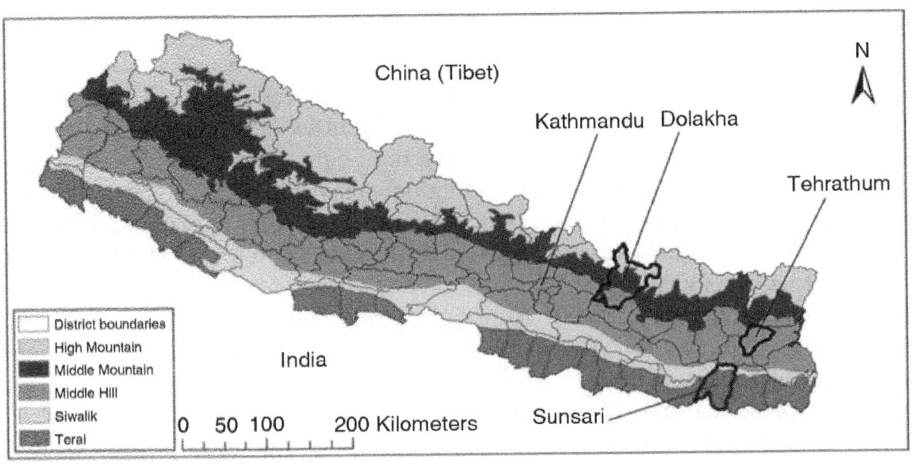

Notes: Study areas in three districts (Dolakha, Tehrathum and Sunsari) are outlined as note, please refer given caption

Figure 1: Physiographic map of Nepal, based on ICIMOD, Menris data 2009

the population lived in the Terai (CBS, 2009) with a continuing population trend of migration from the mountains and hills to the Terai, urban areas and foreign destinations.

As our focus was mainly on landslide affected communities, of the six case studies, four were landslide-affected villages and two were from flood-prone areas in three districts: Tehrathum, Sunsari and Dolakha. The sites were selected to represent a variety of socio-economic compositions from higher social status to illiterate villages; villages with a seemingly high social cohesion; some with conflicts; others, highly affected by out-migration of men for long periods of time.

3.2 *Study Methods*

The methodology of this study combined "bottom-up" qualitative and quantitative participatory approaches with "top-down" quantitative geological assessments, remote sensing and a geographic information system (GIS) database with the goal of triangulating several research approaches (Baxter and Eyles, 1997). The study used a case study approach, combining well-tested participatory qualitative methodologies, typically used in vulnerability and capacity analyses, such as semi-structured interviews with "key informants," transect walks, participatory risk and social resource mapping to understand relations between groups, coping strategies, identify stakeholders, vulnerable households and dangerous areas (Anderson and Woodrow, 1998; Chambers, 1994; Estrella *et al.*, 2000; Kafle and Murshed, 2004; Vajjhala, 2005) (Plate 1).

Plate 1: Social resources mapping, Khariswara village, Dolakha District, Nepal, 2010

The scale of the study is at the community and household level. Field sites were selected to represent high landslide risk situations, yet different land use histories and ethnic compositions. Finally, 168 household surveys were conducted, constituting approximately 50 percent of each village or neighborhood, based on purposeful sampling (Baxter and Eyles, 1997) of households to ensure that households within a perimeter of 100 meters from the landslides or flood-affected zones were questioned. Each household surveyed was geo-referenced using a Geographic Positioning System and located on a high-resolution satellite image from which risk maps were created. Results from the household survey were tabulated in excel tables and open-ended questions were analyzed manually.

3.3 Measuring Resilience

Resilience indicators were developed based on a literature review (Twigg, 2009; Cutter *et al.*, 2008), three years of field observations 2008-2010 and testing of indicators with local populations and local experts. The goal was to develop a methodology for developing locally relevant indicators that could be used for self-monitoring of resilience. Based on this experience, the indicators are relevant for describing resilience within the context of the Middle Hills of Nepal. There are 50 indicators of resilience, modified from the five capitals developed by the sustainable livelihoods approach (Natural, Economic, Social, Human and Physical) (Table I) and validated through community consultations. Values for each indicator were obtained from the household survey questionnaires. Each indicator received a score from 0 to 3, zero being low resilience to three high resilience, consistent with the approach proposed by Kafle (2011). Each of the five resource categories has ten indicators, carrying equal weight, a choice that was made through the participatory process. As the indicator development approach was participatory, a principal component analysis statistical test was not conducted, possibly leading to an overlap in indicators from a statistical viewpoint, something that could be rectified in future research. Likewise, more participatory field testing in different settings will also help to validate and correct the choice of indicators. Thus the maximum resilience score for each household was 150.

3.4 Case Study Results

This section is divided in two parts: the first part provides a general overview of main socio-economic, environmental and disaster loss data for the six case study areas. The second part is a summary of findings on the resilience scores for each village and a comparative analysis of these findings.

3.4.1 General overview of disaster loss data

The four landslide affected villages: Sabra, Thang Thang, Khariswara and Katahare villages had an average of 20-60 households and 5.5 persons per household. Flood-affected places were: Dharan a city of 100,000 and Punarbas with 10,000

Table I: Resilience indicators

	Indicators (50)
Economic resources	Food stocks
	Employment
	Remittance income
	Savings
	Crop diversification
	Access to markets
	House ownership
	Land ownership
	Consumer durables
	Livestock assets
Social resources	Community leadership
	NGO assistance
	Government assistance
	Women's groups
	CFUGs
	Mutual assistance
	Extra kinship ties
	Disaster management committee
	Early warning system/monitoring
	Evacuation plans
Human resources	Population density
	Education level
	Vocational skills
	Access to information
	Previous disaster experience
	Organizational skills
	Household status (health/disabled persons/persons >70years)
	Ethnic group status
	Female headed household
	Ratio working adults: dependents
Natural resources	Forest quality
	Water quality
	Soil productivity
	Ground/air pollution
	Erosion
	Awareness of DRR measures
	Management of land for hazard protection
	Forest management practices
	Grazing management practices
	Access rights to forest resources
Physical resources	Emergency water supply
	Sanitation
	Telephone/mobile
	Electricity
	Emergency health care
	Safe houses, schools and shelters
	Access road
	Means of evacuation
	Search and rescue equipment
	Structural hazard protection

inhabitants, where most-affected neighborhoods (or wards) were surveyed. The elevation and climate varies between 100 meters above sea level (m.a.s.l.) from sub-tropical to temperate, with average rainfalls between 1,800-2,500 mm per year, most occurring during monsoon months June-September. Within the four landslide affected villages, on average 86 percent of households had been affected by landslides, from complete loss of houses or land, to cracks forcing house repairs. For flooding, only neighborhoods affected were surveyed, which included a majority of all households within each neighborhood. The extent of damage created by landslides was calculated as the percent of mean annual household income reduced due to landslides in terms of reported hectares of lost land and destroyed or damaged houses. On average, losses ranged from 2952 percent of annual income for the four landslide affected villages, while economic losses due to flooding were minimal. The most affected village, Khariswara, had recently experienced a 30,000 m^3 landslide (September 15, 2010), which had severely damaged agricultural lands and several houses.

In terms of demographics and socio-economic data, the rural villages are largely agricultural, except for Khariswara where a number of village members are shop keepers, government employees or priests as this is a "high social status" village, whereas, not surprisingly, the two urban areas have a much higher percentage of day laborers, shop keepers and government employees. Literacy rates, on average 29 percent for the four villages is relatively low and largely a function of social status. Thang Thang village has only a handful of literate persons and is mainly composed of an indigenous Thami ethnic group, considered very marginalized. The two urban areas have a large mix of ethnic groups and castes with a relatively high literacy rate of 61 percent. For the rural areas, the divide between high and low social status groups is what marks the "have" and "have nots" for average landholdings, food stocks, access to electricity, mobile phones and remittance incomes.

According to our data, it was primarily the higher or middle status families who could afford to send family members to work abroad, primarily Qatar, Malaysia, Saudi Arabia or India, with Katahare village near the Terai and the two urban areas in the Terai having received in-migrants from the hilly and mountain areas over past decades. Most of out migrants had moved for better economic opportunities but many were also pushed out due to landslides or flooding. Finally, it was found that membership in social organizations was an important factor in most of the villages surveyed. Community forest user groups (CFUGs) was the most common organization except in Dharan and Thang Thang, where there was a CFUG yet a poorly organized one. Instead, the most common organization was a women's savings group. Only the neighborhood in Dharan most affected by flooding had a disaster committee and an evacuation plan. In conclusion, the most impacted communities were from landslide affected villages especially those with "low social status," few community organizations and low access to educational, economic and communications infrastructure, i.e. Thang Thang and Katahare villages (Sudmeier-Rieux *et al.*, 2011).

To sum, landslide affected communities include: Sabra, a relatively well-off high caste community in Tehrathum District; Thang Thang a low status and illiterate community in Dolakha District; Khariswara, a relatively well-off, high caste community; and Katahare, a mixed community mainly comprised of settlers from the higher mountain areas, located in Sunsari District. Punarbas and Dharan are urban or semi-urban areas mainly affected by flooding in Sunsari District.

3.4.2 Resilience score results

Data collected from the household survey on the above indicators gave relative resilience scores for each household and community, which were mapped in a GIS and compared for each resource type (Figure 2). The tool provided a means for obtaining a baseline, useful for a project monitoring and evaluation system against which interventions in all five areas could be measured, or for emphasizing certain interventions over others to maximize resilience. We note that Thang Thang received the lowest relative score (score 59) mainly due to poor human and physical resources, followed by Katahare (score 61). The other four had much higher scores as explained by better access to infrastructure (physical resources) Dharan (score 92), Punarbas (score 94), while Khariswara (score 95) and Sabra (score 101) had the highest scores due to their better access to resources overall as a result of their higher social status.

Another finding from the research was to identify those indicators which had the greatest influence on resilience by order of importance as measured by scores obtained for each indicator:

- ethnic status (percent advantaged population);
- skills training;
- economic: employment and remittances;
- disaster management committee;

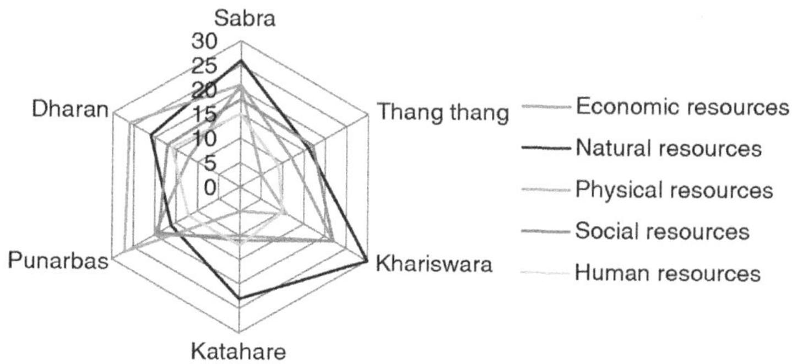

Figure 2: Resilience scores for six communities in central-eastern Nepal, illustrating the higher role played by natural resources for the rural communities, while physical resources played a greater role in increasing resilience in urban or semi-urban areas

- early warning system, monitoring:
- community leadership;
- CFUGs;
- structural hazard protection;
- health care; and
- access to roads.

4. Discussion

The main objective of this paper was to develop an operational framework for measuring resilience and vulnerability as a guidance tool for directing interventions for reducing landslide risk in central and Eastern Nepal. This was a long and iterative process, first based on a thorough literature review, field observations and stakeholder discussions to identify indicators of resilience. The advantages and disadvantages of a quantitative approach to measuring resilience were contemplated. As the goal was to develop a guidance tool for comparison between communities, a decision was made to develop a quantitative method for measuring resilience. The decision was inspired by the Chambers (2007) publication "Participatory numbers," which encouraged more research combining qualitative and quantitative participatory research. Indicators of resilience were thus developed based on existing literature field tested with Nepal expert advice and community feedback. What the above results demonstrate is a relatively straightforward and simple means for obtaining data on the state of a community's resilience as a relatively simple "snapshot" of resilience at one period in time, assuming that resilience is an outcome that can be improved over time with the "right" set of interventions.

The main limitation of this research is that it focussed mainly on outcome indicators; although some process indicators of resilience were identified (i.e. grazing management practices, skills training, organizational skills and learning through education), these need to be more comprehensive and validated through community consultations. Process indicators refer to ability for learning from past experiences, flexibility, early warning and monitoring, risk reduction planning, but can also include ecosystem based processes such as land use management practices, water management, diversification of resources, etc. Examples include:

- sustainable land management: community forest and grazing management for hazard protection, erosion control and improved water quality and quantity;
- community leadership training;
- women's savings groups;
- income diversification;
- water quality and quantity;
- access to information;
- in all cases, special effort to involve women's and minority groups; and
- project flexibility and ability for learning.

This information would then be used for self-monitoring of progress toward resilience, to evaluate the project performance as proposed by Kafle (2011) in an adaptive management process. Furthermore, the indicators identified by this research were developed for a specific context, of which only some could easily be scaled up, depending on data availability and data collection costs. Further research in this field would also need to focus more on identifying the underlying risk factors, institutional issues, power relations and learning processes (Heijmans, 2013). It is, however, one of the few quantifiable examples for measuring resilience at the community level with the exception to Kafle's (2011) research. In replicating this method, it can be considered a "modular skeleton," that can and should be adapted to various situations and for various purposes at relatively low cost. It is very important to keep in mind that resilience is context specific and highly dependent on the type of threat posed.

5. Conclusions

This paper describes empirical research intended to fill the perceived gap in practical guidance methodologies for assessing resilience. To do so, we constituted an interdisciplinary team of researchers to study landslide risk in four different communities of Central and Eastern Nepal using a case study approach. Two case studies on flood-affected communities were developed for comparison sake in more urban areas. Methods combined qualitative participatory approaches to develop indicators of resilience as well as a household survey and focus group discussions for collecting data on the indicators. It identified ethnic and gender discrimination as key root causes of risk, which need to be addressed in order to increase resilience of affected populations. This research provided empirical data for measuring resilience, mainly based on outcome indicators and has thus contributed to the literature, while providing ideas for future research on research on resilience building measures and indicators.

Perhaps one of the most effective measures for resilience building in Thang Thang, the most marginalized village of our study was an NGO program to assist children to stay in school and encourage women to start savings groups. Other notable resilience building factors were the existence of CFUGs, community leadership, skills training, health clinics, health care, sanitation, savings cooperatives and good water quality. These are so-called "soft resilience" factors (Moench and Dixit, 2007) that can be addressed through various government programs and NGO projects as are already underway in many communities across Nepal. Such programs are often very cost-effective with multiplier affects, especially when women are targeted as key actors for resilience building. Last but not least, in Nepal, community forests proved to be essential to decreasing risk and increasing resilience, and have over the past two decades become a major factor for providing communities with vital livelihood support, physical protection from landslides but also a social structure through the CFUGs. There are now tens of thousands CFUGS, some better managed than others, but often the only social organization requiring regular meetings in remote communities. The Federation of community forests of Nepal (FECOFUN) is an independent umbrella organization, often organizing skills training in community organization for improving community forests. There is great potential for FECOFUN to incorporate training on landslide mitigation in its regular training sessions, further increasing the importance of CFUGs for reducing landslide risk.

In spite of our early criticisms against the overuse of resilience as a magic bullet and a passing fashion, the conclusion made by this study is that it did pass the litmus test of communities. Landslide affected persons in Nepal may not use the word "resilience" but they do know which resources are necessary to overcome adversity and which resources are needed to improve everyday lives. Thus, we conclude that it is possible to measure resilience, with several caveats:

RQ1. Resilience needs to be clearly defined in its scope, context and temporality according to a specific threat.

RQ2. Resilience indicators need to be made context relevant and decided upon by stakeholders.

RQ3. Causes of risk need to be carefully analyzed and taken into account into resilience measures.

Resilience has the potential to guide decision makers toward more comprehensive and systemic approaches to risk reduction. If resilience is to become a useful paradigm, then root causes of risk and vulnerability must be included in its definition and only then can resilience be a useful attribute and a valuable decision-making tool for sustainable development and risk reduction interventions.

References

Anderson, M.B. and Woodrow, P.J. (1998), *Rising From the Ashes, Development Strategies in Times of Disaster*, IT Publications, London.

Baxter, J. and Eyles, J. (1997), "Evaluating qualitative research in social geography: establishing 'rigour' in interview analysis", *Transactions of the Institute of British Geographers*, Vol. 22, pp. 505–525.

Bista, B.D. (2004), *People of Nepal*, Ratna Pustak Bhandar, Kathmandu, 309pp.

Bollin, C. and Hidajat, R. (2006), "Community-based risk index: pilot implementation in Indonesia", in Birkmann, J. (Ed.), *Measuring Vulnerability to Natural Hazards, Towards Disaster Resilient Societies*, UNU, Tokyo, pp. 271–299.

Bruneau, M., Chang, S., Eguchi, R.T., Lee, G.C., O'Rourke, T.D., Reinhorm, A.M., Shinouzuka, M., Tierney, K., Wallace, W.A. and von Winterfeldt, D. (2003), "A framework to quantitatively assess and enhance the seismic resilience of communities", *Earthquake Spectra, Earthquake Engineering Research Institute*, Vol. 19 No. 1, pp. 733–752.

Cannon, T. and Müller-Mahn, D. (2010), "Vulnerability, resilience and development discourses in context of climate change", *Nat Hazards*, Vol. 55, pp. 621–635.

CBS (2009), *Statistical Year Book of Nepal 2009*, Government of Nepal Secretariat (Ed.), Central Bureau of Statistics, Kathmandu.

CBS (2011), *Nepal Living Standards Survey III*, press release August 8, 2011, Government of Nepal Secretariat (Ed.), Central Bureau of Statistics, Kathmandu.

Chambers, R. (1994), "Participatory rural appraisal: analysis of experience", *World Development*, Vol. 22, pp. 1253–1268.

Chambers, R. (2007), "Who counts? The quiet revolution of participation and numbers", working papers, Institute of Development Studies, Brighton, 45pp.

Cutter, S.L. and Finch, C. (2008), "Temporal and spatial changes in social vulnerability to natural Hazards", *Proceedings US National Academy of Sciences*, Vol. 105 No. 7, pp. 2301–2306.

Cutter, S.L., Boruff, B.J. and Shirley, W.L. (2003), "Social vulnerability to environmental hazards", *Social Science Quarterly*, Vol. 84 No. 1, pp. 242–261.

Cutter, S.L., Barnes, L., Berry, M., Burton, C., Evans, E., Tate, T. and W., J. (2008), "Community and regional resilience: Perspectives from hazards, disasters, and emergency management", CARRI Research Report No. 1. Oak Ridge National Lab: Community and Regional Resilience Initiative.

DFID (1997), *The UK White Paper on International Development – and Beyond*, Department of Overseas Development (Ed.), DFID, London.

Estrella, M., Blauert, J., Campilan, D., Gaventa, J., Gonsalves, J., Guijt, I., Johnson, D. and Ricafort, R. (2000), *Learning from change. Issues and experiences in participatory monitoring and evaluation*, Intermediate Technology Publications, London.

Gaillard, J.-C., Wisner, B., Benouar, D., Cannon, T., Créton-Cazanave, L., Dekens, J., Fordham, M., Gilbert, C., Hewitt, K., Kelman, I., Morin, J., N'Diaye, A., O'Keefe, P., Oliver-Smith, A., Quesada, C., Revet, S., Sudmeier-Rieux, K., Texier, P. and Vallette, C. (2010), "Alternatives pour une réduction durable des risques de catastrophe", *Human Geography*, Vol. 3, pp. 66–88.

Grünewald, F. and Warner, J. (2012), "Resilience: buzz word or critical strategic concept?" *Humanitarian Aid on the Move*, Vol. 10, October, pp. 1–7.

Harmeling, S. (2010), "Global climate risk index, 2010. Who is most vulnerable? Weather-related loss events since 1990 and how Copenhagen needs to respond", in Watch, G. (Ed.), *Briefing Paper*, German Watch, Munich Re, Bonn, 19pp.

Heijmans, A. (2013), "Handbook resilience", Groupe URD, CARE Nederland (Eds), University of Wageningen, Wageningen, 100pp.

Kafle, S.K. (2011), "Measuring disaster-resilient communities: a case study of coastal communities in Indonesia", *Journal of Business Continuity & Emergency Planning*, Vol. 5.

Kafle, S.K. and Murshed, Z. (2004), *Community-Based Disaster Risk Management for Local Authorities*, Asian Disaster Preparedness Center, Bangkok, 159pp.

Kendra, J.M. and Wachetendorf, T. (2003), "Reconsidering convergence and converger legitimacy in response to the world trade center disaster", in Clarke, L. (Ed.), *Terrorism and Disaster: New Threats, New Ideas (Research in Social Problems and Public Policy, Volume 11)*, Emerald Group Publishing Limited, London, pp. 97–122.

Khanal, P. (2011), "Astonishing decline in absolute poverty to 13 percent", *Republica Daily*, August 4, available at: www.myrepublica.com/ (accessed 15 September, 2011).

Lewis, J. and Kelman, I. (2010), "Places, people and perpetuity: community capacities in ecologies of catastrophe", *ACME: An International E-Journal for Critical Geographies*, Vol. 9, pp. 191–220.

Manyena, S.B., O'Brien, G., O'Keefe, P. and Rose, J. (2011), "Disaster resilience: a bounce back or bounce forward ability?", *Local Environment*, Vol. 16, pp. 417–424.

Mayunga, J.S. (2007), "Understanding and applying the concept of community disaster resilience: a capital-based approach", A draft working paper prepared for the summer academy for social vulnerability and resilience building, UNU-EHS, Bonn, Munich, 22-28 July, 16pp.

Moench, M. and Dixit, A. (2007), *Working with the Winds of Change. Toward Strategies for Responding to the Risks Associated with Climate Change and other Hazards*, ProVention Consortium and Institute for Social and Environmental Transition-International, Geneva and Kathmandu.

MoHA (2009), *Nepal Disaster Report 2009, The Hazardscape and Vulnerability*, Ministry of Home Affairs, Government of Nepal, Kathmandu.

Reghezza-Zitt, M., Rufat, S., Djament-Tran, G., Le Blanc, A. and Lhomme, S. (2012), "What resilience is not: uses and abuses", *Cybergeo: European Journal of Geography*, Environment, Nature, Paysage.

Robert, B., Hémond, Y. and Yan, G. (2010), "L'évaluation de la résilience organisationnelle", *Téléscope*, Vol. 16, pp. 131–153.

Rose, A. (2007), "Economic resilience to natural and man-made disasters: multidisciplinary origins and contextual dimensions", *Environmental Hazards*, Vol. 7, pp. 383–398.

Sudmeier-Rieux, K., Jaquet, S., Derron, M.-H., Jaboyedoff, M. and Devkota, S. (2011), "A case study of landslides and coping strategies in two villages of central-eastern Nepal", *Journal of Applied Geography*, Vol. 32, pp. 680–690.

The Risk to Resilience Team (2009), "Catalyzing climate and disaster resilience: processes for identifying tangible and economically robust strategies: final report in risk to resilience study", in Moench, M. Fajber, E. Dixit, A. Caspari, E. and Pokhrel, A. (Eds), Nepal ISET, Kathmandu, 328pp., available at: http://cybergeo.revues.org/25554 (accessed 15 December, 2012).

Tierney, K. and Bruneau, M. (2007), "Conceptualizing and measuring resilience, a key to disaster loss reduction", *TR News*, Transportation Research Board of the National Academies, Washington, DC, May-June, pp. 14–15.

Twigg, J. (2009), *Characteristics of a Disaster-Resilient Community, Vol. 2*, Version 2, Aon Benfield UCL Hazard Research Centre, London.

UNDP (2009), "Nepal human development report 2009", Tiwari, B.N., Ghai, Y., Levit-Shore, S. and Baral, L.R. in *Human Development Report*, United Nations Development Programme, New York, NY, 214pp.

Vajjhala, S.P. (2005), "Mapping alternatives: facilitating citizen participation in development planning and environmental decision making", *Engineering and Public Policy*, Carnegie Mellon University, Pittsburgh, PA, pp. 177–261.

Further Reading

Haimes, Y. (2009), "On the definition of resilience in systems", *Risk Analysis*, Vol. 29, pp. 498–501.

Social Vulnerability Analysis for Sustainable Disaster Mitigation Planning in Coastal Bangladesh ☆

Bishawjit Mallick, Khan Rubayet Rahaman and Joachim Vogt

Abstract

Purpose – The opportunities and potentials of the coastal zone all over the world have not received much attention, and also the disaster mitigation approaches are seen as a curative measure rather than protective, both of which raise questions about sustainable coastal belt planning and development. What is needed is a multidisciplinary approach to tackle the complexity of social systems, and patterns of vulnerability in those systems. The aim of this paper is to attempt to understand those challenges in context of cyclone SIDR 2007 in Bangladesh.

Design/methodology/approach – The combination of spatial and socio-economic data in this study is based on an empirical analysis. After clustering the geographical boundary, a systematic random sampling technique was applied to identify the respondents for a household survey. A total of 47 percent of the respondents were illiterate and thus required the help of data collectors. In-depth interviews were conducted with the victims of cyclone Sidr to ascertain their experiences during the event.

Findings – The heterogeneous characteristics of the respondents show that the impact of disasters varies from individual to individual, group to group and community to community. It is evident that an affected community waiting for relief and reconstruction materials attracts "dependency on relief works" which makes them more "vulnerable" to other calamities. In the long run it increases the poverty ratio and pressurizes them to stay in a "vulnerability trap" in any type of calamity. Furthermore, it reveals a socio-infrastructural vulnerability

☆ This study is supported by the Karlsruhe House of Young Scientist (KHYS) of Karlsruhe University, Germany under field research grant for the PhD research on "social changes due to increasing vulnerability: analysis of socio-economic factors for spatial planning considerations in coastal Bangladesh".

Reprinted from *Disaster Prevention and Management*
Vol. 20 No. 3, pp. 220–237 (2011). doi:10.1108/09653561111141682

and also the overall "social vulnerability" concepts by using a combination of socio-spatial data.

Originality/value – This paper contains valuable information regarding the adaptation strategies to cyclone hazards resorted to by coastal peoples in Bangladesh.

Keywords: Disasters; Socio-infrastructural vulnerability; Spatial planning; Coastal regions; Bangladesh

Introduction

The linkage between planning, mitigation and adaptation of disastrous situation is critical, thus it requires a test before any intervention. Disasters affect people and places; and thus the first respondents to any crisis situation are the affected residents themselves. Disaster – either natural or man made – are very common in Bangladesh. Almost each and every year the country experiences floods, cyclone or tornadoes, loses a lot of resources and thus struggles for development. The major disasters identified in Bangladesh are: floods, cyclone, storms, tornadoes, drought and desertification, river erosion, earthquakes, arsenic contamination of ground water sources and environmental pollution (Chowdhury, 1998). People of coastal areas are vulnerable because they live in an extremely dynamic estuarine environment facing many natural threats. Besides, there are threats of climate change and upstream land and water uses. These threats affect almost every aspect of life and limit livelihood choices of the people. The coastal zone of Bangladesh, an area covering 47,211 km^2 facing the Bay of Bengal or having proximity to the Bay, and the exclusive economic zone in the Bay, is generally perceived to be a zone of multiple vulnerabilities. Records of last 200 years show that at least 70 major cyclones hit the coastal belt of Bangladesh and during last 35 years nearly 900,000 people died due to catastrophic cyclones. The government of Bangladesh has already identified the zone as "vulnerable to adverse ecological process" and as one of three "neglected regions". The opportunities and potentials of the zone have not received much attention, and also the disaster mitigation approaches are seen as curative measure rather than protective, which make questions for sustainable coastal belt planning and development. What is needed now is a multidisciplinary approach to tackle the complexity of social systems, and patterns of vulnerability in those systems. An attempt has been made in this document to understand those challenges in respect of the context of cyclone Sidr 2007 in Bangladesh. It is intended to analyze the households' situation of a union (local administrative unit) in order to delve into a common view on coastal conditions during cyclone Sidr, especially challenges being faced and or to be faced by the coastal communities. This study provides a synthesized picture of the coastal conditions during cyclone Sidr and hints at issues and areas that need to be addressed for the sustainable well being of the coastal communities of Bangladesh.

Furthermore, vulnerability depends on the interaction of socio-economic and natural factors of a region. Thus, it raises the question of how the societies of the coastal countries react to this menace and risk and how they perceive it, particularly in the field of disaster prevention and spatial planning. In the industrialized countries of the North have established state sponsored programs to respond to the vulnerability issues of their coastal areas – for example, the German coast is secured through extensive embankment construction, and other measures; which are primarily not available in most of the developing countries. On the other hand, knowledge, consciousness and relevant government responsibilities along with appropriate material resources are not available in the developing countries; and some appear as an impossible dream for those poor countries of the South in compare with the highly technical and societal standards of the North. Despite of huge financial expenses in prevention, prediction and protection of the natural disasters, the hi-tech country like the United States also responds to hurricanes with frightening helplessness in their coastal regions. Accordingly, what should happen in developing countries, where almost all the conditions are missing, unplanned and unimplemented? So it is important to know the applicability of the instruments and methods in the South, which are applicable for reducing vulnerability to the North. Are such instruments transferable to them, or not? It is rather important to question: what adjustments are possible in the real social and cultural conditions of the country; which are socially "acceptable" rather than "need" and, therefore, can be implemented with the help of participatory planning; and where and how the critical weaknesses of vulnerability oriented spatial planning can be resolved. This study concentrates on those questions and tries to identify the problem areas with the help of a pilot survey's findings.

Theoretical Debate and Importance of this Study

Newton's theory of "action-reaction" is very operational in planning practices and initiatives as well, if someone does not consider the adverse effect of the taken measures. It appears that in many cases, action taken to the end of the disasters often ends up creating another one. "Flood Action Plan-2000" of Bangladesh is a good example that has been challenged at the court by activists on the grounds that this mitigation plan could create another disaster (Wiebe, 2000). Another important example is that of arsenic contamination in ground water in Bangladesh (Safiuddin and Karim, 2001), people were advised to sink tubewell to get rid of diarrhoeal disease crisis, which was dubbed as a "tubewell revolution". The community never thought about the water quality or contained minerals in the underground water. Thus development delivered disaster due to "unaddressed vulnerability". In both cases the development was perceived as service delivery and inspired by a limited and externally inspired understanding of development (Chowdhury, 1998). In many cases it is providing an excuse for going ahead and to act disregarding the impact on these people with the argument that they will be able to cope.

The concept of "vulnerability" expresses the multidimensionality of disasters by focusing attention onto the complete social system, environmental situation between the intersections of nature and culture of the individual or the group in general (Oliver-Smith, 2004). The modern integrative approach to vulnerability comes from the disaster community and is set out in the Hyogo Framework 2005-2015 and adopted by the UN in 2005. It is defined here as "the conditions determined by physical, social, economic and environmental factors or processes, which increase the susceptibility of a community to the impact of hazards" (Yamin *et al.*, 2005). Although vulnerability is not defined as poverty but today's poverty is yesterday's unaddressed vulnerability (Chambers, 1989; Yamin *et al.*, 2005) and it is shorthand for factors that drive people into poverty, keep them in poverty and block their exit-route from poverty (ActionAid, 2005), it introduces the "social vulnerability" (Braun and Shoeb, 2008; Cannon *et al.*, 2004), and finally "social protection" emerges (Devereux and Sabates-Wheeler, 2004). Accordingly, understanding vulnerability should broaden our understanding of climatic, economical, generational, geographical, political and social processes of society that generate poverty, particularly the poverty traps (Chambers, 1989; Barrett and McPeak, 2004a). Procedural and institutional frameworks are also important because they help to define actors, funding flows and types of policies that must be linked to support successful community-led adaptation strategies (Yamin *et al.*, 2005; Sperling and Szekely, 2005). Thus, "vulnerability" issues were taken into consideration in this work as a concern for disaster mitigation planning.

Numerous research on natural hazards and disasters in recent years focuses increasingly on the society (Wisner and Blaikie, 2004; Dikau and Weichselgartner, 2005; Müller-Mahn, 2007; Gladwin *et al.*, 2007), which interprets the so-called "social disaster" as a result of natural disasters. The effects of such natural disasters can also be determined on the social situation and the affected peoples' capability to adapt. Communities need to be prepared for natural and man-made disasters because these can strike anywhere, regardless of location, culture or society. Communities that are well trained locally, culturally, socially and psychologically are better prepared and are more effective in responding to the aftermath effect of disasters (Matbor, 2007). It is important to mention here that the actual movement towards preparedness at local level during any disaster situation is a real weakness in most of the areas of the world (Light, 2005). Though the resilience of an individual depends on socio-economical and political conditions in the respective community, it explores also the degree of vulnerability of the individual or the family to a disastrous situation. Again, the economic dependence combined with the physical hazards limits the resilience of the poor households to recurring disasters, since it is hard to build up assets or diversify skills. The reasons for the effect of disasters and the increasing vulnerability of individual or even collective groups can become aware about their strategies to reduce risks and to respond to a disaster (Callon and Law, 1989; Bankoff, 2004). This then empowers them and makes them able to identify problems and needs; and increasingly assuming responsibility to plan for them, to manage, to control and to assess the collective action necessary for the situation. It mostly depends on the availability of information regarding the disaster. The poorest are the least likely to hear radio warnings or even understand the meaning of different weather signals. Uneducated people are mostly like to be alienated from scientific system. Women are always lack of knowledge due to their less accessibility outside their homestead, i.e. market places, actually where radio warnings might be heard or news to be discussed. On the other hand, non-participatory or top-down planning implementation can fulfill their agenda of service delivery, but it is only the people who experience disasters or bad impacts of any development interventions, and it is them who have been marginalized or so called "vulnerable" in the process more than others. As a result natural or even man-made disaster experiences along with "social disasters" (Braun and Shoeb, 2008; Cannon *et al.*, 2004) and it seeks for "social protection" (Devereux and Sabates-Wheeler, 2004) and finally the question of "planning" is raised.

We can speak about the concept of "planning with the coping strategies (Mallick *et al.*, 2005)". Yet the concept itself is questioned by some people. They are arguing that what goes by the name of "coping", might be "adjusting" to the inevitable by the sufferers. The fact is that, whatever their natural capacity to cope was, it is diminishing because of the increasing trend of natural disasters, false-planning practice or non-participatory planning, lack of national legal supports and unorganized localized interventions from nongovernmental organizations (NGOs) or community based organizations (CBOs). It seems that development initiatives may cause disasters and interventions in disaster may heighten disaster as well (Najam, 2004). This has largely happened because the victims are not really participants in any of the process, although development practitioners have started their trend with Community Based Management (CBM) approach (Pandey and Okazaki, 2005; Miyan, 2005; Morshed and Huda, 2002; Sumathipala, 2002; Kafle and Morsched, 2001; ISDR, 2000). Or maybe because the policy maker or scientists didn't address the adverse vulnerable issues, although there exist a lots of vulnerability management programs in the world. Taking such discrepancy of disaster mitigation and planning into consideration this study concentrate on the planning problems of coastal regions in Bangladesh with the help of an empirical pilot study in a coastal union.

Pilot Study

Methodology

The Institute for Regional Science (IfR) of the University of Karlsruhe in Germany focuses upon the research related with planning and development of coastal regions. Accordingly, a pre-test of its research concepts was undertaken in cooperation with Urban and Rural Planning Discipline, Khulna University, Bangladesh during February-March 2008.

It particularly helped to learn the experiences of the victims of cyclone Sidr, which hit Bangladesh on November 15, 2007. Reviewing the newspaper information and different media, one of the most devastated unions, namely Baniasanta union of Dacope Upazila in Khulna district was selected as study area. Total area of the studied union is around 29 km^2 with a population of 17,300 and a total 3,331 households (Dacope Upazila Parishad, 2005). Fishing is more favorable occupation rather than agriculture in this area, though most people are also involved primarily or secondarily in agricultural activities. Due to poverty most of them worked as day laborers within and even outside of their locality. There are four primary schools, one high school, two cyclone centers with seven religious centers, where people can take shelter during any emergency like disaster.

The quantitative data collection phase i.e. household survey constituted with a sample size of 124 households. First, as per the "ward" (the lowest administrative unit of local government in Bangladesh) the total sample was distributed based on the total number of households exist. Then, by using systematic random sampling the respondents of the household survey were identified. Usually in Bangladesh, the women are not allowed to talk with strangers or unknown people. It was the main backdrop of the participation of female respondents in this survey. Amongst the total 124 respondents only 14 respondents were female. Mostly half of the respondents (47 percent) were uneducated and thus requires the help of data collectors to complete the household survey. The questionnaire concentrated on the immediate action of the victims of Sidr, which initiatives were taken for their family, success of their initiative, relief and rehabilitation opportunities for them, their housing conditions before and after Sidr, institutional and community involvement as well as their socio-economic solutions to cope with disastrous situations. In-depth interviews with the victims of Sidr were taken and also asked some old people about their experiences with disasters. Results of the questionnaire survey were also verified with qualitative interviews.

Survey Findings

Culture, mentality and perceptions of the studied society. The heterogeneous characteristic of the community shows that the impact of disasters varies from individual to individual, group to group and community to community. Communities are differentiated in terms of access to resources and factors such as gender, age, class and ethnicity and these differences are highly significant to the vulnerability and adaptive capacity of particular individuals (Yamin *et al.*, 2005). This study replied with the similar understanding amongst the respondents with respect to their mitigating approach and response to cyclone Sidr. It is found that educated people (2 percent respondents, who have at least graduate education) invested more capital in constructing their house whereas the illiterate (47 percent of the respondent) group did not invest much money to construct their residence, as they knew that after every disaster somebody would come to rehabilitate their settlements. Such a mentality of waiting for relief materials introduces "dependency" and let them to be more "vulnerable" to any calamities.

Field data show that there are different types of natural calamities like flood, tornadoes (locally called "Kalboishaki"), cyclone, drought, river bank erosion, salinity and even water logging exist in this locality. More than 50 percent of respondents identified "Kalboishaki" as the most frequently experienced disaster in their locality. Every step of managing risk is influenced by the earliest means of receiving information. It is found that radio (50 percent) was the main sources of information during Sidr, following this was the information received from relatives or neighbors (29 percent), community volunteer (17 percent) and television (4 percent). It seems that the information given by the neighbors, relatives and community volunteers can be most rationale for a poor country like Bangladesh, where the poor people are not able to buy a radio or a TV. Unity is strength and for mitigating disasters' risks, people should take combined decisions. Most of the respondents (73 percent) took the decision alone immediately after having the information, whereas 25 percent discussed with their neighbors regarding the problems and tried to repair their own houses and made their own residence safer. It was also found that 60 percent of people who took a decision alone could not implement their immediate action plan and had faced major problems.

What they planned to combat cyclone Sidr? Field data shows, around 86 percent of the respondents decided to stay at their own house to protect their own family, only 11 percent planned to take their old family members and children to other safer places, like a neighbor's or relative's house; and only 3 percent had planed to take their family into a cyclone center (Table I). It was shown that 81 percent of them tried to stay in their own houses, whereas only 19 percent had left their own house and took shelter in cyclone center or neighbors house. Amongst those 19 percent, who left their house, only 4 percent took shelter in cyclone center and 54 percent were in neighbor's houses. The reasons of such decisions are based firstly on the distances of cyclone centers or safer places from their own houses. It was easy to reach their neighbor's house, when they felt at risk in their own house. The spatial and temporal distance of cyclone centers showed that one could reach the cyclone center during a normal period within an average of 10-20 minutes time from any corner of their village (Table I). Thus, one must reach the cyclone center before the beginning of cyclone. The spatial distance is in an average of 1 Kilometre. If the road-network is well planned and constructed with bricks or paved materials, then the spatial distance of a cyclone center is not a problem during any calamities, only if they leave their houses before the calamities strikes. These issues of infrastructural uses and conditions are not well discussed in this study due to the lack of a land use survey. It was also found that 50 percent of the people who live within 1 Kilometre spatial or average 20 minutes temporal distance from a cyclone center (around 50 percent of the respondents) wanted to take their family into a cyclone center (Table I). Is this a positive impression to take shelter in the cyclone center within the community?

It strictly depends on people's motivation and knowledge to handle the crisis with respect to their culture, norms, religion and social strata. Following the field data it is seen that 63 percent of the respondents who left their house (19 percent of total respondents) during Sidr, constructed their house for less than \$145 (likely

Table I: Spatial and temporal distance of cyclone centre in relation to the surviving plan of the respondents' family

Plan to save family	Cyclone shelter distance in meters	Cyclone shelter distance in time: Up to 10 min	10 to 20 min	20 to 30 min	More than 30 min	Respondents (%)
Wanted to take family members in cyclone shelter (3 percent)	250 to 500 meters	25	0	0	0	25
	750 m to 1 km	0	25	0	0	25
	More than 1 km	0	25	25	0	50
	Total	25	50	25	0	100
Wanted to stay at own house (86 percent)	Up to 250 meters	2	0	0	0	2
	250 to 500 meters	13	0	0	0	13
	500 to 750 meters	7	2	0	0	8
	750 m to 1 km	9	21	0	0	30
	More than 1 km	0	22	8	16	46
	Total	31	44	8	16	100
Wanted to send children and old family members to relatives' safe-house (11 percent)	250 to 500 meters	7	0	0	0	7
	500 to 750 meters	7	0	0	0	7
	750 m to 1 km	0	21	0	0	21
	More than 1 km	0	50	0	14	64
	Total	14	71	0	14	100

Source: Field data (2008)

10000 Bangladeshi Taka) and can be termed as poor segment of society. It also depends on their occupational status and sources of income to improve their housing conditions as well as their motivation to mitigate risks. It is found that those who have regular and relatively good income opportunities, mostly the business group, people in jobs, and trading wanted to stay in their own houses and their housing condition is relatively good. Interestingly amongst the day laborers (44 percent of the total respondent) 80 percent wanted to stay in their own houses though 51 percent of them have houses in a poor condition- in terms of monetary investment (Table II). Furthermore, the field data interprets the positive correlation ($r = 0.993$) between the monthly income and the ability of the respondents to implement the plan to save their family. It may complement that those who have enough economic solvency can take better decision in an emergency. In order to judge the significance of this argument, it is important to make use of further research and higher-level statistical analysis.

The middle income groups always tried to preserve their resources, re(de)construct or repair their own shelter, as reported here, that 16 percent tied down the roof of houses with the rope and bamboo into the ground, 31 percent tried to preserve some dried food like fried rice, sweetmeat etc. using mud-pot or poly-packet under the ground. Interestingly those people who preserved food (31 percent respondents) had also collected relief foods (74 percent of who preserved food). Thus in one hand it raises the issue of "dependency on relief works" and on the other hand it accuses the sources of income. It shows that mostly day laborers (93

Table II: Plan to save their family in respect to occupation and housing conditions

Occupation of family-head	Plan to save family	Cost of construction of the residential house before Sidr in US$ (1 US$ = 69.75 BDT, dated 19 June 2008) Up to $145 (%)	$145-290 (%)	$290-435 (%)	$435-725 (%)	$725 + (%)	Total (%)
Farming	Wanted to take family members to cyclone shelter	6					6
	Wanted to stay at own house	66	6	6		5	83
	Wanted to send children and old family members to other relatives, who were in relatively safer position		11				11
	Total	72	17	6		5	100
Fishing	Wanted to stay at own house	56	20	8	4	4	92
	Wanted to send children and old family members to relatives	8					8
	Total	64	20	8	4	4	100
Hunting	Wanted to stay at own house	50					50
	Wanted to send children and old family members to other relatives, who were in relatively safer position	50					50
	Total	100					100
Timber business	Wanted to stay at own house	34		33			67
	Wanted to send children and old family members to other relatives, who were in relatively safer position	33					33
	Total	67		33			100
Trading/shop/small business	Wanted to stay at own house	40		20	20	20	100
	Total	40		20	20	20	100
Day labor	Wanted to take family members in cyclone shelter	2	2	2			6
	Wanted to stay at own house	40	29	7	4		80,0
	Wanted to send children and old family members to other relatives, who were in relatively safer position	9	3	2			14
	Total	51	34	11	4		100
Job	Wanted to stay at own house	20	20	20	20	20	100
	Total	20	20	20	20	20	100
Housewife	Wanted to stay at own house	50			50		100
	Total	50			50		100
Others	Wanted to stay at own house	11	56	11	11	11	100
	Total	11	56	11	11	11	100

Source: Field data (2008)

percent), fishermen (80 percent), people in small businesses like hunting, trading etc. were dependent on relief foods. A further 53 percent reported that they had faced food shortages during Sidr, amongst them 14 percent didn't receive any relief at all. Whereas, 84 percent, who didn't face any food shortages, had received relief foods. This shows misappropriation of relief works thus weakens the community resilience to risks management, increases corruption, favoritism, conflict, and makes the poor deprived. It also indicates the sign of individuality and individual strategies to cope with risks, which in total could strengthen the community resilience to the risk, if it is properly managed (Gupta, 2002). Otherwise, in the long run it will increase the poverty ratio and pressurize them to stay in a "vulnerability trap" in any type of calamity.

It is also seen that more than 85 percent of the respondents had received relief during Sidr amongst them around 90 percent had below secondary level educational qualifications. Though it helps to expand the income opportunities and changes the mentality of the person, it was reported that 50 percent of those who had minimum secondary level education, had taken the chance to collect relief goods and materials although most of them have regular income sources (Table III).

Previously, it was seen that 81 percent respondents did not want to leave their house during Sidr, though most of their houses and trees were damaged severely. This convergence surely interprets the issue of self-resilience, religion and cultural belief. Usually, the Muslims don't like to take shelter in common place with their female and children because of their religious beliefs and norms, whereas other religions are relatively more flexible during any unnatural situations. Although 76 percent of respondents were Hindus, the rate of taking shelters in a cyclone center was also very minimal (4 percent of the total). It raises the questions of not only the social beliefs but also the personal habits and customs or particular issues of social segregation due to local political power exercises.

For example, it is reported that the middle-income group didn't receive enough relief as they felt shy to collect relief standing behind the poor people in a queue. It led them to sell their own property, or to take credit from other sources. Such continuous trends of taking loans from different sources due to natural disasters makes them more susceptible to poverty traps (Barrett and McPeak, 2004b). And in the long run it will introduce a community without middle class, and in general it hinders the capabilities of the community to respond to disasters as well as the rate of development of the country.

Institutional and infrastructural facilities of the study area. In Bangladesh the Cyclone Preparedness Program (CPP) set up by the Red Cross Society is charged to spread the message through the community via hand-held microphones. In 1991, though there was ample warning that a cyclone might strike, few people were convinced of the imminent danger until they saw the embankment overtopped or the wave advancing. Analysts of the '91 cyclone event concluded that the warning system in place was not really designed to convey information to local people. Further investigations showed that many people did not believe the warning in 1991 because the number 10 warning (which means "Great Danger") had been issued on several occasions prior to this event, with no cyclone occurring. In 1991, the "Great

Table III: Stands of receiving relief in respect to education and occupation

Education of family head	Occupation of head of family	Did you receive any relief? Yes (%)	No (%)	Total (%)
Illiterate (47%)	Farming	12		12
	Fishing	15	4	19
	Timber business	3		3
	Trading/shop/small business	2	2	4
	Day labour	43	4	48
	Housewife	3		3
	Others	10	2	12
	Total	88	12	100
Primary (31%)	Farming	13	5	18
	Fishing	16	5	21
	Hunting	5		5
	Timber business	3		3
	Day labour	45	5	50
	Job	3		3
	Total	85	15	100
Secondary (14%)	Farming	18		18
	Fishing	23		23
	Trading/shop/small business	18		18
	Day labour	35		35
	Job		6	6
	Total	94	6	100
SSC (6%)	Farming		12	12
	Fishing	13	12	25
	Day labour	37		37
	Job		13	13
	Others		13	13
	Total	50	50	100
Graduate and more (2%)	Job	50	50	100
	Total	50	50	100

Source: Field data (2008)

Danger" warning was broadcast well in advance of the cyclone but when it increased in intensity and a new, more urgent warning needed to be broadcast, the imminent arrival of the storm could not be communicated to the public (EU, 1998). This experience of 1991 helped to make people aware of during cyclone Sidr. Field study shows that the community level efforts were not too satisfactory as the respondents waited for more initiatives from the community volunteers. The messengers, local volunteers, were shouting through loud speakers or megaphones to warn the people about the impending cyclone and let them to bring people to cyclone shelters. Many of the affected people, who had mobile phones, maintained contact with the rest of the country. Of the respondents, 25 percent replied that they received support from their community initiative, as in information distribution, rescue and relief work. However, there were few rooms in the cyclone shelter they were hardly accessible for all the people and a majority of people didn't leave their own houses. It was very common in the coastal belt that people did not want to leave their houses. They tried to reconstruct their houses or shelter and wanted to preserve their food and other resources; but most of them never wanted to take shelter in a cyclone center. One of the problems was a scarcity of resources and the other was the lack of coordination, favoritism, nepotism by the local chairmen and ward commissioners. The women and children were somewhat lagging behind in securing relief materials. Although the government of Bangladesh with Red Cross Society (RCS) had implemented the project "Cyclone Preparedness Program" to reduce the communication problem, there also existed the problems with social status and relationship, which explored that middle-class farmer and fishermen in the cyclone-prone areas suffered the most.

As the infrastructure, health and education system of Bangladesh lag far behind, people who live in the cyclone's path had their homes and livelihoods destroyed, with no safety net to help them recover. Effective disaster risk management relies on a strong legal policy, an inter-institutional coordination mechanism and of course community participation. After the devastating cyclone of 1970, the government and other agencies undertook construction of multi-purpose cyclone shelters. During 1972-1979, a sum total of 238 shelters were constructed in coastal districts out of which 11 appeared to have been washed away. Each center was capable of accommodating about 2,000 people during cyclone and tidal surge. After 1985 cyclone, Bangladesh Red Crescent Society constructed 62 shelters and Caritas and other NGO's constructed 20 shelters. These shelters are two-storied frame building with free ground floor three meter height on RCC columns, which can accommodate 800 people during a cyclone and tidal surge. After the devastating cyclone of 1991, various organizations like Bangladesh Red Crescent Society, Ministry of Education with a Saudi grant, EEC, local Government Engineering Bureau as well as several NGO's have constructed considerable number of cyclone shelters, which are of different types and design. At present about 2,400 cyclone shelters are available in the country for the use of the coastal people (Karim, 2000).

After the 1991 cyclone, the government had planned to develop multipurpose cyclone centers in the coastal belt. During a normal period these cyclone centers are used as a primary school and high school. In the study area, it was found that two cyclone centers were constructed near to the existing primary school, without improving the conditions of those schools (Figure 1). The primary school has not yet moved into this cyclone center, although the condition of the primary school buildings was very vulnerable, and it still didn't supports to take shelter during Sidr. The catchment areas of the cyclone centers show the lack of adequate support for all the inhabitants in the study area.

To support this argument, there requires an analysis of the proximity of another cyclone centers in the adjacent unions. The religious places like the mosques, temple, and church have very little capacity of accommodating people during a disaster and most of them are not well constructed. In this respect, it is very difficult to estimate whether the present institutional support is effective for the local population or if more support is needed there.

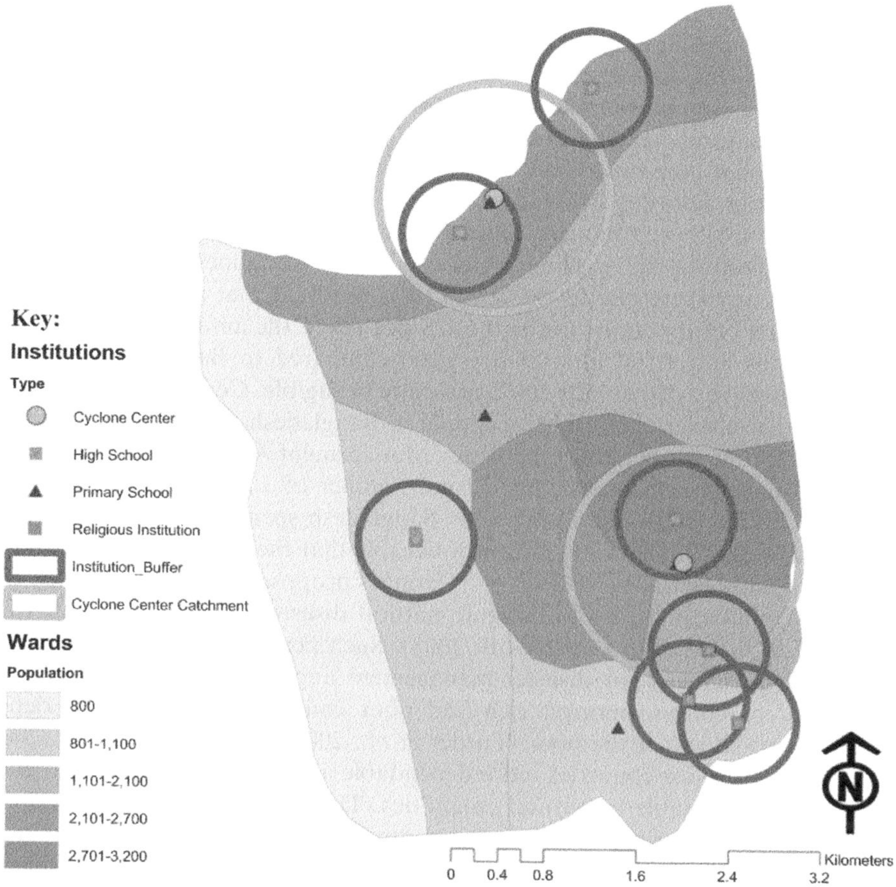

Source: Field data (2008)

Figure 1: Catchment areas of available institutions

It seems that all the population had a chance to take shelter in a safer place. However, from household survey it was found that only 19 per cent of the total respondents had left their houses and taken shelter in safer places, like cyclone centers (only 16 percent of the 19 percent). This result raises not only the question of adequate institutional support but also the question of their socio-cultural motivation to leave their house in an emergency. Why they didn't like to leave their own house, as it was risky to remain in their house during any natural calamities? Why they didn't like to improve their housing conditions, as they frequently face such natural disasters? Are these problems really related to their lack of knowledge or motivation? Or there are some other indigenous strategies, knowledge, norms or customs, which influence their lifestyles, their communication, behavior and their ways of thinking. This study cannot reply to all of these questions. It requires further field based intensive analysis, especially with the methods of endogenous and exogenous approaches of fact-finding analysis. That may help to design or plan a sustainable resilience for community based disaster mitigation.

Differences are seen in forecasting, detection, communications and public awareness regarding natural hazards everywhere in the world. As for example, a shift from the traditional "top-down" approaches (Victoria, 2002) as emphasized by the Bangladesh Urban Disaster Mitigation Project (BUDMP, 2002). And still up to $2.2 trillion of the US economy are believed to be affected annually by weather and climate events (Dutton, 2001). Though the cyclones or tornadoes are more common in the US than anywhere else in the world (it is reported that an average of 1,000 tornadoes are reported nationwide in the US per year), the amount of damage and losses (70 deaths and 1,500 injuries per year) compared to Bangladesh (death of 3,406 human lives in cyclone Sidr 2007) are quite negligible. Conversely, the amount paid out for the recovery per affected people in Bangladesh is very little, compared to the investment of the Federal Emergency Management Assistance of the US government. During the last decade, for a total number of 102 tornados the US disbursed $1.72 billion (SDR, 2003), whereas Bangladesh spends $1 billion emergency help during cyclone Sidr 2007. It is also noticeable that the Joint Damage Loss and Needs Assessment (JDLNA) Mission of 11 donors proposed to the Bangladesh government a $4 billion program to mitigate natural disasters like cyclone Sidr to be implemented in the next 15 years (GoB, 2008). Such perception between developed and developing countries for disaster management augments the intra-dependency of disaster preparedness amongst rich and poor countries and leads the rich to spend for the problems of the poor (Turner *et al.*, 2003; Pettit and Wheeler, 2005). Thus, it makes the poor countries more dependable and redundant upon rich countries and more vulnerable to natural calamities. Therefore, it is urgent to develop strategies that will be originated from the community itself and will be sustainable in the long run. This point leads the expert community to enlarge the "risk-hazard model" to a "vulnerability model" (Wisner and Blaikie, 2004; Cutter, 1996) and it ultimately adds up the environment with population in order to determine resilience (Adger *et al.*, 2005; Turner *et al.*, 2003). Accordingly, during any disaster, people at the community level must use coping and survival strategies to respond the situation long before the arrival of outside help from NGOs or the government.

Again in extreme emergencies, some women have gone to cyclone centers once or twice, but in the center, women find that no separate facilities are provided for their needs (EU, 1998). In the past, some women were rejected by their husbands if Pardah (one kind of dress in Muslim religion only for female that help the women to hide herself from outsider of the family) is seen to be compromised by going to an unlit and crowded cyclone center. When cyclone centers are used for exclusively male activities (mosques in particular) women do not believe themselves to have sanctioned access and will not enter. This suggests that future cyclone centers should be designated as gender-neutral places for multi-purpose, community use. Access to such centers is dominated by the elite and inactive center management committees. Minority groups and others may not be granted entry and at the same time, religious centers of minority groups are often not open to outsiders. Unless these issues are addressed in a community-managed plan, it may be futile to construct further refuges.

Planning: "Necessity" or "Acceptance"?

The frequent cyclones cannot be stopped in future due to a rise of sea level, increased temperature of sea, and the greenhouse effects from climatic change. To mitigate such unavoidable natural disasters it is now needed to draw up a sound plan for the people. Community Based Disaster Management (CBDM) requires the importance of people's participation (ADPC, 2006; Pandey and Okazaki, 2005; Steins, 2001; ISDR, 2000) and technical improvement which can provide an early warning for the successful evacuation of people from vulnerable areas prior to cyclones. Thus, it results in fewer casualties, but it could not resist the damages done to houses, crops and trees', proving it is imperative that measures should be planned to curb the possibility of such damage. With risk embedded in the vulnerability concept, a more vulnerable population is one that is frequently exposed to, is easily harmed by, and has low levels of recovery, buffering, and an adaptation to a hazard (NRC, 2007). Therefore, we should consider the approach of "what is accepted by the community" rather than "what is necessary for the community".

"What is accepted by the community?" is not easy to determine as the level of acceptance of any plan varies community-to-community, or even individual to individual. This study refers the acceptance of locally adopted and inherited strategies to combat with disasters i.e. empowering the indigenous knowledge of disaster mitigation. As the disastrous situation is no more new and the people have some inherited practices to fight against different disasters, it should identify those practices before any external interventions. Therefore, it will be very useful to utilize the social capital, i.e. social integration, social cohesion, solidarity, networking, multiple-way communication between and among the members of the community. This can foster the leadership qualities, empower the local knowledge and give a hand to other community members to initiate locally managed and adoptable strategies to combat with unnatural situations. Finally, different actors of the communities, the government and other voluntary organizations, financial institutions will be able to assist in mitigating the consequences of natural disasters. Their effectiveness in working together may improve through mobilizing community's strength and resources, expertise, professionals and volunteers, before any disaster strikes and in the recovery work that takes place during and aftermath of the events. Though, there are many obstacles to preparedness and survival strategies in a community: religious beliefs, superstition, gender roles, lack of protective infrastructure, economic vulnerability, and local insecurity all play a part. But without credible and acceptable planning systems for pre-and post disaster periods, even the available resources and option are under-utilized and caused more damages and losses than it was expected.

Therefore, a holistic approach with vulnerability and local knowledge as a concept of assessing disasters within their cultural, socio-economic, political and environmental context is now very important for disaster mitigation and planning. This concept provides a helpful guide in formulating approaches and policies in hazard management. In spite of that, there exists lack of methodological and conceptual advances of this approach. It is still hampered by a one-dimensional construction of the processes that transform a hazard into a disaster (Bankoff, 2004). In particular, the relationship between society's vulnerability and the adaptation of its culture in terms of local strategies and knowledge has not been adequately explained. The absence of a holistic approach to vulnerability that assesses it different characteristics – seems to have contributed to a decrease in the effectiveness of disaster management. An approach – combining exogenous and endogenous methods for vulnerability research – would help to improve the effectiveness of management and to identify and to prioritize factual and efficient measures for the adequate reduction of risks by the local communities and authorities, who are undoubtedly the fundamental actors in achieving a preventive attitude.

Numerous reports and news on Sidr reported that the villages behind the Sundarbans (the biggest mangrove forest in the world) were saved! Can we think of having such mangrove trees planted on the water edge throughout the length and breadth of the coastal area? Can we motivate the villagers who live near the rivers and seashore to plant them on their own? Are there leaders to undertake the task?

This study goal undertakes research to know the methods and strategies already exist within communities for the capacity building for the common people to cope with disasters rather than focusing in a way to take on pre-determined initiatives. It also aims to strengthen the local government's institutions, and above all on enhancing the government's capacity for negotiation with the developed countries that had pledged assistance for developing nations. It also must be asked whether the individual and collective learning processes inhibit and how they are sustained after a disaster, and in particular whether the provision for the next disaster victims to or reaches the typical pattern of individual or collective displacement processes. Public policies must be geared to local policies and must secure the social changes, rather than to call by technical means of prevention from foreign experts.

There are many best practices to mitigate cyclone disaster in the world, but a sustainable mitigating approach should always be developed within the community and by the community considering the aim of "accepted by the community rather than necessary for the community" (Pandey and Okazaki, 2005). Therefore, the proposed research work considers "society" as the key element for understanding acceptable approaches for preventing the causalities and damages of natural hazards by the community and then tries to develop alternative sustainable local strategies for mitigating natural disasters through an endogenous approach of research (Clausen *et al.*, 2003). Technical supports and development works can be supported exogenously but at first we should identify the local strategies endogenously. Considering the cultural manifestation and people's beliefs within a community, the proposed research will try to find out the sustainable local strategies for mitigating natural calamities in the coastal region of Bangladesh. Local experiences during cyclone Sidr will result in designing the endogenous methods of aimed work.

Conclusion

A sustainable community is one that balances: social equality and equity, economic vitality, environmental responsibility and infrastructural effectiveness. Such an infrastructural effectiveness as well as community resilience is absent in the studied areas. Obtaining funds to provide sufficient shelters in the future may be a forlorn hope. It may be necessary to consider alternative community-based solutions in the intermediate term. Access to shelters is dominated by the élite and inactive shelter management committees. Minority groups and others may not be granted entry and at the same time, religious centres of minority groups are often not open to outsiders. Unless these issues can be addressed in a community-managed plan, it may be futile to construct further refuges. This might require some resisting of important community infrastructure in more valuable coastal areas but could be planned with local people to determine the optimum placement of these refuges. It sounds good in theory, but it does not come easily. There are many barriers to a community coming to consensus around the common good, but there are also conditions that can be fostered that make such consensus more likely. Finally, the "community-accepted disaster mitigation plan" may be a platform to learn from others that have faced similar hazards and developed mechanisms to cope with difficult situations over the years. And with the stronger local, regional and international partnerships, effective practices for intervening disaster situations both in the long and short terms can be built and implemented.

References

ActionAid (2005), *Participatory Vulnerability Analysis: A Step by Step Guide for Field Staff*, Action Aid International, International Emergencies Team, London, pp. 6–12.

Adger, W.N., Hughes, T.P., Folke, C., Carpenter, S. and Rockström, J. (2005), "Social-ecological resilience to coastal disasters", *Science*, Vol. 309 No. 5737, pp. 1036–9.

ADPC (2006), *Community Based Disaster Risk Management 2006*, Asian Disaster Preparedness Center, available at: www.sheltercenter.org/shelterlibrary/items/pdf/ADPCCriticalGuidelines.pdf (accessed October 3, 2007).

Bankoff, G. (2004), "The historical geography of disaster: vulnerability and local knowledge", in Bankoff, G., Freks, G. and Hilhorst, D. (Eds), *Mapping Vulnerability: Disaster, Development and People*, Earthscan, Sterling, VA, pp. 25–37.

Barrett, C. and McPeak, J. (2004a), *Poverty Traps and Safety Nets*, available at: http://aem.cornell.edu/faculty_sites/cbb2/papers/BMT_povertytraps_june2004.pdf (accessed January 14, 2008).

Barrett, C. and McPeak, J. (2004b), "The economics of poverty traps and persistent poverty: an asset-based approach", *BASIS and CRSP*, p. 14, available at: www.nric.net/poverty/pubs/CarterBarrett.pdf (accessed January 14, 2008).

Braun, B. and Shoeb, A.Z.M. (2008), "Naturrisiken und Sozialkatastrophen in Bangladesch-Wirbelstürme und Überschwemmungen", in Felgentreff, C. and Glade, T. (Eds), *Naturrisiken und Sozialkatastrophen*, Spektrum Akademischer Verlag, Berlin, pp. 381–94.

BUDMP (2002), "Hazard mapping and vulnerability assessment for flood mitigation, Asia case study 1", Bangladesh Urban Disaster Mitigation Programme, available at: www.provention-consortium.org/themes/default/pdfs/CRA/Bangladesh.pdf (accessed December 18, 2007).

Callon, M. and Law, J. (1989), "On the construction of socio-material networks: content and context revisited", *Knowledge and Society: Studies in the Sociology of Science Past and Present*, Vol. 8, pp. 57–83.

Cannon, T., Twigg, J. and Rowell, J. (2004), *Social Vulnerability, Sustainable Livelihoods and Disasters*, DFID, London.

Chambers, R. (1989), "Editorial introduction: Vulnerability, coping and policy", *IDS Bulletin*, Vol. 20 No. 2.

Chowdhury, A. (1998), "Disasters: issues and responses", in Gain, P. (Ed.), *Bangladesh Environment: Facing the 21st Century*, SHED, Dhaka, pp. 203–20.

Clausen, L., Geenen, E.M. and Macamo, E. (Eds) (2003), "Entsetzliche soziale Prozesse", *Theorie und Empirie der Katastrophe*, LIT-Verlag, Münster, pp. 23–30.

Cutter, S.I. (1996), "Vulnerability to environmental hazards", *Progress in Human Geography*, Vol. 209, pp. 529–39.

Dacope Upazila Parishad (2005), *Union Statistics of Dacope Upazila Parishad up to 2005*, Dacope Upazila, Khulna, Bangladesh.

Devereux, S. and Sabates-Wheeler, R. (2004), "Transformative social protection", IDS Working Paper No. 232, Institute of Development Studies, Brighton.

Dikau, R. and Weichselgartner, J. (2005), *Der unruhige Planet*, Der Mensch und die Naturgefahren, Darmstadt.

Dutton, J. (2001), *Weather Impact on USA Economy*, November, NOAA, available at: www.noaanews.noaa.gov/magazine/stories/mag4.htm/ (accessed December 23, 2004).

EU (1998), *Cyclone Shelter Preparatory Study (CPSP) Stage I: Feasibility Study, Draft Final Report*, Supp. Vol. 3, Community Development Studies, Part A, Supp. Vol. 8; Environmental Analysis, Field visits and other notes, EC/Sener Ingenieria Sistemas SA.

Gladwin, H., Lazo, J.K., Morrow, B.H., Peacock, W.G. and Willoughby, H.E. (2007), "Social science research needs for the hurricane forecast and warning system", *Natural Hazards Review*, Vol. 8 No. 3, pp. 87–95.

GoB (2008), *Damage, Loss and Needs Assessment for Disaster Recovery and Reconstruction*, Ministry of Food and Disaster Management, Government of Bangladesh.

Gupta, M. (2002) "Empowered individual: caring neighbours make the best disaster managers", *Proceedings of the Regional Workshop on Best Practices in Disaster Mitigation in Bali, Indonesia*.

ISDR (2000), *Mobilizing Local Communities in Reducing Disasters*, International Strategy for Disaster Reduction, United Nations, available at: www.unisdr.org/eng/public_aware/world_camp/2001/pdf/Kit_4_Mobilizing_Local_Communities_in_Reducing_Disasters.pdf (accessed January 12, 2008).

Kafle, S.K. and Morshed, Z. (2001), *Participants' Workbook, Community-Based Disaster Management for Local Authorities*, Asian Disaster Preparedness Center (ADPC), Bangkok, pp. 16–24.

Karim, N. (2000), *Options for Cyclone Protection: Bangladesh Context*, available at: www.climate.org/PDF/Bangladesh.pdf (accessed April 12, 2008).

Light, P. (2005), "Lessons learned: Hurricane Katrina and Wilma hit US Gulf coastal states", *Boston Globe*, September 4.

Mallick, D.L., Rahman, A., Alam, M., Juel, A.S. Md., Ahmad, A.N. and Alam, S.S. (2005), "Floods in Bangladesh: a shift from disaster management towards disaster preparedness. Case study 3: Bangladesh", *IDS Bulletin*, Vol. 36 No. 4, pp. 53–70.

Matbor, G.M. (2007), "Enhancement of community preparedness for natural disasters – the role of social work in building social capital for sustainable disaster relief and management", *International Social Work*, Vol. 50 No. 3, pp. 357–69.

Miyan, M.A. (2005), "Cyclone disaster mitigation in Bangladesh", *Proceedings of the 2nd Regional Technical Conference on Tropical Cyclones, Storm Surges and Floods*, Secretariat of the World Meteorological Organization, Geneva, available at: www.fao.org/forestry/webview/media?mediaId=11285&langId=1 (accessed February 2, 2008).

Morshed, M. and Huda, N. (2002), "Community participation in urban flood mitigation under Bangladesh Urban Disaster Mitigation Project (BUDMP)", *Proceedings of the Regional Workshop on Best Practices in Disaster Mitigation in Bali, Indonesia.*

Müller-Mahn, D. (2007), "Perspektiven der geographischen Risikoforschung", *Geographische Rundschau*, Vol. 59 No. 10, pp. 4–11.

Najam, A. (2004), "The environmental challenge to human security in South Asia", in Takhur, R. and Wiggen, O. (Eds), *South Asia in the World: Problem-Solving Perspectives on Security, Sustainable Development and Good Governance*, United Nations University Press, Hong Kong, pp. 225–47.

NRC (2007), *Tools and Methods for Estimating Populations at Risk from Natural Disasters and Complex Humanitarian Crises*, The National Academies Press, Washington, DC, pp. 17–20.

Oliver-Smith, A. (2004), "Theorizing vulnerability in a globalised world: a political ecological perspective", in Bankoff, G., Freks, G. and Hilthrost, D. (Eds), *Mapping Vulnerability: Disaster, Development and People*, Earthscan, Sterling, VA, pp. 10–24.

Pandey, B. and Okazaki, K. (2005), *Community-Based Disaster Management: Empowering Communities to Cope with Disaster Risks*, United Nations Center for Regional Development, Japan, available at: http://unpan1.un.org/intradoc/groups/public/documents/un/unpan020698.pdf (accessed January 18, 2008).

Pettit, J. and Wheeler, J. (2005), "Developing rights? Relating discourse to context and practice", *IDS Bulletin*, Vol. 36 No. 1, Institute of Development Studies, Brighton, pp. 1-8.

Safiuddin, M. and Karim, M.M. (2001), "Groundwater arsenic contamination in Bangladesh: causes, effects and remediation", *Proceedings of the 1st IEB International Conference; Institution of Engineers, Bangladesh.*

SDR (2003), *Reducing Disaster Vulnerability through Science and Technology – An Interim Report*, Subcommittee on Disaster Reduction, National Science and Technology Council, Washington, DC, p. 12, available at: www.sdr.gov/SDR_Report_ReducingDisasterVulnerability2003.pdf (accessed January 12, 2008).

Sperling, F. and Szekely, F. (2005), "Disaster risk management in a changing climate", discussion paper, prepared for the World Conference on Disaster Reduction on behalf of the Vulnerability and Adaptation Research Group, Kobe, Japan, 18-22 January.

Steins, N. (2001), "New directions in natural resource management: the offer of actor-network theory", *IDS Bulletin*, Vol. 32 No. 4.

Sumathipala, G. (2002), "Community participation in disaster mitigation in Nawalapitiya Urban Council, Sri Lanka", *Proceedings of the Regional Workshop on Best Practices in Disaster Mitigation in Bali, Indonesia.*

Turner, B.L. II, Kasperson, R.E., Matson, P., McCarthy, J.J., Corell, R.W., Christensen, L., Eckley, N., Kasperson, J.X., Luers, A., Martello, M.L., Polsky, C., Pulsipher, A. and Schiller, A. (2003), "Framework for vulnerability analysis in sustainability science", *Proceedings of the National Academy of Sciences of the United States of America*, Vol. 100 No. 14, 8 July, pp. 8074-9.

Victoria, L.P. (2002), "Community-based approaches to disaster mitigation", *Proceedings of the Regional Technical Workshop on Coastal Protection in the Aftermath of the Indian Ocean Tsunami: What Role for Forests and Trees in Khao Lak, Thailand?*

Wiebe, H. (2000), "Flood action plan in Bangladesh", *Dams and Development*, available at: www.dams.org/docs/kbase/contrib/opt174.pdf (accessed January 12, 2008).

Wisner, B. and Blaikie, P.M. (2004), *At Risk: Natural Hazards, People's Vulnerability and Disasters*, 2nd ed., Routledge, Oxford, p. 464.

Yamin, F., Rahman, A. and Huq, S. (2005), "Vulnerability, adaptation and climate disasters: a conceptual overview", *IDS Bulletin*, Vol. 36 No. 4, pp. 1–14.

Critical Success Factors for Community-based Post-disaster Housing Reconstruction Projects in the Pre-construction Stage in Indonesia ☆

Taufika Ophiyandri, Dilanthi Amaratunga, Chaminda Pathirage and Kaushal Keraminiyage

Abstract

Purpose – The purpose of this paper is to investigate the critical success factors (CSFs) of community-based post-disaster housing reconstruction projects (CPHRP) during the pre-construction stage.

Design/methodology/approach – An extensive literature review and interviews were undertaken to establish selected factors contributing to the success of community-based post disaster housing reconstruction projects. Following this, a questionnaire survey was administered to key stakeholders in order to perceive their view on CSFs of CPHRP. Data were analysed by deploying statistical software.

Findings – It was found that 12 factors are considered to be the CSFs: transparency and accountability, appropriate reconstruction policy/strategy, an understanding of the community-based method, gathering trust from the community, facilitator capacity, good coordination and communication, sufficient funding availability, implementer capacity, having a significant level of community participation/control, government support, involvement of all community members, and successful beneficiary identification.

Practical implications – The establishment of CSFs in CPHRP helps key stakeholders to identify factors that must exist and go well during pre-construction of CPHRP, in order to ensure the success of the programme.

Originality/value – The paper is very specific as it attempts to discover the CSFs of CPHRP during the pre-construction stage.

Keywords: Disasters; Housing; Indonesia; Critical success factors; Housing reconstruction; Community-based

☆The research is funded by DIKTI scholarship, Directorate General of Higher Education, Ministry of National Education, Republic of Indonesia.

Reprinted from *International Journal of Disaster Resilience in the Built Environment*
Vol. 4 No. 2, pp. 236–249 (2013). doi:10.1108/IJDRBE-03-2013-0005

1. Introduction

Post-disaster reconstruction has been seen as an opportunity to build back better (Labadie, 2008; Amaratunga and Haigh, 2011), in other words, what has been affected by disaster should be built better than before and be able to withstand future disasters. However, the implementation of this simple goal is not straightforward, particularly in the housing sector. The increasing number of large earthquake occurrences in the last decade has led to massive housing reconstruction projects which unfortunately have been found to be the most challenging sector (Lambert, 2007; World Vision, 2008).

Several approaches in post-disaster housing reconstruction are available to be implemented (Jha *et al.*, 2010; da Silva, 2010) and one of them is the community-based method. In this type of reconstruction, the community have a significant amount of control over the project (Ophiyandri *et al.*, 2010). The affected community are not just consulted about their needs and expectations, but they can be an owner, a supervisor, or even a contractor of their own housing reconstruction project. This method has gathered a lot of success in the reconstruction of many affected areas, for instance in Bam, Iran (Fallahi, 2007), the Maldives (Lawther, 2009), Gujarat (Barenstein, 2008), and Indonesia (Dercon and Kusumawijaya, 2007; MacRae and Hodgkin, 2011; Ophiyandri *et al.*, 2011). However, some problems still remain with this method (Davidson *et al.*, 2007; Dercon and Kusumawijaya, 2007) which can lead to cost overrun, delays in delivery, quality degradation, and dissatisfaction. The level of success of community-based post-disaster housing reconstruction projects (CPHRP) can be increased through the identification of critical success factors (CSFs), about which the research has been well established, begun by Rockart (1979). Many models of CSFs in different types of projects have been developed (Belassi and Tukel, 1996; Chan and Chan, 2004). However, little attention has been paid to the CSFs in post-disaster housing reconstruction. Given the above background, this paper aims to investigate the CSFs of CPHRP during the pre-construction stage in Indonesia.

2. Literature Review

Earthquakes and their Impact

Indonesia is a highly disaster prone country, particularly to earthquakes. The frequency of occurrence of large earthquakes has increased significantly in the last ten years in Indonesia. The earthquake which triggered the tsunami in Aceh on 26 December 2004 measured 9.1 on the Richter scale, followed by an earthquake in Nias Island on 28 March 2005. In 2006, a large earthquake which measured 6.3 on the Richter scale struck Yogyakarta, affecting two provinces: Yogyakarta and central Java. A large earthquake (7.6 on the Richter scale) hit the West Sumatra province on 30 September 2009. These earthquakes have created considerable losses to

Indonesian communities. A summary of the fatalities, economic losses and number of houses heavily damaged are given in Table I.

As can be seen from Table I, earthquakes have left hundreds of thousands of houses destroyed or heavily damaged. Housing is the most affected sector by earthquakes, and often is the most challenging sector of the entire reconstruction programme. In Aceh and Nias (referred to as just Aceh), losses in the housing sector were over 30 per cent of total damage and loss assessment (BRR, 2006). In Yogyakarta and Central Java (referred to as just Yogyakarta) and West Sumatra, the total losses were dominated by the housing sector – 53 and 74 per cent of the total losses, respectively, (Bappenas *et al.*, 2006; BNPB *et al.*, 2009). These figures indicate the severity of damage caused by earthquake in the housing sector in these affected areas.

Practices of the Community-based Approach

According to Abarquez and Murshed (2004), community in the context of disaster management is:

> [...] a group that may share one or more things in common, such as living in the same environment, having similar disaster risk exposure, or having been affected by a disaster.

A similar definition, though more closely related to the built environment, is proposed by Ginige and Amaratunga (2011). They define community as:

> [...] individuals and groups sharing a natural and built environment that is vulnerable to hazards. In other words, community is the general public; the users and occupants of the built environment and the beneficiaries of post-disaster reconstruction.

Table I: Number of fatalities, economic losses and housing damage because of earthquake in Aceh and Nias, Yogyakarta and Central Java, and West Sumatra

No.	Disaster location	Fatalities	Economic losses (US$)	Housing destroyed/heavily damage
1	Aceh and Nias, 2004 and 2005	127,720	4.9 billion	139,195
2	Yogyakarta and Central Java, 2006	5,716	3.1 billion	250,000
3	West Sumatra, 2009	1,117	2.3 billion	115,000

Source: BNPB *et al.* (2009), BRR (2009), Bappenas *et al.* (2006) and JRF (2010)

Drawing from the above definitions, in this context, the authors define community as "groups of beneficiaries for housing reconstruction in which their houses are affected by a disaster".

Davidson *et al.* (2007) categorized the level of community participation in post-disaster housing reconstruction into five aspects; the level to which the community can manipulate, inform, consult, collaborate, and empower, where in the last category the community have more power to control the reconstruction project. To be considered as being the community-based method, Ophiyandri *et al.* (2010) suggest that the level of participation of the community should be at least at the level of collaboration. The practice of the community-based method in post disaster housing reconstruction in Indonesia has been conducted in the reconstruction of Aceh and Nias, Yogyakarta and Central Java, and West Sumatra. In the reconstruction of Aceh, the Government of Indonesia (GOI) established an agency called BRR (agency for the rehabilitation and reconstruction) to coordinate and implement a community-driven reconstruction programme. The policy adopted for the new housing was to provide the beneficiaries with a type-36 house, which means the minimum area was 36 m^2. However, despite the spirit of a community-driven programme being clearly stated in the policy, few projects were categorized as being "real" community-based. However, the implementation of CPHRP in Aceh has shown its superiority to the contactor-based method in many ways, notably that it can achieve high satisfaction among beneficiaries.

Learning from the success of CPHRP in Aceh and particularly its advantages to the beneficiaries, the GOI committed to implement this approach in the reconstruction of Yogyakarta. The reconstruction of Yogyakarta was very different from the reconstruction in Aceh, particularly in terms of funding and implementation agencies. While in Aceh the main source of funding came from donors, the main source of funding in Yogyakarta was provided by the GOI (80 per cent) (Bappenas *et al.*, 2008). For coordination and implementing agencies the GOI did not establish a new agency like BRR, but appointed a national technical team (TTN) for coordination and technical departments in local government for the implementing agencies. The GOI could not construct a full house like in Aceh, because of budget limitations, but provided cash grants of Rs 15 million (US$1,500) for a heavily damaged house and adopted the community-based method for its implementation. There was also a reconstruction program called Community-based Settlement Reconstruction and Rehabilitation Project (CSRRP) from which the funding was provided by a group of seven international donors called Java Reconstruction Fund (JRF), and it successfully built 15,153 houses (JRF, 2010). Both programmes were acknowledged to be successful, although some aspects needed to be enhanced (Bappenas *et al.*, 2008; MacRae and Hodgkin, 2011).

The policy of reconstruction of West Sumatra also implemented the community-based approach and replicated the Yogyakarta reconstruction model. The GOI established a technical support team (TPT) for coordination and the implementation was carried out by local government. However, the funding available for reconstruction was insufficient (Pranoto *et al.*, 2011) and contributed to the slow progress of housing reconstruction. After almost four years following the disaster, housing reconstruction is still taking place. The block grant provided for beneficiaries was the same for Yogyakarta victims, Rs 15 million, for a heavily damaged house.

Critical Success Factors

Rockart (1979), in his seminal paper, defines CSFs as:

> [...] the limited number of areas in which results, if they are satisfactory, will ensure successful competitive performance for the organization. They are the few key areas where "things must go right" for the business to flourish.

Similarly, according to Boynton and Zmud (1984), CSFs are:

> [...] those few things that must go well to ensure success for a manager or an organization, and, therefore, they represent those managerial or enterprise areas that must be given special and continual attention to bring about high performance.

Synthesizing from these two definitions, both mention the "few factors" and the words "satisfactory/well". In this context, the meaning of CSFs adopted in this paper is the few factors that must go well in order to ensure the successful implementation of CPHRP.

Many scholars have investigated CSF models or frameworks. For instance, the CSFs for a general project were developed by Belassi and Tukel (1996), Chua *et al.* (1999) and Pinto and Slevin (1988), and for general construction projects such as Chan and Chan (2004). Specific CSF models in construction projects have also been researched by scholars, such as in construction research and development (Kulatunga *et al.*, 2009), competitiveness of contractors (Lu *et al.*, 2008), performance of safety programs (Aksorn and Hadikusumo, 2008), labour-intensive construction sub-contractors (Ng and Tang, 2010), and construction project briefing (Yu *et al.*, 2006). However, those models already developed cannot be implemented or adopted directly to the CPHRP, since the circumstances of post-disaster housing reconstruction projects are different compared to construction projects in normal situations. The uniqueness is increased further by the implementation of being community-based, which is also extremely different compared to the traditional procurement method in construction projects.

The success factors can be indicated by identifying a specific factor that creates a problem or an area having a risk that affects the success of the project. Manelele and Muya (2008) reveal that many critical risks of community-based construction projects are found in the pre-construction stage, such as unconfirmed sources of funds, lack of technical advice, lack of consensus, lack of cooperation, non-conformity to standard specifications, incompetency in recruiting skilled labour, unavailability of skilled labour, incompetent labour, lengthy tender processes, and lack of work schedules. In line with this, many problems with the implementation of the community-based approach in the post disaster context has also been found in the pre-construction stage, such as inappropriate policies on reconstruction strategy, lack of understanding on the meaning of the community-based programme, coordination and communication problems, and lack of a database system (Dercon and Kusumawijaya, 2007; Davidson *et al.*, 2007; Ganapati and Ganapati, 2009). In addition, there are many specific activities of post disaster housing reconstruction taking place in this stage, such as damage assessment, beneficiary identification, facilitator recruitment, forming a community organisation and community training. Accordingly, this research focuses on the pre-construction stage of CPHRP.

3. Methodology

A questionnaire survey was conducted aiming to investigate the degree of influence of selected success factors (SSFs) on the success of CPHRP. The identification of SSFs was carried out through extensive literature review and interviews conducted in Indonesia. Following this step, a structured questionnaire was developed and piloted in November 2011. The results from the pilot study meant that minor revisions were made to the format of the questionnaire and additions made to the SSFs. The finalized questionnaire consists of 32 SSFs and is drafted in two languages, English and Bahasa Indonesian. In the questionnaire, respondents were invited to rate the level of influence of SSFs based on a five-point Likert scale, varying from:

(1) not influential at all;
(2) slightly influential;
(3) influential;
(4) very influential; and
(5) extremely influential.

To be classified as a CSF, each SSF rating mean has to be equal or more than four, which indicates that the level of influence has to be more than "influential". In the case of more than one factor having the same mean value, the factor having the lower standard deviation would be classified as more influential.

The questionnaire was administered in December 2011 and completed in February 2012. The survey applied the snowball sampling technique where some respondents informed the researchers' other potential respondents. The questionnaire was emailed to 92 potential respondents and 73 completed questionnaires were received by the researchers, representing a 79 per cent feedback rate. The response rate was considered very satisfactory. Among these 73 questionnaires, 65 questionnaires were categorized as valid. The validity criterion was based on two factors: respondents having had experience in CPHRP, and one of the project locations being in Indonesia.

The nature of respondents' organisations and working experience is shown in Figure 1. It can be seen that most of the respondents' demographic background comes from international NGOs. Respondents were working in various positions during the CPHRP, ranging from facilitators (29 per cent), consultants (29 per cent), advisors (28 per cent), project staff (23 per cent) and project managers (20 per cent). Analysing the respondents' experience in terms of duration and location, Figure 1(b) shows that most of the respondents have been working for more than six years (80 per cent), whilst on the other hand their working experience in reconstruction was less than six years (75 per cent). This implies that most post-disaster reconstruction projects are a recent phenomenon in Indonesia. The majority of respondents have worked on the reconstruction of Aceh followed by Yogyakarta and Padang. 43 respondents have only worked in one location, while 13 respondents and four respondents have worked in two and three different locations, respectively. The overlap of respondents' locations in reconstruction projects is shown in Figure 2. In addition, 91 per cent of respondents have worked in Indonesia, while 9 per cent of them have also worked outside Indonesia, such as in Sri Lanka, Pakistan and Haiti.

4. Analysis and Discussion

Data was analysed using statistical package for social sciences (SPSS) 16.0, including descriptive statistics, and a one sample t-test was also conducted at a 95 per cent significance level with a test value of zero, in order to evaluate the significance level of success factors statistically. The results of descriptive statistics and the one sample t-test are shown in Table II. It can be seen that 12 from 32 SSFs can be considered as CSFs since the average is equal to, or more than four. The highest CSF is:

- transparency and accountability (mean value = 4.406), followed by;
- appropriate reconstruction policy/strategy;

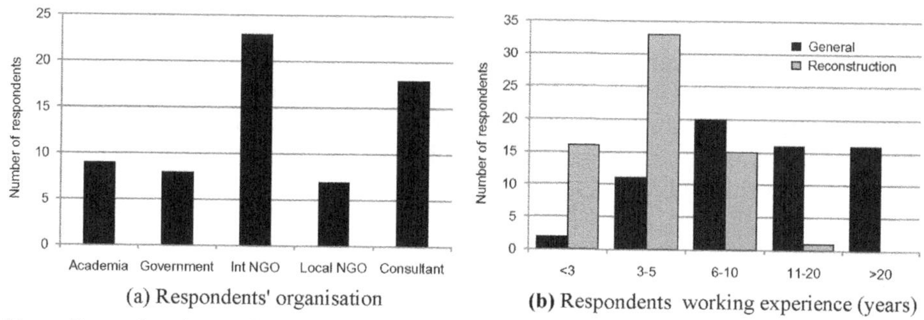

Note: General and post-disaster reconstruction

Figure 1: Respondents' organisations and working experience

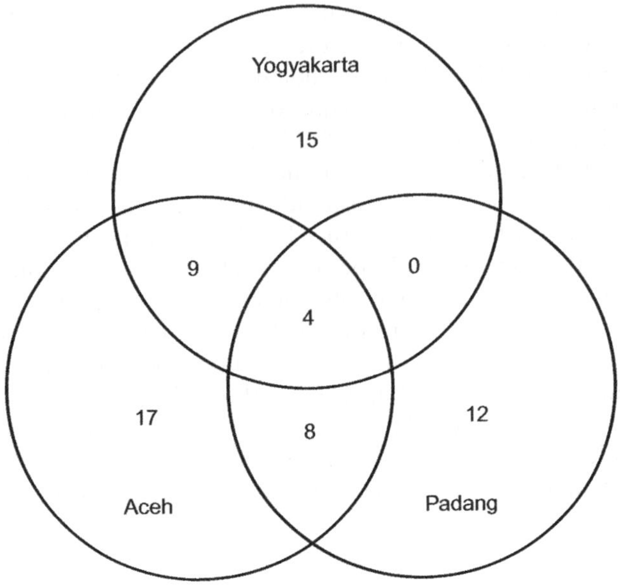

Figure 2: Number of respondents based on project location in Indonesia

- understanding the community-based method;
- gathering trust from the community;
- facilitator capacity;
- good coordination and communication;
- sufficient funding availability;
- implementer capacity;
- significant level of community participation/control;
- involvement of all community members;
- successful beneficiary identification; and
- government support.

Details of each CSF can be seen in Table II. The low standard deviation suggests that there is not much variability between samples and the population mean. Further, the results of the *t*-test in Table II strengthen the findings by indicating that all success factors are statistically significant as the significant value is very high at 0.00 (less than 0.05).

Transparency and Accountability

Transparency and accountability is perceived by respondents as the most critical factor for the success of CPHRP. Dasgupta and Beard (2007) and Labadie (2008)

Table II: Success factors in CPHRP as perceived by different stakeholders

SSFs	Mean	SD	*t*	Test value = 0 Sig. (two-tailed)	95% confidence interval of the difference Lower	Upper	Rank
Transparency and accountability	4.385	0.744	47.541	0.000	4.200	4.569	1
Appropriate reconstruction policy/strategy	4.323	0.589	59.158	0.000	4.177	4.469	2
Understanding on community-based method	4.262	0.668	51.438	0.000	4.096	4.427	3
Gathering trust from community	4.215	0.780	43.545	0.000	4.022	4.409	4
Facilitator capacity	4.185	0.748	45.118	0.000	3.999	4.370	5
Good coordination and communication	4.169	0.720	46.713	0.000	3.991	4.348	6
Sufficient funding availability	4.169	0.858	39.167	0.000	3.957	4.382	7
Implementer capacity	4.154	0.755	44.369	0.000	3.967	4.341	8
Significant level of community participation/control	4.077	0.835	39.367	0.000	3.870	4.284	9
Government support	4.015	0.820	39.502	0.000	3.812	4.219	10
Involvement of all community members	4.015	0.820	39.502	0.000	3.812	4.219	11
Successful beneficiaries identification	4.015	0.838	38.614	0.000	3.808	4.223	12
Minimising bureaucracy	3.954	0.779	40.908	0.000	3.761	4.147	13
Successful land tenure identification	3.908	0.897	35.139	0.000	3.686	4.130	14
Appropriate project organisation	3.877	0.801	39.045	0.000	3.679	4.075	15
Materials availability	3.862	0.827	37.653	0.000	3.657	4.066	16
Successful community training	3.846	0.734	42.258	0.000	3.664	4.028	17
Good written contract between community and implementer	3.800	0.987	31.027	0.000	3.555	4.045	18
Success on forming community organisation	3.785	0.838	36.395	0.000	3.577	3.992	19
Conducive social environment	3.769	0.806	37.720	0.000	3.570	3.969	20
Sufficient numbers of facilitators	3.754	0.751	40.318	0.000	3.568	3.940	21
Access to affected community	3.677	0.986	30.066	0.000	3.433	3.921	22
Successful damage assessment	3.615	0.860	33.875	0.000	3.402	3.829	23
Conducive physical environment	3.600	0.787	36.898	0.000	3.405	3.795	24
Project duration	3.585	0.950	30.415	0.000	3.349	3.820	25
Government capacity	3.539	0.903	31.602	0.000	3.315	3.762	26
Having a pre-reconstruction plan (scenario based) before disaster	3.539	0.985	28.949	0.000	3.294	3.783	27
Conducive economical environment	3.492	0.850	33.122	0.000	3.282	3.703	28
Conducive political environment	3.477	0.986	28.431	0.000	3.233	3.721	29
Project location	3.354	0.943	28.687	0.000	3.120	3.587	30
Design flexibility	3.339	0.871	30.902	0.000	3.123	3.554	31
Project size	3.339	0.923	29.153	0.000	3.110	3.567	32

highlighted the importance of these factors in community-based projects. Moreover, Labadie (2008) argued that with transparency and accountability, the chance of success of post-disaster reconstruction can be increased. Transparency and accountability are required not only in terms of funding, but in all aspects of the housing reconstruction. Transparency in information, programme details and objectives, decision making processes, funding availability and its disbursement, and time scales, are some aspects that are important. It is also required in every stage of the reconstruction process, from planning to implementation.

In post disaster reconstruction, traumatic conditions often make survivors become suspicious to people coming from outside their community. Sometimes there are hidden agendas brought by outside organisations and this manipulates the community in achieving their own objectives. Transparency and accountability can also minimize corruption. Failure to address this issue can lead to high dissatisfaction from beneficiaries. Hence, it is not surprising that this factor became the highest critical factor to ensure the success of CPHRP.

Appropriate Reconstruction Policy/Strategy

The second factor that contributes to the success of CPHRP is appropriate reconstruction policy and strategy. Inappropriate policy or strategy can be very costly and waste time. One reason for this is because the government is forced into making quick decisions on reconstruction strategy in order to provide houses for beneficiaries as soon as possible.

In Aceh, for example, the initial blue print for reconstruction required a safety zone, or a non built area 2 km from the coastline and survivors were not allowed to go back to their destroyed land. This policy was later revised, as no buffer zone was implemented and the community could rebuild their houses in the exiting location. In Sri Lanka, the introduction of a buffer zone was also reduced from 100-200 m to 35-50 m. The changing policy in these two tsunami affected areas has delayed the reconstruction process. As suggested by Davidson *et al.* (2007), it is impossible to develop a single best approach of CPHRP that can be adopted universally, since it is very contextual. The level of destruction, level of capacity of affected stakeholders, funding availability, and culture will be different from one affected area to another. Thus, da Silva (2010) highlighted that the key consideration in establishing reconstruction strategy is by understanding the geography, society, economics, politics, climate and hazards of the affected area.

Understanding of the Community-based Method

The community-based method is a form of high level community participation in a reconstruction programme. Reconstruction which only consults the community about their needs and expectations with no guarantee that it will be implemented, and with no contribution from the community afterwards, cannot be classified as community-based or community-driven methods.

External organisations sometimes underestimate the capacity of the affected community and often assume that they know what is best for the community. In reality, it is the community that know what is best for them, and what they need. Thus, without involving the community from the very beginning of a reconstruction project, makes it very unlikely that the reconstruction project will be successful. As a result, the community should be engaged from the very beginning until the end of the CPHRP. Every effort of post-disaster reconstruction should benefit the beneficiaries, people should be at the heart of the programme.

As survivors in a community become passive in post-disaster situations, there are four basic strategies required in order to increase the level of participation (Johnston, 1982): build mutual trust between community members, leaders, and external organisations; give the community an opportunity to participate; encourage communities to welcome the project since it provides something of value to them; and promote a strong sense of ownership and responsibility for the programme within the community.

Gathering Trust from the Community

This is a must for a community-based approach. The CPHRP requires external agencies to work closely together with the affected community. Without having a mutual trust between parties involved in the reconstruction process, it would be unlikely that the programme would be successful. There are many ways to gather trust from the community, such as through transparency and accountability, understanding the local culture and religious aspects in the community, showing respect to the community, and by showing that the implementers are competent and capable of carrying out the programme successfully.

Facilitator Capacity

Success and failure of the housing reconstruction programme will also depend on the capacity of the facilitator. The facilitator is the one who is directly involved and works together with the community in the housing reconstruction project. Facilitators guide the community in the process of housing reconstruction, from the concept, planning, construction and through to completion. Facilitators are also responsible for upgrading community capacity through training programmes. It is not only technical skills required to become a good facilitator, soft skills are also important.

Good Coordination and Communication

Coordination and communication have become one of the major issues in post-disaster reconstruction. This issue emerged in Aceh, Yogyakarta and Central Java, and West Sumatra reconstruction programmes (BRR, 2009; MacRae and Hodgkin,

2011; Sugimin *et al.*, 2011). MacRae and Hodgkin (2011) state that the greatest problem in post-disaster housing reconstruction is to coordinate three main stakeholders: international NGOs, local NGOs and governments.

Uncoordinated reconstruction can lead to programmes overlapping and competition between implementing agencies. In Aceh, for example, the availability of huge funding and lack of coordination have made some NGOs compete for beneficiaries, not for sources of funds. Thus, it is important to administer who is doing what, where, when and how. For effective coordination, Moe and Pathranarakul (2006) suggested to group the coordination into five levels: international, national, regional, organisational, and project level. A mode of fast and effective communication between stakeholders also has to be established in order to ensure the success of CPHRP. As a result, the implementation of information systems for fast, accurate, reliable and up to date information is crucial.

Sufficient Funding Availability

Funding availability obviously is very important in any kind of project. In a post-disaster housing reconstruction context, the amount of money available to be spent will determine the type of house that can be delivered and to what extent government/organisation can provide assistance to beneficiaries. As described elsewhere, with sufficient funds, a full house reconstruction (more than $4,500) can be provided to beneficiaries, while in Yogyakarta and Padang, with a limited government budget, the amount of money that could be allocated was only around US$1,500 per household. The challenges in funding, according to da Silva (2010) are the total amount of availability, the time scales over which it can be spent and specific requirements from donors. Llyod-Jones (2006) also highlighted that funding for reconstruction is too inflexible and focused on the short-term plan.

The huge funding availability in Aceh was a very rare case in a post-disaster situation (Steinberg, 2007; da Silva, 2010), as in normal scenarios funding is only sufficient for emergency and provision of temporary shelters (da Silva, 2010), such as in Yogyakarta and West Sumatra. To fulfil the post-disaster reconstruction needs, loan or grants from donors are needed by non-developed countries (Freeman, 2004). As a result, governments have to start designing an innovative way to fund the post-disaster housing reconstruction.

Implementer Capacity

The reconstruction of Aceh has witnessed many organisations failing to adopt the community-based approach. Excessive funding availability has made some organisations which originally were humanitarian organisations to get involved in housing reconstruction projects (Steinberg, 2007). For many organisations it was their first experience and as a result many of them stopped their programme during the process or failed in producing good quality houses (Dercon and Kusumawijaya, 2007). Kennedy *et al.* (2008) suggest that implementing organisations should evaluate their own capacity, and if found to be low then partnerships or collaboration with other organisations should be sought. This shows how important the implementer capacity is in CPHRP.

Significant Level of Community Participation/Control

The role of the community in the post-disaster reconstruction process can vary, but basically they should be engaged in every stage of the reconstruction process. Their level of participation should be at the level of collaboration and empowerment. Davidson *et al.* (2007) in their research in four case studies, have found that empowerment of the community in post-disaster housing reconstruction achieved higher satisfaction among beneficiaries compared to projects in which community participation was minimal.

However, assuming that the higher the level of community participation, the better the result of reconstruction can be misleading. The level of community control on post-disaster housing reconstruction will much depend on the capacity of the community itself and considering the local context. For example, it is inappropriate to engage all communities to construct their own houses by themselves (as labourers) as there might be some of them just willing to only supervise their house reconstruction. Moreover, Kennedy *et al.* (2008) suggest that community participation does not necessarily mean communities have complete control over the reconstruction process.

Government Support

The support from government is very important. Inevitably the reconstruction effort is within the government domain and the government is responsible for providing better housing for beneficiaries. Hence, the government should support any effort to provide assistance for beneficiaries.

Involvement of all Community Members

Involvement of community members is important in implementing CPHRP. Although the nature of community participation can reduce the possibility of marginalisation, sometimes it happens (Dercon and Kusumawijaya, 2007). All community members have to contribute in the reconstruction process, particularly in the pre-construction stage. The voice of vulnerable or marginalised groups such as women, orphans, disabled or the elderly has to be heard, in order to capture all community needs and expectations.

Successful Beneficiary Identification

Although this factor was found to be the lowest ranked CSF, successful beneficiary identification is the path to producing speedy housing reconstruction and can lead to high satisfaction. Problems in beneficiary identification actually can be minimised if the government has an adequate data base system, which can identify the owner of affected houses, numbers of occupants, or the tenant of the house quickly and accurately. Yet, this type of system is not available. As a result, beneficiary identification and verification take a lot of time to be completed and can be costly.

In addition, the government also has to establish clear eligibility criteria for survivors to receive funding. In cases where budget is limited and reconstruction has to be carried out in stages, other criteria on who is entitled first also has to be informed for community transparently. This can reduce conflict between community members.

5. Conclusions

This research reveals there are 12 factors classified as critical in CPHRP. The top three critical factors that contribute to the success of CPHRP are transparency and accountability, appropriate reconstruction strategy/policy, and understanding of the community-based method.

The CSFs identified are not impartial factors, but are interconnected. For instance, by ensuring the accountability and transparency particularly to the beneficiaries, gathering trust would not be a challenging task; the implementer capacity factor is closely related to their understanding of the community-based approach; or the reconstruction strategy could affect the coordination/communication mechanism and degree of community involvement. With the establishment of the CSFs, it is expected that key stakeholders in post-disaster housing reconstruction projects to be informed of the factors and ensure that these factors are monitored during the reconstruction process.

References

Abarquez, I. and Murshed, Z. (2004), *Community-based Disaster Risk Management: A Field Practioners' Handbook*, ADPC, Pathum Thani.

Aksorn, T. and Hadikusumo, B.H.W. (2008), "Critical success factors influencing safety program performance in Thai construction projects", *Safety Science*, Vol. 46 No. 4, pp. 709–727.

Amaratunga, D. and Haigh, R.P. (2011), "Introduction", in Amaratunga, D. and Haigh, R. P. (Eds), *Post-disaster Reconstruction of the Built Environment: Rebuilding for Resilience*, Wiley, Chichester, pp. 1–12.

Bappenas, the Provincial and Local Governments of D.I. Yogyakarta, the Provincial and Local Governments of Central Java and International Partners (2006), "Preliminary damage and loss assessment Yogyakarta and Central Java natural disaster", paper presented at the 15th Meeting of The Consultative Group on Indonesia, Jakarta, 14 June.

Barenstein, J.D. (2008), "From Gujarat to Tamil Nadu: owner-driven vs. contractor-driven housing reconstruction in India", i-Rec, available at: www.sheltercentre.org/sites/default/files/IREC_OwnerDrivenVsContractorDrivenHousingReconstruction.pdf (accessed 5 May 2009).

Belassi, W. and Tukel, O.I. (1996), "A new framework for determining critical success/failure factors in projects", *International Journal of Project Management*, Vol. 14 No. 3, pp. 141–151.

BNPB, BAPPENAS, and the Provincial and District/City Governments of West Sumatra and Jambi and International Partners (2009), *West Sumatra and Jambi Natural Disasters: Damage, Loss and Preliminary Needs Assessment*, BNPB, Jakarta.

Boynton, A.C. and Zmud, R.W. (1984), "An assessment of critical success factors", *Sloan Management Review*, Vol. 25 No. 4, pp. 17–27.

BRR (2006), *Aceh and Nias, 2 Years After Tsunami: 2006 Progress Report*, BRR, Jakarta.

BRR (2009), *Housing: Roofing the Pillars of Hope*, BRR, Jakarta.

Chan, A.P.C. and Chan, A.P.L. (2004), "Key performance indicators for measuring construction success", *Benchmarking: An International Journal*, Vol. 11 No. 2, pp. 203–221.

Chua, D.K.H., Kog, Y.C. and Loh, P.K. (1999), "Critical success factors for different project objectives", *Journal of Construction Engineering and Management*, Vol. 125 No. 3, pp. 142–150.

Dasgupta, A. and Beard, V.A. (2007), "Community driven development, collective action and elite capture in Indonesia", *Development and Change*, Vol. 38 No. 2, pp. 229–249.

da Silva, J. (2010), *Lessons from Aceh: Key Considerations in Post-disaster Reconstruction*, Practical Action, Rugby.

Davidson, C.H., Johnson, C., Lizarralde, G., Dikmen, N. and Sliwinski, A. (2007), "Truths and myths about community participation in post-disaster housing projects", *Habitat International*, Vol. 31, pp. 100–115.

Dercon, B. and Kusumawijaya, M. (2007), "Two years of settlement recovery in Aceh and Nias: what should the planners have learned?", paper presented at 43rd ISOCARP Congress, Antwerp, Belgium, 19-23 September.

Fallahi, A. (2007), "Lessons learned from the housing reconstruction following the Bam earthquake in Iran", *The Australian Journal of Emergency Management*, Vol. 22 No. 1, pp. 26–35.

Freeman, P.K. (2004), "Allocation of post-disaster reconstruction financing to housing", *Building Research and Information*, Vol. 32 No. 5, pp. 427–437.

Ganapati, N.E. and Ganapati, S. (2009), "Enabling participatory planning after disasters: a case study of the World Bank's housing reconstruction in Turkey", *Journal of the American Planning Association*, Vol. 75 No. 1, pp. 41–59.

Ginige, K. and Amaratunga, D. (2011), "Capacity development for post-disaster reconstruction of the built environment", in Amaratunga, D. and Haigh, R.P. (Eds), *Post-disaster Reconstruction of the Built Environment: Rebuilding for Resilience*, Wiley, Chichester, pp. 13–29.

Jha, A.K., Barenstein, J.D., Phelps, P.M., Pittet, D. and Sena, S. (2010), *Safer Homes, Stronger Communities: A Handbook for Reconstructing after Natural Disasters*, The World Bank, Washington, DC.

Johnston, M. (1982), "The labyrinth of community participation: experience in Indonesia", *Community Development Journal*, Vol. 17 No. 3.

JRF (2010), *Progress Report 2010: Enhancing Community Resilience for a Self Sustaining Future*, JRF, Jakarta.

Kennedy, J., Ashmore, J., Babister, E. and Kelman, I. (2008), "The meaning of build back better: evidence from post-tsunami Aceh and Sri Lanka", *Journal of Contingencies and Crisis Management*, Vol. 16 No. 1, pp. 24–36.

Kulatunga, U., Amaratunga, D. and Haigh, R. (2009), "Critical success factors of construction research and development", *Construction Management and Economics*, Vol. 27 No. 9, pp. 891–900.

Labadie, J.R. (2008), "Auditing of post-disaster recovery and reconstruction activities", *Disaster Prevention and Management*, Vol. 17 No. 5, pp. 575–586.

Lambert, B. (2007), *UNHCR's Response to the Tsunami Emergency in Indonesia and Sri Lanka, December 2004-November 2006: An Independent Evaluation*, UNHCR's Policy Development and Evaluation Service (PDES), Geneva.

Lawther, P.M. (2009), "Community involvement in post-disaster re-construction – case study of the British Red Cross Maldives recovery programme", *International Journal of Strategic Property Management*, Vol. 13 No. 2, pp. 153–169.

Llyod-Jones, T. (2006), *Mind the Gap! Post-disaster Reconstruction and the Transition from Humanitarian Relief*, RICS, London.

Lu, W., Shen, L. and Yam, M.C.H. (2008), "Critical success factors for competitiveness of contractors: China study", *Journal of Construction Engineering and Management*, Vol. 134 No. 12, pp. 972–982.

MacRae, G. and Hodgkin, D. (2011), "Half full or half empty? Shelter after the Jogjakarta earthquake", *Disasters*, Vol. 35 No. 1, pp. 243–267.

Manelele, I. and Muya, M. (2008), "Risk identification on community-based construction projects in Zambia", *Journal of Engineering, Design and Technology*, Vol. 6 No. 2, pp. 145–161.

Moe, T.L. and Pathranarakul, P. (2006), "An integrated approach to natural disaster management: public project management and its critical success factors", *Disaster Prevention and Management*, Vol. 15 No. 3, pp. 396–413.

Ng, S.T. and Tang, Z. (2010), "Labour-intensive construction sub-contractors: their critical success factors", *International Journal of Project Management*, Vol. 28 No. 7, pp. 732–740.

Ophiyandri, T., Amaratunga, D. and Pathirage, C. (2010), "Community based post-disaster housing reconstruction: Indonesian perspective", *Proceeding of CIB World Congress, Salford, 10-13 May 2010*.

Ophiyandri, T., Amaratunga, D. and Pathirage, C. (2011), "Community-based post-disaster housing reconstruction: examples from Indonesia", in Amaratunga, D. and Haigh, R.P. (Eds), *Post-disaster Reconstruction of the Built Environment: Rebuilding for Resilience*, Wiley, Chichester, pp. 91–116.

Pinto, J.K. and Slevin, D.P. (1988), "Project success: definitions and measurement techniques", *Project Management Journal*, Vol. 19 No. 1, pp. 67–72.

Pranoto, S., Sentosa, S., Kayo, R.B.K.P., Karimi, S., Fauzan, Ermiza, Z. and Antoni, S. (2011), *Lesson Learned, Pembelajaran Rehab Rekon Pasca Gempa di Sumatera Barat 30 September 2009, Building Back Better*, TPT RR, Padang.

Rockart, J.F. (1979), "Chief executives define their own data needs", *Harvard Business Review*, Vol. 57 No. 2, pp. 81–93.

Steinberg, F. (2007), "Housing reconstruction and rehabilitation in Aceh and Nias, Indonesia – rebuilding lives", *Habitat International*, Vol. 31 No. 1, pp. 150–166.

World Vision (2008), *World Vision Indonesia Tsunami Response, Final Report: December 2004-December 2007*, World Vision, Monrovia, CA.

Yu, A.T.W., Shen, Q., Kelly, J. and Hunter, K. (2006), "Investigation of critical success factor in construction project briefing by way of content analysis", *Journal of Construction Engineering and Management*, Vol. 132 No. 11, pp. 1178–1186.

Further Reading

Shaw, R. (2006), "Indian Ocean tsunami and aftermath: need for environment-disaster synergy in the reconstruction process", *Disaster Prevention and Management*, Vol. 15 No. 1, pp. 5–20.

Framing Responses to Post-earthquake Haiti: How Representations of Disasters, Reconstruction and Human Settlements Shape Resilience

Lisa Bornstein, Gonzalo Lizarralde, Kevin A. Gould and Colin Davidson

Abstract

Purpose – The aim of this paper is to add a new dimension to urban resilience by exploring how representations of disasters, reconstruction and human settlements are made, and how, by shaping plans and programs, they ultimately influence resilience.

Design/methodology/approach – The paper draws on James Scott's notion of "legibility" to ask how different representations simplify complex realities and how they are transformed into plans and programs. The paper first outlines the various broad analytic lens used to examine legibility to portray post-disaster reconstruction, drawing on international literature and policies. The paper then focuses on post-earthquake Haiti and analyzes eight reconstruction plans and reviews design proposals submitted for the Building Back Better Communities program to explore how different stakeholders portrayed the disaster, identified the reconstruction challenges and proposed to address human settlements.

Findings – Representations of the disaster, the reconstruction challenge and the housing problem were quite varied. While the plans assumed a very broad view of the reconstruction challenge (one that goes beyond the representations found in the literature), the BBBC program adopted a very narrow view of it (one that the literature condemns for failing to achieve sustainable resilience).

Research limitations/implications – The empirical research is exploratory, suggesting an approach that throws a new light on the analysis of plans and programs for improved resilience.

Practical implications – The study suggests that the representations that decision makers, institutions and organizations make of the world ultimately establish the framework in which resilience is constructed.

Reprinted from *International Journal of Disaster Resilience in the Built Environment*
Vol. 4 No. 1, pp. 43–57 (2013). doi:10.1108/17595901311298991

Originality/value – The lens of legibility confirms that the expression of different representations makes the world legible in different ways and therefore transforms the way in which resilience can be improved.

Keywords: Resilience; Legibility; Plans; Human settlements; Disaster response; Haiti; Disasters

1. Introduction

This paper explores how representations of disasters, reconstruction and human settlements are put forward at critical junctures in the recovery process, and how, in shaping plans and programs, thereby influence urban resilience.

Much of the literature on disasters and reconstruction has focused on the technical challenges of immediate emergency response to basic needs of shelter, food, and health services, the balance between short-term responses and those oriented towards long-term reconstruction, and such key dilemmas as the political and economic rights of displaced people, the means to assure meaningful bottom-up participation, and the roles of international, national and local actors.

The framing of a disaster and subsequent reconstruction in a specific way, and its ultimate translation into policy, plans and programs, is intimately related to the consolidation of the state, its relations to the polity and local development trajectories. As such, it is also directly related to the dynamics of local resilience, the latter understood as both the ability of a system to survive a shock and, importantly, to adjust to make such future shocks less damaging (Polese, n.d.). The theoretical literature underpinning such an analytic approach is presented in the following section.

To make sense of how representations matter in post-disaster planning, first the contours of the disaster/post-disaster reconstruction field are sketched, roughly in chronological sequence, reviewing the four international approaches to disasters that have dominated the field. For each approach, we outline the "nature of disaster", the principal aims of intervention, and the best means to do so (Section 3). At the empirical level, we examine official plans (Section 4a) and competing proposals (Section 4b) for reconstruction in Haiti following the earthquake of January 12, 2010.

Problem-framing and representational narratives affect policy (Schön and Rein, 1994; Roe, 1994); plans and proposals reflect struggles over the definition of state-civil society relations as each consolidates (Scott, 1998; Ferguson, 2005); and, crucially, the process of disaster planning – from representation of needs to community reconstruction – defines new roles and relations for the state, international actors, local residents, NGOs, businesses, etc. that are as important to future community resilience as the technical planning of physical structures, participatory inputs, or services.

2. Policy Frames and "Legibility"

The analytical approach advanced here rests on three inter-related observations.

First, the narrative, representational and discursive levels are important to understanding formulation and adoption of policies, programs and plans, including those after disasters. Policy framing can be understood as "a way of selecting, organizing, interpreting and making sense of a complex reality to provide guideposts for knowing, analyzing, persuading, and acting" (Rein and Schön, 1993, p. 145); as such, it "socially constructs the situation, defines what is problematic about it, and suggests what courses of action are appropriate to it" (Rein and Schön, 1993, p. 153). Especially when the situation is characterized by complexity, uncertainty and contention, the resulting narratives underpin "the assumptions for decision-making" and thus tend to persist, even in the face of contradictory evidence (Roe, 1994, p. 2).

Second, the processes of framing, adopting and implementing policies are highly political and occur in a context where power is not evenly shared. We draw here first on Scott's (1998) work on state planning and bureaucratization; governments historically introduced tools such as cadastral maps and standard measurements to enhance administrative capacity to tax, monitor and control, thereby consolidating state power. The process of simplifying a complex reality, of replacing local systems of knowledge with those that met the needs of the state, renders particular characteristics of populations and environments "legible". Importantly, as Scott asserts, this typification is not only about a particular sort of vision or representation, but also produces new material relations – states transmit these ways of seeing into institutions, laws, and norms, such as housing types, building codes, or standards. Advancing a particular representation of reality, and implementing these in policies and practices in homogenizing and standardized ways, is what allows the state to act effectively.

The context in which such dynamics operate in the contemporary world are also shaped by extreme inequalities at a global level and by states that have not consolidated power, that are instead weak, fractured, or resource-constrained (Bornstein, 2008). In this respect, Ferguson (2005) notes current constraints on state power, namely: the neo-liberal attack on the state; the influence of international bodies (corporate and governmental) relative to national ones; the on-going usefulness of disorder to divisions within the state (Reno, 1998); and the consequent fracturing of the national territory, in which localities become the relevant boundary for consolidation, standardization and global integration rather than the nation. In sum, while the forms of legibility imposed by a modernizing state may still be important, studies of such processes of simplification and standardization in poor countries may need to consider state power vis-à-vis both local and international players.

Klein (2007, p. 49) provides a relevant example of the way in which international interests may impose new policy frames and forms of legibility, arguing that:

> [...] disasters have become the preferred moments for advancing a vision of a ruthlessly divided world, one in which the very idea of a public sphere has no place at all [...]. Every time a new crisis hits – even when the crisis itself is the direct by-product of free-market ideology – the fear and disorientation that follow are harnessed for radical social and economic re-engineering.

In her analysis, post-disaster periods offer an opportunity to advance a particular political and economic agenda, that of neo-liberalism. Privatization, entry of foreign investment and firms, and reshaping of local political and financial institutions ensue. State capacity may diminish rather than be strengthened during post-disaster reconstruction. While neo-liberal policies are not the only ones that may be imposed or encouraged post-disaster, Klein's analysis is particularly relevant in the case of Haiti where a neo-liberal arrangements were already well entrenched even before the earthquake (Schuller, 2009).

A third observation relates to the way that historical, cultural and racial narratives become articulated in processes of framing, adopting and implementing policies. Of particular relevance here are stories about the vulnerability of Caribbean and Latin American countries. Often framed by tropes of the primitive, the traditional, the lawless, etc. these narratives serve to justify the authority of outsiders and especially Europeans and North Americans in the affairs of Latin American and Caribbean nations (Berger, 1995; Escobar, 1995). In the context of Haiti for example, Farmer (1994) documents how US interventionist and imperialist policies towards Haiti were justified according to just such tropes: the "isolation" and "primitivism" of Haiti and Haitians. Other authors have highlighted how similar trophes have been employed in post-earthquake Haiti (Bellegarde-Smith, 2010; Farmer, 2011; Lundy, 2010; Zanotti, 2010). In brief, policy frames, discourse and the resulting plans and practices draw upon and reproduce varied understandings of race, culture and history with implications for local level recovery and resilience.

These observations, taken together, can be used to analyze how the challenge of post-disaster reconstruction is understood and pursued. For instance, in the wider field of post-disaster studies, the focus on legibility throws into relief the shifts in the tectonics of post-disaster reconstruction response (Table I). Four generations of approaches are apparent. Throughout the 1980s, the United Nations and international agencies considered disasters as "interruptions of the regular order of societies" and the reconstruction process as "actions taken to re-establish a community" that "would include construction of permanent housing, full restoration of services, and complete resumption of the pre-disaster state" (UNDHA, 1992). By narrowly defining pre-disaster situations as the norm, the international agencies were able to focus on actions that were "time-bound and sector-specific". A revised definition of disasters as a product of vulnerabilities emerged in the 1990s (UN/ISDR, 2009). Vulnerabilities were defined as the physical, social, economic and environmental factors that lead a community to a certain level of "weakness", such that, stricken by a hazard, a considerable level of destruction follows. There were two immediate implications of such an approach: recognition of the social construction of disaster,

Table I: Representations of disaster, reconstruction and human settlements in the international literature

Approaches	View of the disaster	View of reconstruction process	View of human settlements
1. Disaster management (UNDHA, UN-ISDR)	As an interruption of the regular order of societies	Moment to resume the pre-disaster state	Improved by returning to the previous state
2. Vulnerability	As a result of root causes of vulnerabilities	Moment to reduce vulnerabilities	Improved through the reduction of social and physical vulnerabilities
3. Capability	As a result of insufficient freedoms and scarce capacity to choose	Moment for increasing capabilities	Improved through household's increased freedom to choose
4. Resilience	As an inability of the system to absorb and adapt to external stresses	Moment to reduce risk and increase preparedness	Improved through preventative and reactive measures

and a search for "root causes" of vulnerability (Blaikie *et al.*, 1994; Pelling, 2003). More recent framings of disasters and reconstruction have emphasized capabilities, drawing on Sen (1999); vulnerabilities are linked to insufficient freedoms and scarce capacity to choose; reconstruction, in this frame, is seen as a "process of improvement of pre-disaster capabilities, targeted to achieving long-term local development and disaster risk reduction, through the pairing of local and external resources" (Lizarralde and Raynaud, 2011, p. 2). Finally, a fourth strand of meanings was propelled by the widespread adoption of the concept of resilience, which contributes to a representation of the causes of disasters as complex interactions between society and the physical environment (McEntire *et al.*, 2002). It encompasses both the principles of preparedness and reaction within dynamic systems (Bosher, 2008) and focuses responses on bridging the gap between pre-disaster actions and post-disaster interventions, and between structural (e.g. strengthening of buildings) and non-structural (e.g. better urban planning) mitigation (Bosher, 2008; McEntire, 2011).

As these examples suggests, the analytical approach used here shows how a particular policy frame simplifies and renders the world legible in ways that allow disaster response to happen, and which also functions so that certain complexities of the world are forgotten (rendered illegible).

3. Methods

The three observations above provide a theoretical and methodological framework for analysis of policies, plans and practices related to disaster. Narrative analysis of plans, policies and practices is well-established (Roe, 1994; Escobar, 1995; Scott, 1998) as a methodology in the social and policy sciences.

The empirical investigation was designed as an exploratory study of how plans for local redevelopment in Haiti following the 2010 earthquake reflected particular ways of "seeing a disaster, local recovery, and longer-term resilience". It examines two levels of post-earthquake response: plans for reconstruction of settlements (Section 4), and proposals submitted in a competition, covered in Section 5.

Printed documentation about the following six plans was collected and analyzed: the Plan for National Development and Recovery (Government of Haiti, March 2010); the strategic Plan for the Re-founding of Haiti (Government of Haiti, March 2010); the "Haiti Tomorrow" plan (*Haiti Demain*) produced by the Inter-ministerial Committee on Territorial Planning (Republique d'Haiti – CIAT, 2010); the Strategic Plan for National Salvation (civil society document); The Plan of Action for a New Haiti (international civil society document); and the "Plateforme de patriots haitiens" (PLAPH) (a political party). In addition, between February 2010 and July 2011, one author attended six major meetings related to disaster response at which key Haitians (e.g. mayors, representatives of local institutions, Haitian expatriates, and experts) played a significant role; plans were both elaborated and presented, and participant observation of these events supplements our analysis of the written plans.

The plans above, while revealing, do not permit detailed analysis of the transmittal of policy frames to specific projects and practices. To remedy this, we conducted analysis of Building Back Better Communities (BBBC), a program to improve human settlements in Haiti. The core of this program was an international request for proposals (RFP) for housing solutions. Our examination of the various proposals at the level of building and site reconstruction allowed for assessment of a narrower, and also pragmatic, framing of the disaster and reconstruction challenges.

The BBBC program was initiated by a partnership of local and international, public and private, stakeholders to "discover and promote" the best solutions for post-earthquake reconstruction. The competition for best housing designs began in early 2010 with a RFP that closed with over 360 submissions, arguably one of the world's most successful competitions of its kind.

We examined the RFP itself and documentation of several entries that were successful in the competition (entries were extensively documented by the proponents, architects and construction companies in online plans, photos and descriptions). In addition, a special issue of *The Gazette*, a Canadian newspaper, documented several proposals, providing photos of each of the housing prototypes, videos, interviews and technical description of the units ((*The*) *Gazette*, 2011).

The plans and proposals were analyzed with respect to:

- the definition of the problem;
- policy initiatives (sectors addressed, scale of intervention, key actors to be involved); and
- depiction of desired human settlements attributes and resilience.

Importantly, the aim was not to critique the content of the plans and proposals *per se*. Rather, following Scott's (1998) approach to legibility, analysis addressed the framing of the documents – what they put into focus and what they left obscure – and the implications of this framing for programs, practices and settlements. Indeed, as Bar (2011, p. 14) observes:

> [...] we do not interpret our world merely by analyzing incoming information, but rather we try to understand it using a proactive link of incoming features to existing, familiar information (e.g. objects, people, situations).

Bearing in mind the importance of framing as a motor for actions is of crucial importance.

4. Results and Discussion

(a) A Haitian "State of Disaster"

Four distinct approaches to the framing of post-disaster recovery are apparent in the proposed plans, situated in the diagnosis of the central problem: the weak state, weak conditions for development, weak governance and planning, and lack of adequate shelter.

1. The weak state

The strategic Plan for the Re-founding of Haiti, prepared by Haitian civil society organizations, centers on reform of the state as the key to recovery. It identifies the key problem in post-earthquake recovery as a structural failure of the state, manifest visibly in the physical damage to the presidential palace and several ministries, but principally oriented towards urgent *Restauration de l'état* (Restoration of the State) that would allow for the "overall reconstruction of the country". Three aspects were required for the re-establishing the foundations of the Haitian state: "the consolidation of a legitimate political force capable of defending the national sovereignty; the development of the civil society; and the reinforcement of education and training." Plan proponents contend that "re-founding" should become a project of the society at large. The disaster was seen as an excuse to recreate national institutions, define "Haitian" values and claim the sovereignty of the Haitian republic, a partial response to a long history of international aid and domination. Political decentralization was seen as indispensable, whereby concentration of power and resources in what many call the "Republique de Port-au-Prince" would be contained. In this approach, culture – understood as traditional cultural representations – was also seen as a fundamental vehicle for the regeneration of local values. The interventions needed thus went beyond the reconstruction of settlements, buildings and infrastructure. Disaster becomes, in this plan, a catalyst for a re-calibration of political power away from international actors and Port-au-Prince elites.

2. Weak conditions for development

The official response of the Haitian Government to the disaster was published in March 2010 under the title of *Plan d'action pour le relèvement et le développement d'Haïti* (Action Plan for Recovery and Development) (Gouvernement de la République d'Haïti, 2010). This plan focused on the implications of the earthquake and subsequent settlement difficulties in terms of its impacts on humans, infrastructure and the environment. The problem becomes one of reversing arrested development so that negative impacts can be resolved through growth. Four areas of intervention are outlined:

(1) economic reconstruction though decentralized poles of economic activity, infrastructure development and land management;
(2) modernization of the agriculture, manufacturing and tourism, and the development of a formal construction sector;
(3) social development (with an emphasis on education and public health); and
(4) institutional reform of the legal system and governance structures.

This approach draws on both international disaster management and vulnerability approaches. It corresponds to the former in its attention to solving the immediate problems. Root causes of vulnerability, and impediments to recovery and future resilience, are seen as long-term impoverishment of the country, shortages of jobs and economic opportunities, weaknesses in economic sectors and human resource development thus are considered, as the conditions for economic development are seen as patently insufficient (a form of vulnerability).

3. Weak governance and planning

Three plans – the Strategic Plan for National Salvation, the Plan of Action for a New Haiti, and *Haiti demain* – can be roughly grouped together, based on their call for structural reforms and improved planning as key elements in reconstruction and recovery. The former focuses on reforms, while the other two take a systems' approach to planning, however all target modernization, and social contracts for progress and prosperity.

The Strategic Plan for National Salvation was presented by retired politicians, civil society and private sector groups. It proposes to save the country from itself. The document blames bad politics and inefficient governments for the poor post-earthquake situation. The country is to collectively combat "corrupt, vicious, authoritarian and autocratic political leaders" as a means to redemption and recovery. The plan describes "the reform and modernization of the state as a fundamental pillar of tomorrow's society" and, claiming to be a national consensus on fundamental values, proposes an inter-generational social contract for progress and prosperity. In addition to reforming government, key objectives are "development" and "progress", with a strong emphasis on economic growth. The cost of the plan is estimated at $100 billion (US) over 25 years, with a call for international contributions towards the Haitian Marshall-like plan. The heavy emphasis on solving the problem of the state sets this approach apart from international literature on disaster recovery.

The Plan of Action for a New Haiti was produced by the Haitian community living abroad which, following the earthquake, undertook an international effort to mobilize Haitians professionals living abroad in support of recovery (Groupe de Réflexion et d'action pour une Haïti nouvelle, 2010). On-going effects of the disaster are, in this plan, seen as exacerbated by the deeply rooted practice in Haiti and the aid community of pursuing isolated and uncoordinated interventions. A comprehensive plan of interventions was developed through extensive meetings and exchanges. The plan proposed a partnership between those with Haitian resources within the country and abroad, promoted a systems view of inter-dependencies between various sectors, and advocated participatory approaches to addressing local challenges.

A similar plan based on a structural revitalization of practices and institutions was proposed by the Government of Haiti's Inter-ministerial Committee on Territorial Planning (CIAT) in the "Haiti Tomorrow" plan (*Haiti Demain*), published in March 2010 (Comité Interministériel D'aménagement Du Territoire, 2010). In the view of the CIAT, the disaster was largely caused by a "spiral of environmental degeneration" (Republique d'Haiti – CIAT, 2010, p. 23). Disaster is portrayed as an opportunity for change in local practices, both within and outside of government; for example, population displacement of population caused by the disaster should be exploited to reduce the concentration of resources and power in the capital; "the redundancy of actions" that contributed to environmental degradation and deforestation should be avoided; and "a consensus on mutual interest" promoted. The emphasis is on coordinated territorial planning and land management (as opposed to the state reform, socio-economic or cultural-moralistic aspects), with attention to regional and urban planning, infrastructure, drainage, community buildings and public space.

4. Lack of adequate shelter

The "*Plateforme des Patriotes Haïtiens*" (PLAPH) plan did not emphasize structural reforms and instead concentrated on the pragmatic solutions to the pressing challenges of inadequate shelter. The plan emerged from a local political party, which responded to the governmental plan with strong criticism; it accused the government plan of being "incoherent" and "manipulative" and causing "deception, shame and reservations". The PLAPH proposed an approach focused on projects, immediate needs, and fast recovery, with two priorities: providing sheltering to affected people, and creating jobs.

Several international specialists and local mayors also assumed a pragmatic approach targeted at identifying short-, medium- and long-term projects to reduce vulnerabilities and increase urban resilience. Rather than proposing fundamental structural reforms, emphasis was placed on projects and specific programs (housing, infrastructure, community services, training, etc.) that were could lead to manageable, pragmatic solutions.

Table II summarizes how the Haitian plans made legible their views of the disaster, the reconstruction and the human settlements.

Table II: Disaster, reconstruction and human settlements in Haiti made legible

	View of the disaster	View of reconstruction process	View of human settlements
1. Weak state (refounding)	As a failure of the state	Moment to recreate state institutions and values	Improved as a consequence of (modern) institutions and values[a]
2. Weak conditions for development (development and recovery plan)	As the result of insufficient structural development	Moment for development, consensus and international partnership	Improved through regional, economic social and institutional reforms[a]
3. Weak coordination and poor planning (salvation and reform plans)	As a result of fragmented practices and institutions	Moment for a systemic view of interconnected changes	Improved through interconnected planning[a]
4. Inadequate shelter (PLAPH and other pragmatic approaches)	As a result of vulnerabilities and root causes	Moment to reduce vulnerabilities and increase resilience through access to soft and hard resources	Improved through manageable projects of infrastructure, services and housing[b]

Notes: [a]Emphasis on policy; [b]emphasis on the program and project levels of intervention

There are some commonalities across the different frames. Natural disaster, even that causing massive displacement of human populations and destruction of the built environment, is treated as entwined with governance failures (weak state, weak coordination) and the historical legacies of concentrated power (spatial and economic), impoverishment, inadequate shelter, and environmental degradation. The documents, aside from those prepared within government, reflect a fundamental lack of confidence in the capacity of the state in its current form to act on behalf of "a public good", even one as pressing as providing shelter for displaced earthquake victims, and even the ones prepared by the government identify areas for improved state action.

More telling, however, are the differences across and omissions from the plans. While the state and its functioning are in the limelight, the widespread and immediate need for shelter and services in areas affected by the earthquake is not. Only in the pragmatic approaches is shelter (together with employment) a primary focus. Instead, review of the plans and their emphasis suggests that most of these plans are pitched at too high a level, are too ambitious, to address these immediate needs for shelter, or indeed for longer-term resilience. Polarized interests – within and between each of these frames – are apparent; potential partners are vilified in some of the documents. Efforts to scale down interventions, to address policy and institutional reforms and the implementation of new programs, provide possible directions forward. However, it is interesting that they are neither linked to the expanded legitimacy and capacity of the state (as per historical precedents documented by Scott) nor do they relate strongly to the post-disaster reconstruction approaches dominant in the literature. Indeed, it is further important to note that few approaches were linked explicitly to urban structures or city-level governance mechanisms; the exceptions are the CIAT plan (with its few pages on territorial and urban planning), and political or economic decentralization in several of the others.

(b) From Policy Frames to Housing Frames

To detail the transmittal of policy frames to specific projects and practices, we analyzed the BBBC program, which had at its core an international competition for housing solutions. A RFP generated over 360 proposals at the level of building and site reconstruction, submitted by local and international, private and non-profit groups. Analysis of the competition documents, the resulting submissions, and those selected for merit permits assessment of how the framing of reconstruction affects specific projects.

The program documents reflect a dual framing of the challenges. The RFP stress the importance of both:

(1) improving poor construction practices as a means to achieve resilient human settlements; and
(2) responding to urgent needs for shelter.

For example, the program claimed to be interested in "best-practice solutions alongside wider urban themes such as green energy, transportation and use of local materials and production". Its emphasis on shelter pointed to the development of high-design: "The approach ... will be holistic, focusing on home designs, incorporation of green technologies and the development of model communities". At the same time, the urgency of shelter delivery was a strong message in the RFP:

> With the rainy season on-going, a key priority for the Haitian government and its international relief partners is to relocate those sheltering in camps to transitional forms of shelter prior to permanent housing. Transitioning displaced camp residents presents not only a huge logistical challenge but also a unique opportunity to make vital advancements to Haiti's social and economic infrastructure.

A prototype of selected entries had to be built in a housing exhibition, located on the outskirts of Port-au-Prince. According to the RFP the exhibition was to be:

> [...] a planned settlement for 125 families in Port-au-Prince that will define a template for rebuilding housing developments and as a road map for the inclusion of renewable energy, education, culture and livelihoods.

Performance specifications placed emphasis on shelter for domestic activities. Specifications were for prefabricated or easy-to-erect units (an even narrower option of housing solutions). They included such elements as: transportation (specifying the option of prefabricated elements), codes (with specific reference to disaster-resistance), production (a direct reference to manufacturing), durability, cost and floor area (a maximum cost of \$5,000 and an area of 35 m^2 were established), and culture. About 70 prototypes were chosen and by mid-June, about 60 were on site, preparing for the official opening at the end of July.

Considering the RFP specifications for easy-to-erect sheltering solutions, it is not surprising that a large number of awarded projects opted for high-tech designs of independent units. For the most part, units were quite costly and relied on materials unavailable in Haiti. For example, commended projects included: a 40 m^2 unit built of foam panels and aluminum post and beams (\$43,000); "the Lego House," a 14 m^2 shelter (without washroom and kitchen) made of plastic panels (\$7,500); "the plastic house", a 45 m^2 unit built with hollow panels of PVC (\$20,000); the "Straw house": a 60 m^2 unit built with panels of compressed straw and steel posts and beams (\$20,000); and the "Foam house", built of ten-inch thick polystyrene wall panels fitted into a steel frame. Low-tech solutions included a house made of wood posts and panels, which cost about \$25,000, and a steel-frame house with cement panels.

Both high- and low-tech proposals failed to provide a comprehensive "template for housing developments" or a holistic approach to the design of human settlements, as called for in the RFP. Designs emphasized the dwelling over other aspects of settlement, such as the potential for income-generation (home-based shops, workshops, retail, etc.) public and collective space, infrastructure, services and economic activities incremental construction, desired urban density, or social development. In so emphasizing, the proposals responded to some aspects of the RFP but neglected best practices well-known in the field of post-disaster reconstruction, for instance, the need to address: subsidies and financing (Ferguson and Navarrete, 2008; Gilbert, 2004), infrastructure development (Huchzermeyer, 2001; Choguill, 2007), optimization of public and transit services (Choguill, 2007; Zanetta, 2001), potential for income generation activities (Lizarralde *et al.*, 2009), and participation of stakeholders (Lizarralde, 2010; Barenstein *et al.*, 2010).

Improving construction techniques is a crucial component in improving the resilience of settlements to disasters, but these proposals did not address whether the techniques could be used easily and would function well in Haitian cities. In the BBC program, the dual emphasis on innovative "best practice" design and needs for shelter, coupled with design specifications biased towards the former, meant that the "frame" ended up leading to costly solutions inappropriate to the shelter needs of uprooted Haitians. Even the local architectural firms, who opted for traditional cinderblock and concrete technologies, neglected a holistic response to the housing challenge.

5. Conclusion: Can Post-disaster Recovery be Framed to Promote Resiliency?

In this article, we built upon three observations about the power and importance of representations of disasters, reconstruction and human settlements. We drew particularly on Scott's notion of "legibility" to ask how disaster response plans represent and simplify complex urban realities and how those representations could create conditions for more (and less) resiliency.

The empirical study explores how plans and proposals advance particular conceptions of the causes of the disaster, the type of reconstruction to be pursued, and measures necessary to be taken to improve resilience to future shocks, in other words, a definition of the problem, the solutions, and means to achieve them. Despite the simple language, the implications of such acts are profound. In simplifying complex dynamics, a plan, proposal or project addresses and emphasizes some social, political, economic and environmental relations, and leaves others out. Portrayal of a "crisis" and "desired and appropriate responses" may entail new roles for the private sector, the weakening or strengthening of specific elements of the state apparatus, expanded powers for international bodies within national or local boundaries, and, indeed, propagation of specific images – of the rescuers, the victim, the deserving, the venal, etc. – that have long-term implications for all involved.

The political expediency of policy framing is apparent in the analysis of the Haitian plans, in ways that are not clear in the international literature. Different views were created by stakeholders currently in power (the developmental frame), stakeholders susceptible to gain or regain power (the state frame), and stakeholders interested in playing an active role in the process without necessary being in power (the pragmatic planning frame). This is certainly not the first time that disasters are used in politics or by those in power to lead nation-wide policy making (Klein, 2007; (*The*) *Economist*, 2011). However, the analysis suggests that – in a country of widespread destruction that went beyond the capital city itself – stakeholders represented the disaster, the reconstruction challenges, and human settlements objectives according to views that responded to their own position, regardless of the limits of municipal governance.

Discussion here turns to how the framing of disaster and recovery both in Haiti and the international literature – the ways in which some relations and structures are made legible and others obscured – relates to the resilience of cities. Resilience – including in urban areas – is affected by the actions and inactions of numerous players. The role of local government may be especially important, as discussed in other articles of this issue; it is usually the level of government that comes face-to-face with citizen demands most frequently, and often local officials and staff are particularly aware of community needs and dynamics.

Our review of the Haitian plans suggests an addendum to such observations: resilience with respect to the three key components analyzed (disaster, reconstruction, and human settlements) is not necessarily built at the municipal or urban level. The Haitian plans framed the difficulties as extending beyond the level of communities or cities, and cited local supra-local measures, indeed, even supra-national ones, as needed for recovery and long-term resilience. Given Haiti's poverty and historical legacies, and their perpetuation at both local and international levels, the focus on national and international dimensions of contemporary challenges may well be crucial. At the same time, it may well be that the potential of the local – whether of local government or alliances of local residents – is one of the arenas that has been obscured. In contrast to the international literature on disasters and recovery, all of which outlined an important role for local actors, only a few of the Haitian plans did so.

Attention to the way that our conceptions frame our actions may seem tangential to the discussions of how to construct more resilient cities, especially for areas in which "natural disasters" occur with devastating effects. Our suspicion, in putting forward this exploratory material, is that international attention could productively be directed to how disasters and resilience are framed at a local level. Processes of disaster response make sense of and transform the world in particular ways. Planners, policy-makers and experts do more than "objectively" analyze disasters, their causes and the appropriate responses. They act as agents, shaping disaster and disaster preparedness responses through the visions of the world that they create. The different frames at the international level – and the corresponding shifts in disaster and preparedness programming – are illustrative of this agency. The different frames apparent in the Haitian plans and competition further point to the political import of such dynamics, with effects at all levels: discursive (who or what is blamed, vilified or extolled), organizational (what is reformed, strengthened or abolished), and material (what resources are accorded to what programs, places or groups). These frames may leave out – or make illegible – other elements (the local government, the role of nation-building and centralized power, the potential of local groups, or the potential negative effects of international NGOs, all points present in the academic literature on Haiti).

Equally importantly, these frames outline the desired future – a return to the past, a resolution of past inequalities, a nation founded on local values – that will be pursued. This desired future may be one in which resilient cities are promoted, in which people can live in pleasant, just and productive environments, but it is by no means certain. It is thus important to understand the ways in which disasters, reconstruction, and the human settlements are made legible, and how those ideas shape reconstruction and resilience.

References

Bar, M. (2011), "The proactive brain", in Bar, M. (Ed.), *Predictions in the Brain: Using Our Past to Generate a Future*, Oxford University Press, Oxford, pp. 13–26.

Barenstein, J.D., Phelps, P.M., Pittet, D. and Sena, S. (2010), *Safer Homes, Stronger Communities: A Handbook for Reconstruction After Natural Disasters*, World Bank, Washington, DC.

Bellegarde-Smith, P. (2010), "A man-made disaster: the earthquake of January 12, 2010 – a Haitian perspective", *Journal of Black Studies*, Vol. 42 No. 2, pp. 264–75.

Berger, M.T. (1995), *Under Northern Eyes: Latin American Studies and US Hegemony in the Americas, 1898-1990*, Indiana University Press, Bloomington, IN.

Blaikie, P., Cannoon, T., Davis, I. and Wisner, B. (1994), *At Risk: Natural Hazards, People's Vulnerability, and Disasters*, Routledge, New York, NY.

Bornstein, L. (2008), "Planning and peacebuilding in post-war Mozambique: from narratives to practices of development", *Journal of Peacebuilding and Development*, Vol. 4 No. 1, pp. 1–15.

Bosher, L. (2008), *Hazards and the Built Environment: Attaining Built-in Resilience*, Taylor & Francis Group, New York, NY.

Choguill, C.L. (2007), "The search for policies to support sustainable housing", *Habitat International*, Vol. 31, pp. 143–9.

Comité Interministériel D'aménagement Du Territoire (2010), *Haïti demain*, CIAT et République d'Haïti, Port-au-Prince.

(*The*) *Economist* (2011), "Colombia economy: post-flood emergency mode", *The Economist*, January 26.

Escobar, A. (1995), *Encountering Development: The Making and Unmaking of the Third World*, Princeton University Press, Princeton, NJ.

Farmer, P. (1994), *The Uses of Haiti*, Common Courage Press, Monroe, ME.

Farmer, P. (2011), *Haiti After the Earthquake*, Public Affairs, New York, NY.

Ferguson, B. and Navarrete, J. (2008), "A financial framework for reducing slums", in Sernau, S. (Ed.), *Contemporary Readings in Globalization*, Sage, London.

Ferguson, J. (2005), "Seeing like an oil company: space, security and global capitalism in neoliberal Africa", *American Anthropologist*, Vol. 107 No. 3, pp. 377–82.

(*The*) *Gazette* (2011), "Haiti: after the quake", *Montreal: The Gazette*, available at: www.montrealgazette.com/news/haiti-quake/index.html (accessed July 15).

Gilbert, A. (2004), "Helping the poor through housing subsidies: lessons from Chile, Colombia and South Africa", *Habitat International*, Vol. 28, pp. 13–40.

Gouvernement de la République d'Haïti (2010), *Plan d'action pour le relèvement et le développement d'Haïti*, Gouvernement de la République d'Haïti, Port-au-Prince.

Groupe de Réflexion et d'action pour une Haïti nouvelle (2010), *Plan d'action*, Montreal, Document of presentation.

Huchzermeyer, M. (2001), "Housing for the poor? Negotiated housing policy in South Africa", *Habitat International*, Vol. 25, pp. 303–31.

Klein, N. (2007), "Disaster capitalism: the new economy of catastrophe", *Harper's*, October, pp. 47–58.

Lizarralde, G. (2010), "Stakeholder participation and incremental housing in subsidized housing projects in Colombia and South Africa", *Habitat International*, Vol. 35, pp. 175–87.

Lizarralde, G. and Raynaud, M.M. (2011), "The capability approach in housing development and reconstruction", *Post Earthquake Reconstruction – Lessons Learnt and Way Forward. Government of Gujarat*, Government of Gujarat, Ahmedabad.

Lizarralde, G., Davidson, C. and Johnson, C. (2009), *Rebuilding After Disasters: From Emergency to Sustainability*, Taylor & Francis, London.

Lundy, G. (2010), "The Haiti earthquake of 2010: the politics of a natural disaster", *Journal of Black Studies*, Vol. 42 No. 2, pp. 127–30.

McEntire, D. (2011), "Understanding and reducing vulnerability: from the approach of liabilities and capabilities", *Disaster Prevention and Management*, Vol. 20 No. 3, pp. 294–313.

McEntire, D., Fuller, C., Johnston, C. and Weber, R. (2002), "A comparison of disaster paradigms: the search for a holistic policy guide", *Public Administration Review*, Vol. 62, pp. 267–81.

Pelling, M. (2003), *The Vulnerability of Cities: Natural Disasters and Social Resilience*, Earthscan, London.

Polese, M. (n.d.), "The resilient city: on the determinants of successful urban economies", in Paddison, R. and Hutton, T. (Eds), *Cities and Economic Change*, Sage, London.

Rein, M. and Schön, D. (1993), "Reframing policy discourse", in Fischer, F. and Forester, J. (Eds), *The Argumentative Turn in Policy Analysis and Planning*, UCL, London.

Reno, W. (1998), *Warlord Politics and African States*, Lynne Rienner, Boulder, CO.

Republique d'Haiti – CIAT (2010), *Haiti Demain, Objectifs et Strategies Territoriales Pour la Reconstruction*, Republique d'Haiti – CIAT, Port-au-Prince.

Roe, E. (1994), *Narrative Policy Analysis*, Duke University Press, Durham.

Schön, D. and Rein, M. (1994), *Frame Reflection: Toward the Resolution of Intractable Policy Controversies*, Basic Books, New York, NY.

Schuller, M. (2009), "Gluing globalization: NGOs as intermediaries in Haiti", *PoLAR: Political and Legal Anthropology Review*, Vol. 32, pp. 84–104.

Scott, J. (1998), *Seeing Like a State: How Certain Schemes to Improve the Human Condition Have Failed*, Yale University Press, New Haven, CT.

Sen, A. (1999), *Development as Freedom*, Anchor Books, New York, NY.

UNDHA (1992), *Glossary: Internationally Agreed Glossary of Basic Terms Related to Disaster Management*, United Nations Department of Humanitarian Affairs, Geneva.

UN/ISDR (2009), *UNISDR Terminology on Disaster Risk Reduction*, UN/ISDR, Geneva.

Zanetta, C. (2001), "The evolution of the World Bank's urban lending in Latin America: from sites and services to municipal reform and beyond", Vol. 25, pp. 513–33.

Zanotti, L. (2010), "Cacophonies of aid, failed state building and NGOs in Haiti: setting the stage for disaster, envisioning the future", *Third World Quarterly*, Vol. 31 No. 5, pp. 755–71.

Further Reading

Cannon, T. (2008), "Vulnerability, 'innocent' disasters and the imperative of cultural understanding", *Disaster Prevention and Management*, Vol. 17 No. 3, pp. 350–7.

Collier, D. (1976), *Squatters and Oligarchs: Authoritarian Rule and Policy Change in Peru*, John Hopkins University Press, Baltimore, MD.

Davis, I. (1978), *Shelter After Disaster*, Oxford Polytechnic, Oxford.

Davis, I. (1981), *Disasters and the Small Dwelling*, Pergamon Press, Oxford.

Gasper, D. (2007), "What is the capability approach? Its core, rationale, partners and dangers", *Journal of Socio-Economics*, Vol. 36, pp. 335–59.

Li, T.M. (2005), "Beyond 'the state' and failed schemes", *American Anthropologist*, Vol. 107, pp. 383–94.

Lizarralde, G., Johnson, C. and Davidson, C. (2003), "Houses of candied sugar: comparative research on controversial temporary housing after earthquake disasters in Colombia and Turkey", *Proceedings from the International Association for Housing Science 31st World Congress on Housing Process and Product, Montréal, Canada, June 23-27*.

Lyons, M. (2009), "Building back better: the large-scale impact of small-scale approaches to reconstruction", *World Development*, Vol. 37, pp. 385–98.

Maskrey, A. (1989), *Disaster Mitigation: a Community Based Approach*, Oxfam, Oxford.

Mason, C. (2011), "Foreign aid as a gift", *Critical Studies in Media Communication*, Vol. 28 No. 2, pp. 94–112.

Norris, F.H., Stevens, S.P., Pfefferbaum, B. and Wyche, K.F. (2008), "Community resilience as a metaphor, theory, set of capacities, and strategy for disaster readiness", *American Journal of Community Psychology*, Vol. 41, pp. 127–50.

Pierre-Louis, F. (2011), "Earthquakes, nongovernmental organizations, and governance in Haiti", *Journal of Black Studies*, Vol. 42 No. 2, pp. 186–202.

Turner, J.F.C. (1977), *Housing by People: Towards Autonomy in Building Environments*, Pantheon Books, New York, NY.

UNDRO (1982), *Shelter After Disaster: Guidelines for Assistance*, UNDRO, New York, NY.

About the Authors

Lisa Bornstein teaches Planning and International Development at McGill University and directs a community-university alliance researching mega-projects in North America. She has worked as an NGO consultant, planner and researcher in Latin America and Southern Africa. She has published on community development, urban planning, poverty, donor-NGO relations, governance, conflict, and dynamics of cities in the global economy.

Gonzalo Lizarralde is a Professor at the School of Architecture of Université de Montréal. He has long experience in consulting for architecture and construction projects and has published important research in the fields of low-cost housing and project management. He has taught at the University of Cape Town (South Africa); McGill University, Université de Montréal, and Universidad Javeriana (Colombia). He conducted Post Doctorate research in the Department of Construction Economics and Management of the University of Cape Town. He is the Director of the IF Research Group (grif) of Université de Montréal, which studies the processes related to the planning and development of construction projects. He is the co-author of the book *Rebuilding After Disasters: From Emergency to Sustainabiity*. Gonzalo Lizarralde is the corresponding author and can be contacted at: gonzalo.lizarralde@umontreal.ca

Kevin A. Gould is an Assistant Professor in the Department of Geography, Planning and Environment at Concordia University. He completed his PhD at the University of British Columbia in 2009. His dissertation analyzes the material and ideological production of a rural land market in contemporary Guatemala. He has broad research interests in critical development studies, political ecology, and economic geography. His current work examines how race, nature, and markets are produced through economic development policies.

Colin Davidson is a Professor Emeritus of Architecture, founder of the programs installation and management of development projects (University of Montreal), and founder of the Research Group IFgrif. He is a specialist in the field of innovation and technology transfer. His research interests also include communication in the construction sector, and in particular on the use of knowledge from research. After a career in Britain, Italy and the USA, he joined the Faculty in 1968 (he was Dean of the Faculty from 1975 to 1985). He has also taught in the USA (including Harvard and Washington University), Brazil (at the University of Rio Grande do Sul) and Italy (University Institute of Architecture of Venice). He holds a Master's of Architecture from MIT. He was a member of the IBC from 1972 to 2010 and is recipient of "Distinguished Professor" of the Association of Collegiate Schools of Architecture.

Implementation of Hyogo Framework for Action in Makati City, Philippines☆

Yuki Matsuoka, Yukiko Takeuchi and Rajib Shaw

Abstract

Purpose – The purpose of this paper is to review the challenges for disaster risk reduction (DRR) by local governments and local implementation of the Hyogo Framework for Action (HFA) as the global DRR guideline.

Design/methodology/approach – Based on a survey on 20 tasks identified in "A guide for implementing HFA by local stakeholders", HFA implementation by local government is analyzed to identify priorities and the gaps. The target group for the detail analysis was the Makati city DRR coordinating council (MCDRRCC).

Findings – The survey reviewed how multi-stakeholders involved in local DRR perceive these HFA 20 tasks, which revealed trends and gaps within their work. The result showed that Makati currently places more emphasis on HFA 1, but revealed some gaps in the area of HFA 4. While suggesting a set of recommended actions for Makati, the analysis also revealed how these gaps were addressed in its recent action plan. MDRRCC demonstrated a case for local platform for DRR in terms implementing the actions and addressing the challenges through proper coordination among stakeholders.

Research limitations/implications – Since local HFA implementation is relevantly new area, its applicability needs to be examined further considering linkages between national and local governments.

Originality/value – This paper is unique since the original data were collected from the survey. Makati city case proposes a model of local platform for comprehensive DRR actions along with HFA, which provides value added approach contributing to the ISDR Campaign. The case of Makati provides an

☆The authors acknowledge Makati City Government for cooperation to the survey. The Global COE Program "Human Security Engineering for Asia Megacities" for supporting the work.

Reprinted from *International Journal of Disaster Resilience in the Built Environment*
Vol. 4 No. 1, pp. 23–42 (2013). doi:10.1108/17595901311298982

on-going model process of a local platform for DRR which can be leant by other local government for possible replication.

Keywords: Disaster prevention; Capacity; Governance; Case studies; Coordination; Disasters; Philippines

1. Introduction

1.1 Importance on Local Level DRR and HFA Implementation at Local Level

At the 2nd United Nations World Conference on Disaster Reduction (WCDR) in January 2005 in Kobe City, Japan, the *Hyogo Framework for Action (HFA) 2005-2015: Building the Resilience of Nations and Communities to Disasters* (UNISDR, 2005) was adopted. The United Nations secretariat for the International Strategy for Disaster Reduction (UNISDR) is the focal point within UN system to promote increased commitment to disaster risk reduction (DRR) and strong linkages to sustainable development. UNISDR served as the secretariat for this process of the WCDR and the process to develop the HFA.

Since the inception of HFA, the international efforts on DRR coordinated by UNISDR have begun to recognize the importance of localizing DRR activities. This is because impacts of disasters are most immediately and intensely felt at the local levels; therefore, the crucial and effective process in which the HFA would be implemented is also required at the local level, adapted and owned by the citizens and officials of the local government. Through this process, the local/city governance in DRR activities is strengthened, and stakeholder roles and responsibilities are identified, clarified, and eventually carried out. The most important set of actors are governments and local institutions. Local governments bear the ultimate responsibility for the safety of their citizens and communities. Aid is far from sufficient to play more than a complementary role in addressing the challenges of risk management (Christoplos, 2003).

As hazards usually occur locally and many of the most effective tools to reduce vulnerability to hazards, such as land use regulation and building code enforcement are at the local level, local governments are perhaps best-positioned to implement DRR (McBean and Rodgers, 2010). Local level is of fundamental importance, not only because it is closer to the citizens but because it is the repository of the basic environmental management and regulatory governance functions that is essential for effective DRR (Jackson, 2011).

These literature reviews supported the strong importance of DRR at local government levels, and at the same time identified several major obstacles and challenges to be encountered and raised the question on how can these be overcome. During the year 2010, the mid-term review of the HFA implementation was conducted by UNISDR. Since the adoption of the HFA in 2005, a certain progress has been made in HFA implementation by national governments with support from international and regional agencies. At the same time, the need for comprehensive DRR approach, thus HFA implementation at local level, has been strongly recognized. The report for the HFA mid-term review (UNISDR, 2011b) admitted that there was still insufficient level of implementation of the HFA at the local level. In addition, ISDR Global Assessment Report for DRR 2011 mentions that the strong recognition to the central role of local governance in disaster risk management acknowledge by most countries, and also added that a failure to strengthen local governments and make progress in community participation means that the gap between rhetoric and reality is widening (UNISDR, 2011a). These findings clearly demonstrate that the HFA implementation by local governments is one of the important areas for the international community to support and work together. Such recognition and efforts are also being promoted through international initiatives such as the ISDR World Campaign for DRR "Making Cities Resilient" (UNISDR, 2010), which promotes local governments from around the world to take action in implementing DRR activities. This paper aims at reviewing the challenges and identifying gaps for DRR by local governments and local implementation of the HFA.

1.2 What are the Challenges on Local Level DRR?

As the above literatures review identified, the major challenge is limited capacity of local governments where local capacity does not match local government responsibilities. Capacity building on DRR of local governments is the key area to enhance local DRR actions and to address challenges (UNISDR, 2011b). What are the major elements and obstacles in terms of capacity of local governments? It was pointed out that they are challenges due to the priority issues at local levels (McBean and Rodgers, 2010). The primary goal of any politician is re-election. In the process of ensuring political success, however, preventative and preparatory measures are often under-emphasized due to the fact that they may not provide immediate results (McBean and Rodgers, 2010). Due to this priority issues, budget allocation is one of the challenges for DRR by local governments.

It was noted in the mid-term review of HFA that a number of countries had passed laws assigning local government's legal responsibility for DRR management without passing budget allocations for this responsibility. Thus, the problem of local level action for DRR remains a serious concern (UNISDR, 2011b).

Progress in HFA implementation is monitored by UNISDR through the two-year reporting cycle for HFA national progress report by countries. During the reporting cycle of 2009-2011, 133 countries participated and 82 countries submitted their national progress report to UNISDR by May 2011 (UNISDR, 2011b). Initial data from 2009 to 2011 HFA reporting cycle indicated that only 20 countries reported dedicated budget allocations to local governments; these include most Caribbean countries. While there are few examples of budget allocations to local governments, many countries (65 per cent of all reporting countries and 80 per cent of lower-middle income countries) report that local governments have a legal responsibility for DRR management. However, some governments, especially of high-income countries or those with very decentralized systems, may not have reported budget allocations to local governments because local administrations have independent revenue sources from direct taxation and receive limited amounts of funding from the national level (UNISDR, 2011b). In the absence of a fiscal grant system that explicitly puts DRR on the agenda of local governments, it is unlikely to achieve the mainstreaming required for effective action unless local voices are sufficiently strong to advocate for a prioritization of resources at the local government level in favour of DRR (Gupta and Leung, 2011).

Decentralization also affects DRR by changing funding arrangements, which in turn affect the overall level of finance available for DRR. In order to mainstream DRR, it makes sense to incorporate it across all areas of a local budget, rather than concentrating DRR finance within a particular fund. However, evidence from Mozambique, South Africa and Colombia shows that un-earmarked funds for DRR are frequently diverted to other areas that have a higher political profile, or where there are apparently more pressing needs (Scott and Tarazona, 2011). The policy literature tends to assume that decentralization automatically increases participation which, in turn, is inherently beneficial. There is little empirical evidence to support this view, and it is increasingly being questioned by decentralization experts. In relation to DRR, the presence of decentralized governance systems does not automatically lead to participatory DRR. Effective decentralization of DRR can be constrained by low capacity at a local level (Scott and Tarazona, 2011).

The other key element for local DRR capacity is the coordination on DRR activities. Implementation of the HFA at local level, or lack thereof, and the capacity of governments to coordinate it with other efforts, such as socio-economic development plans at local level, was also raised consistently throughout the mid-term review. The brief review of national-level progress suggests that action at local level was consistently noted as in need of improvement (UNISDR, 2011b). As DRR is a cross-cutting issues, it is crucial to have a multi-stakeholder consultation among relevant sections and divisions within a local government from comprehensive approach. Social demand for DRR, especially at the local level, is closely linked to an effective use of truly multi-stakeholder consultative mechanisms and the involvement of community organizations (Serra and Chibay, 2011). Limited capacity of local governments on DRR is the central issue to be addressed in this paper, with specific focus on two major challenges within their capacity, that are challenges in terms of budget allocation and coordination.

2. A Guide for the HFA Implementation for Local Stakeholders

When the HFA was adopted in 2005, the instrument was largely intended as a guideline for national governments while acknowledging the enabling support of international and regional players, to take action so that disaster losses, in terms of lives, social, economic and environmental assets, are substantially reduced by 2015. To help attain that outcome, HFA identified five specific priorities for action. The five priorities were not mutually exclusive, especially when focusing on the processes since each country has different situation. HFA implementing guideline for national governments titled *Words into Action: A Guide for Implementing the Hyogo Framework* (UNISDR, 2007) was produced in 2007 by UNISDR together with partners.

Considering the importance of local government DRR actions and challenges in terms of their limited capacity, to support local governments to take comprehensive DRR actions, the HFA implementation guideline for local governments called *A Guide for Implementing the Hyogo Framework for Action by Local Stakeholders* (Kyoto University and UNISDR, 2010) was developed (Matsuoka *et al.*, 2009). The guide is for local governments and other local stakeholders to implement DRR in their cities.

It interpreted "Words into Action" to use for local level implementation by customizing the guidelines made for national level. By using this guideline, stakeholders may identify the gaps in its DRR plans and activities, which will allow them to then seek appropriate partnerships and networks to work together for safer communities. Thus, putting this guide to use requires an arena or forum by which people of different backgrounds and affiliations can share experiences, uncertainties, knowledge, and success stories of others. This forum is referred to as a "platform" which should be coordinated by a local government with other relevant stakeholders.

The guide consists of introduction and five chapters, detailing recommended actions and processes of local implementation for each key priority area of HFA:

- Chapter 1 – "Priority for Action 1 (HFA-1): ensure that DRR is a national and local/city priority with a strong institutional basis for implementation" (making disaster reduction a priority; governance).
- Chapter 2 – "Priority for Action 2 (HFA-2): identify, assess and monitor disaster risks and enhance early warning" (improving risk information and early warning; risk assessment and early warning).
- Chapter 3 – "Priority for Action 3 (HFA-3): use knowledge, innovation and education to build a culture of safety and resilience at all levels" (building a culture of safety and resilience; knowledge management).
- Chapter 4 – "Priority for Action 4 (HFA-4): reduce the underlying risk factors" (reducing the risks in key sectors; vulnerability reduction).
- Chapter 5 – "Priority for Action 5 (HFA-5): strengthen disaster preparedness for effective response at all levels" (strengthening preparedness for response; disaster preparedness).

In the "Words into Action", 22 tasks are identified to implement HFA Priority for Action. The 22 tasks of "Words into Action" were adapted to be used at local/city levels, and a slightly modified version of the list of 20 tasks was used in the guide for local government's use. The guide provides tools for implementation, evaluation, and monitoring at a local level.

20 tasks drawn from HFA five priorities for local governments and stakeholders (*A Guide for the HFA Implementation for Local Stakeholders*, 2010):

(1) Local/city governance (HFA priority 1 related):
- Task 1. Engage in multi-stakeholder dialogue to establish foundations for DRR.
- Task 2. Create or strengthen mechanisms for systematic coordination for DRR.
- Task 3. Assess and develop the institutional basis for DRR.
- Task 4. Prioritize DRR and allocate appropriate resources.

(2) Risk assessment and early warning (HFA priority 2 related):
- Task 5. Establish an initiative for community risk assessment to combine with country assessments.
- Task 6. Review the availability of risk-related information and the capacities for data collection and use.
- Task 7. Assess capacities and strengthen early warning systems.
- Task 8. Develop communication and dissemination mechanisms for disaster risk information and early warning.

(3) Knowledge management (HFA priority 3 related):
- Task 9. Raise awareness of DRR and develop education programme on DRR in schools and local communities.
- Task 10. Develop or utilize DRR training for key sectors based on identified priorities.
- Task 11. Enhance the compilation, dissemination and use of DRR information.

(4) Vulnerability reduction (HFA priority 4 related):
- Task 12. Environment: incorporate DRR in environmental management.
- Task 13. Social needs: establish mechanisms for increasing resilience of the poor and the most vulnerable.
- Task 14. Physical planning: establish measures to incorporate DRR in urban and land-use planning.
- Task 15. Structure: strengthen mechanisms for improved building safety and protection of critical facilities.
- Task 16. Economic development: stimulate DRR activities in production and service sectors.
- Task 17. Financial/economic instruments: create opportunities for private sector involvement in DRR.
- Task 18. Emergency and public safety; disaster recovery: develop a recovery planning process that incorporates DRR.

(5) Disaster preparedness (HFA priority 5 related):
- Task 19. Review disaster preparedness capacities and mechanisms, and develop a common understanding.
- Task 20. Strengthen planning and programming for disaster preparedness.

3. Research Methodology

To review gaps and challenges in local implementation of HFA, analysis of HFA implementation from local perspectives by using a questionnaire survey was conducted. The survey aimed at reviewing how multi-stakeholders involved in local DRR perceive these HFA local 20 tasks, and identifying trends and gaps within their work on DRR. The survey questions canvassed the 20 tasks identified in the guide and analysed existing trends and gaps in local level DRR approaches towards HFA requirements. The survey was targeted at multi-stakeholders which are engaged in disaster related activities and working from local context and with local governments.

3.1 Survey on the 20 Tasks for Local HFA Implementation

The questionnaire consisting of two questions based on these 20 tasks were administered. The first question asked city officials to rank tasks in terms of its relevance to their responsibilities as a city official (A – most relevant, B – some relevant, and C – not relevant). Then, in the second question, they were asked to look at the tasks that they had marked most relevant, then were again asked to rank the relevance among them within their responsibilities (1-5, 1 being highest priority and 5 being lowest priority).

The survey was conducted at 107 multi-stakeholders. Figure 1 shows the diverse backgrounds of all 107 respondents to the survey. About 50.5 per cent of respondents consist of 54 individuals from local government officials. About 49.5 per cent of respondents consist of 53 individuals from national government officials (18.7 per cent); and actors from civil society (15 per cent), international organizations (6.5 per cent), academic institutions (4.7 per cent) and other groups that include the private sector (4.7 per cent).

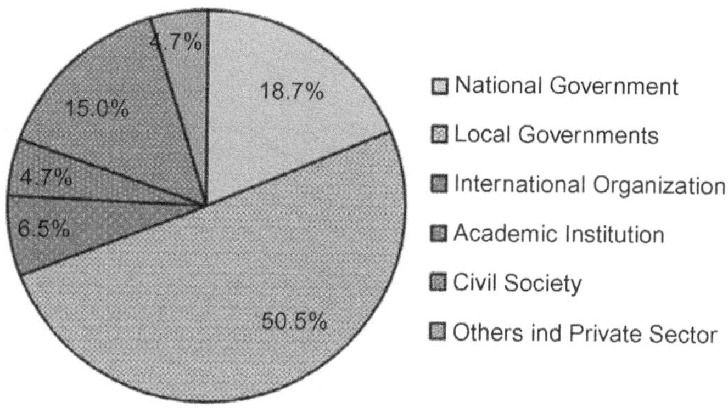

Figure 1: Distribution of respondents to the questionnaire (total 107)

This survey included a target group of Makati City (the Philippines) in order to explore deeper analysis for a specific city and also to conduct comparative analysis. The description of respondents (total 107 individuals) to the questionnaire is as follows. In the total number of respondents ($n = 107$), the Group of Makati City had 32 individuals (29.9 per cent), and the Group of non-Makati had 75 individuals (70.1 per cent) (Figure 2). The survey were administered to the Group of Makati City ($n = 32$) and the Group of non-Makati ($n = 75$). For the Group of non-Makati, the questionnaires were administered at several meetings and conferences focusing on DRR at local government levels.

3.2 *Makati as the Target Group*

Makati City is part of Metro Manila and the financial capital of the Philippines. Makati City is exposed to two physical characteristics in terms of risks. First, a part of the valley fault system, a potential generator of a large magnitude earthquake in Metro Manila, is located at the Eastern part of Makati City. Second, the Western portion of the city is composed of former tidal flats. There are seven low-lying barangays (villages) at this portion of the city that are flood-prone (Kyoto University, CITYNET, UNISDR, and UNU, 2009).

Makati City has been active in DRR efforts and has strong recognition to HFA as an internationally agreed DRR framework. The analysis of the survey explores the case of Makati Group and diagnoses the gaps and areas where greater prioritization must occur by identifying the areas in which Makati City are currently placing low priority. It explores the common trends and distinctions in prioritization between Makati Group and non-Makati Group under the assumption that Makati City has been heralded in its DRR efforts and has been considered as relatively an

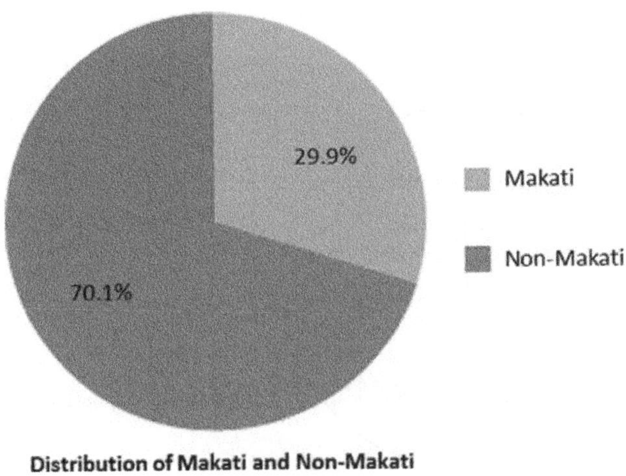

Figure 2: Distribution of Makati and non-Makati (total 107)

Table I: Composition of Makati City respondents ($n = 32$)

City government	Budget department
	Department of Education (Dep-Ed Makati) Department of Engineering and Public Works (DEPW) Department of Environmental Services (DES) Human Resource Development office (HRDO) Liga ng mga Barangay Makati C3/Rescue Makati Health Department (MHD) Makati Social Welfare Department (MSWD) Office of the Mayor (OM) Opital (Hospital) ng Makati Public Employment Service Office (PESO) Urban Development Department (UDD)
National government	Metro Manila Development Authority (MMDA)
Private sector	Manila Water, Inc.

Note: Members of the MCDRRCC

example which integrates DRR into various sectors and considers comprehensive DRR perspectives.

For the Group of Makati, the questionnaires were distributed among the focal points of Makati City DRR Coordinating Council (MCDRRCC) (Table I). 32 officials responded to the questionnaire from the below 15 sections, which were members of the MCDRRCC. At least two officials from these 15 sections participated in the survey in order to take the balance of the participation from various sections.

4. Results of the Survey

4.1 Analysis of the Makati Group

By analyzing the responses from the Makati Group, it revealed gaps and missing areas for Makati City in terms comprehensive DRR and HFA implementation. Figure 3 shows HFA tasks in terms of relevancy and priority by the Group of Makati City with following major observations; a majority of tasks that Makati Group regarded as most relevant to their work are related to HFA1 and HFA5. About 50 per cent or more of officials identified all four tasks under HFA1 as most relevant, with more than 70 per cent identifying T4 (prioritize DRR and allocate appropriate resources) as the most relevant. HFA5 was regarded as the most relevant with 60 per cent of officials selecting T20 and over 50 per cent of officials selecting T19. HFA2 and HFA4 tasks were regarded as lesser relevance with an exception of T18 (HFA4) which was the only task considered as most relevant by over 50 per cent of officials under HFA4. Of the HFA4 tasks, the least relevant were T16 (19 per cent) and T17 (25 per cent), relating to economic development and the use of financial or economic instruments to encourage private sector participation in DRR were ranked

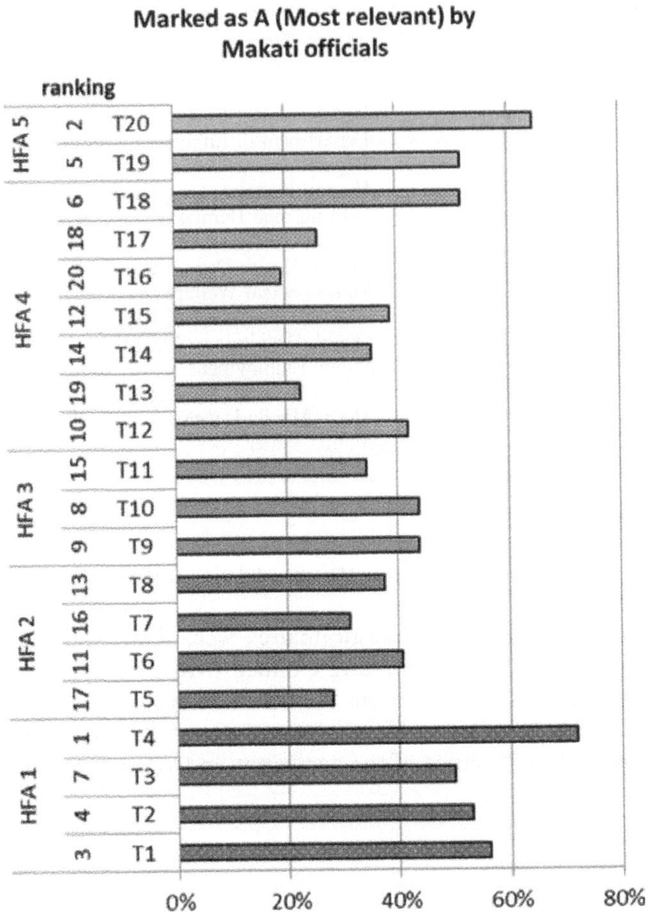

Figure 3: Tasks marked as most relevant by Makati officials

least relevant. HFA4-T13 (22 per cent), which relates to addressing social needs of vulnerable groups, also ranked low. This implied that government coverage of DRR activities did not encompass enough all sectors or demographics. All HFA3 tasks were ranked as most relevant by over 30 per cent of respondents but with low priority. T9 (43 per cent) and T10 (43 per cent) had relatively higher relevancy than T11 (34 per cent) which showed the lowest under HFA3 relates to the collection and dissemination of DRR information. HFA2 tasks were dispersed with T5 (28 per cent) and T7 (31 per cent) ranking lower in relevancy compared to T8 (37 per cent) and T6 (40 per cent). The relative rankings of the HFA2 suggest that risk assessment and early warning activities may need further attention.

Figure 4 shows HFA tasks with rankings in priority by Makati Group among the tasks marked with relevant tasks. Over 40 per cent of officials regarded HFA5-T20 as

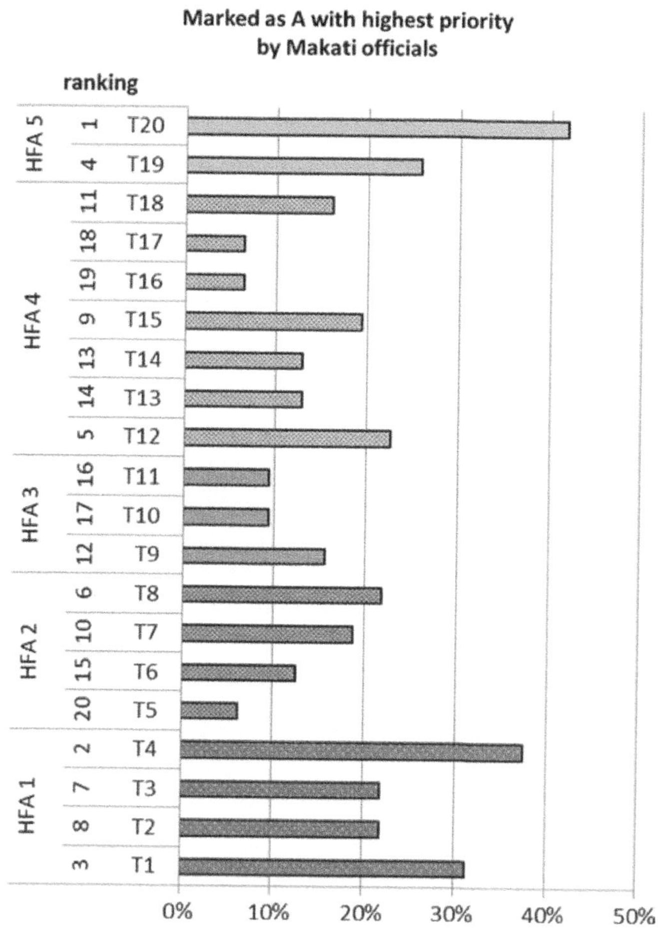

Figure 4: Tasks marked as most relevant with highest priority by Makati officials

the high priority task. Over 30 per cent of officials regarded HFA1-T1 and T4 as the next tasks which take priority. Over 25 per cent of officials regarded HFA5-T19 (review disaster preparedness capacities and mechanisms) as a priority task.

The responses from Makati Group can be inferred that work in these officials' divisions currently relate more to governance (HFA1) and planning activities for disaster preparedness (HFA5), with less attention on risk assessment and early warning (HFA2), knowledge management (HFA3) and vulnerability reduction (HFA4).

4.2 Comparative Analysis Between Makati Group and Non-Makati Group

It is also informative to compare the two results as there are some similarities in what officials deem relevant, and some distinctions between the results obtained from Makati and non-Makati Group. Figure 5 shows the comparison between the

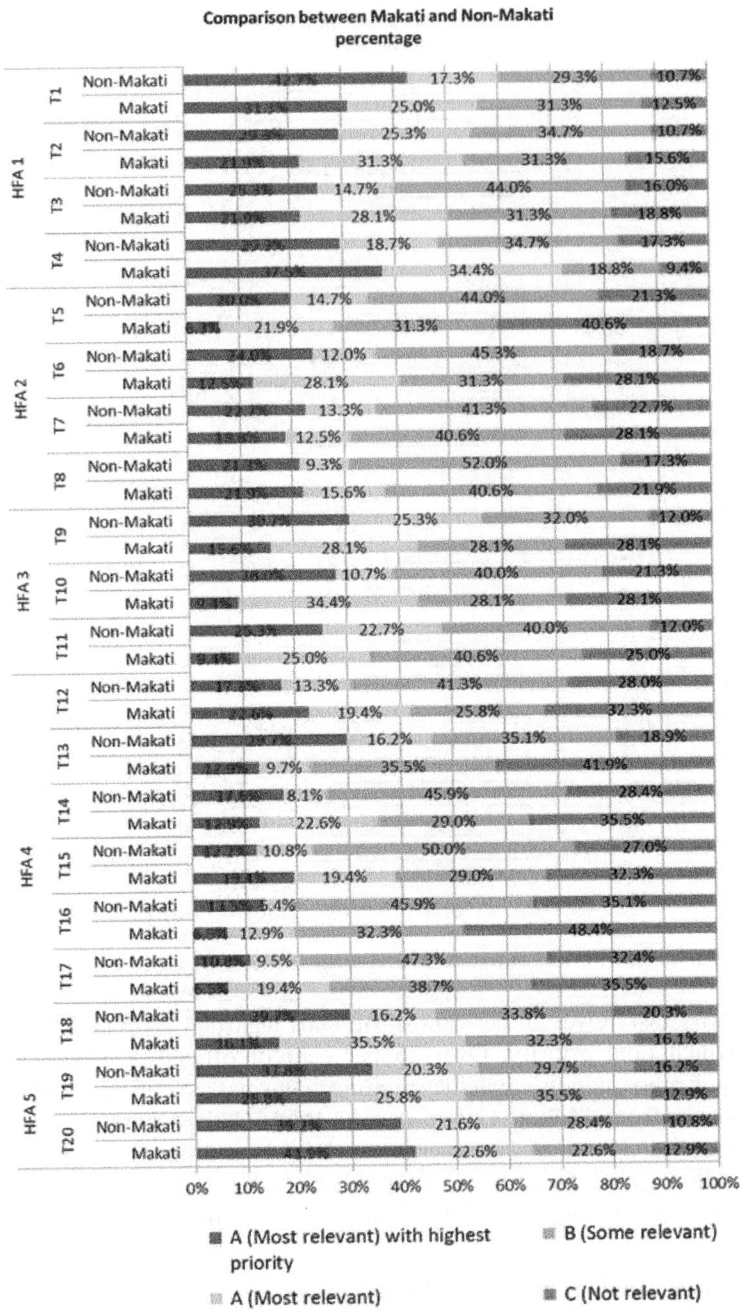

Figure 5: Comparison between Makati and non-Makati regarding the percentage of relevance and the highest priority tasks

two groups according to the relevancy of the tasks and the tasks marked as the highest priority (highlighted with the darkest color).

Table II shows the comparison between the two groups of five tasks with highest relevance and highest priorities. Both groups regarded same four tasks (T1, T2, T19 and T20) as one of five highest relevance and priorities. There were some distinctions. The majority (71.9 per cent) of Makati Group considered T4 (allocate appropriate resources on DRR) as the most relevant task. Among them, 37.5 per cent regarded T4 as the highest priority task. However, in the non-Makati Group, T4 was not regarded as either most relevant or highest priority (its rank is 7th among 20 tasks).

Table II showed that for Makati Group the five highest relevant or five highest priority tasks did not include any task from HFA3. Non-Makati Group regarded T9 from HFA3 as one of the five more relevant tasks, and T9 from HFA3 and T18 from HFA4 as one of the five highest priorities.

Table II: Comparison between Makati and non-Makati Groups in terms of five tasks marked with highest relevance and priority

	Makati Group		Non-Makati Group	
	Task	Percentage	Task	Percentage
Highest relevance				
1	T4 (HFA1)	71.9	T20 (HFA5)	60.8
2	T20 (HFA5)	64.5	T1 (HFA1)	60
3	T1 (HFA1)	56.3	T9 (HFA3)	56
4	T2 (HFA2)	53.1	T2 (HFA1)	54.7
5	T19 (HFA5)	51.6	T19 (HFA5)	54.1
Highest priority				
1	T20 (HFA5)	41.9	T1 (HFA1)	42.7
2	T4 (HFA1)	37.5	T20 (HFA5)	39.2
3	T1 (HFA1)	31.3	T19 (HFA5)	33.8
4	T19 (HFA5)	25.8	T9 (HFA3)	30.7
5	T12 (HFA4)	22.6	T18 (HFA4)	29.7

Table III: Comparison between Makati and non-Makati Groups in terms of average percentages of tasks as highest relevance and highest priority

	Makati Group Average of %		Non-Makati Group Average of %	
	Most relevant	Highest priority	Most relevant	Highest priority
HFA1	57.8	28.15	50.6	31.7
HFA2	34.4	14.8	34.3	22
HFA3	40.6	11.5	47.6	28
HFA4	33.6	13.8	30.0	18.7
HFA5	58.1	33.9	57.45	36.5

Table III shows the average of percentage of Figure 5 according to the five HFA priorities. The comparison between the two groups shows also that Makati Group has less emphasis on HFA3.

While both groups placed strong emphasis on HFA5, both groups had less prioritization of HFA2 and HFA4, and low prioritisation of tasks 16 and 17 under HFA4. This implies these tasks are common challenged areas. Regarding observed distinction, Makati City officials were more committed to T4 compared to non-Makati Group. Makati City placed greater relevance on incorporating the environment into DRR policies (T12). Non-Makati Group placed greater emphasis on T13 and HFA3 in general. T13 is important in catering to the social needs of the city, which Makati Group placed much less priority and relevance. From the results obtained from this questionnaire (Figure 5), it appears that Makati Group should focus more on the awareness raising and social needs of the residents. While the analysis was conducted under the hypothesis that Makati City, being a forerunner in localizing DRR, would have a more well-rounded focus on the 20 tasks, the results show that that was not necessarily the case. Makati City, like the other cities, prioritizes some tasks more than others.

Comprehensive DRR approaches need balanced approach by covering all the five HFA priority areas. For the purpose of taking comprehensive DRR approaches, recommended area for actions for the next five years to Makati City can be drawn from the result of the 20 tasks survey. Makati City should place more emphasis and priority to HFA2, HFA3 and HFA4. In particular, below several tasks among 20 tasks shown in Table IV should be paid more attention by Makati City, since the current understanding and situation revealed by the 20 tasks survey revealed that these tasks have not yet been covered enough as relevant or priority tasks by members of Makati DRRCC. Not many individuals regard these tasks as relevant tasks or priority tasks. This implies that these tasks could be gaps or missing areas of work within Makati City.

4.3 *Makati Action Plan*

Through the training programme which was jointly conducted between February and April 2010 by UNISDR, Kyoto University, CITYNET, World Bank Tokyo Development Learning Center, SEEDS, Makati City developed a set of actions by using the Guide (UNISDR and Kyoto University, 2010). Through the pilot training program, Makati itself developed a series of action plans using the Guide and the 20 tasks. Makati City developed a total number of 90 actions were developed by ensuring all the 20 tasks are covered. In the Makati Action Plan (MAP), HFA1 actions totalled 14 with emphasis on short-term actions. HFA2 actions totalled 10 with actions dispersed by timeframe. HFA3 actions totalled 6 and are also well dispersed. HFA4 actions totalled 48, with emphasis on mid- and long-term actions. HFA5 actions totalled 12 with some focus on short-term actions. The largest number of actions (48 actions) was developed under HFA4 (Table V).

Table IV: A set of tasks requiring further attention and actions by Makati City, considering that they are regarded as most relevant by less individuals and as highest priority by less individuals of Makati Group

	Tasks regarded as most relevant by less than 30 per cent of Makati Group	Tasks regarded as highest priority by less than 15 per cent of Makati Group
HFA2 (risk assessment and early warning)		
Task 5. Establish an initiative for community risk assessment to combine with country assessments	□	□
Task 6. Review the availability of risk-related information and the capacities for data collection and use		□
HFA3 (knowledge management)		
Task 10. Develop or utilize DRR training for key sectors based on identified priorities		□
Task 11. Enhance the compilation, dissemination and use of DRR information		□
HFA4 (vulnerability reduction)		
Task 13. Social needs: establish mechanisms for increasing resilience of the poor and the most vulnerable	□	□
Task 14. Physical planning: establish measures to incorporate DRR in urban and land-use planning		□
Task 16. Economic development: stimulate DRR activities in production and service sectors	□	□
Task 17. Financial/economic instruments: create opportunities for private sector involvement in DRR	□	□

The joint training program by using the guide and the 20 tasks survey demonstrated the case of useful combination towards the concrete action planning process to make sure comprehensive DRR actions and HFA priority areas are covered. This case of Makati City makes the case where an internally agreed instrument like HFA can drill into local level and support its action planning through a concrete set of guideline by presenting these concrete 20 tasks.

5. Discussion for Budget Allocation and Coordination Issues

The two major challenges identified by the literature review for local government capacity on DRR are coordination mechanism and budget allocation. It was also pointed out that the issue of budget allocation is due to the priority issues and

Table V: Makati action plan and HFA local 20 tasks

Priority area	Task	Short term Between now and next two years (number of action)	Mid term Between next two to five years (number of action)	Long term Beyond five years (number of action)	Total number of actions
HFA1	Task 1	2	0	0	2
	Task 2	2	0	2	4
	Task 3	0	2	2	4
	Task 4	4	0	0	4
Sub-total		8	2	4	*14*
HFA2	Task 5	2	0	0	2
	Task 6	0	2	0	2
	Task 7	0	0	2	2
	Task 8	2	0	2	4
Sub-total		4	2	4	*10*
HFA3	Task 9	2	0	0	2
	Task 10	0	2	0	2
	Task 11	0	0	2	2
Sub-total		2	2	2	*6*
HFA4	Task 12	0	4	4	8
	Task 13	4	6	8	18
	Task 14	0	2	2	4
	Task 15	2	0	0	2
	Task 16	2	2	0	4
	Task 17	2	4	4	10
	Task 18	0	2	0	2
Sub-total		10	20	18	*48*
HFA5	Task 19	4	4	0	8
	Task 20	2	0	2	4
		6	4	2	*12*
Grand-total		30	30	30	*90*

decentralization. Complete decentralization of budgeting and reporting can also generate problems. Although it may ensure that spending is in line with local priorities, it almost inevitably leads to divisions with national and sector policies and programmes (Benson, 2011). Therefore, the issues related to coordination mechanism, budget allocation, priority issues and decentralisation are interconnected and need to be addressed in an integrated manner to overcome their challenges. One of the studies conducted for the HFA mid-term review on effective financial mechanisms at the national and local levels for DRR highlighted some of the structural factors and hierarchical constrains within resource allocation mechanisms to explain why national budgets and financial allocations at the local level remain stubbornly difficult to influence when it comes to DRR (Jackson, 2011; Nagamatsu *et al.*, 2005). This challenge in terms of hierarchical structure could be better addressed by an effective coordination mechanism which facilitates vertical coordination and overcome difficulties surrounding the hierarchical structure.

In addition to identifying specific fiscal and regulatory opportunities for improving and increasing the allocation of funding for DRR at the local level, the above mentioned study recommends decentralizing authority and resources to appropriate administrative levels in support of local multi-stakeholder partnerships (including equitable representation from the most vulnerable) to coordinate and manage policy execution on risk reduction, poverty alleviation, development, and climate change adaptation (Jackson, 2011).

From this context, efforts and support from national governments are crucial to support capacity building of local governments together with proper budget allocations earmarked to DRR and incremental decentralization. Competent and accountable local government is a precondition for effective disaster risk management. Unless local governments have the capacities and resources to fulfil their functions, decentralization of responsibilities may be counter-productive. Therefore, in decentralization processes, more attention needs to be paid to the appropriate layering of functions, where higher administrative levels financially and technically support local implementation. If the decentralization of relevant functions and resources cannot be fully realized due to extremely weak local capacities, an incremental approach may be the most effective way forward (UNISDR, 2011a). Incremental decentralization accompanied by clear mandates, budgets and systems of subsidiarity, promotes ownership and improved risk governance capacities at all levels. Scaling up community initiatives can be enabled by local planning, financial and investment that build on civil society partnerships (UNISDR, 2011a). Effective local action requires human capacity, financial resources and political authority. Central policy responsibility for DRR must be complemented by adequately decentralized and layered risk management functions, capacities and corresponding budgets (UNISDR, 2011a).

In terms of "what must be added to decentralization to strengthen DRR?", the below points were suggested to be in place so that decentralization can strengthen DRR (Scott and Tarazona, 2011):

- incentives that create strong political interest in and engagement with DRR issues (for example high disaster risk levels, personal liability of mayors, pressure from the electorate, media engagement, academic influence, or convincing financial analysis on the cost effectiveness of DRR);
- adequate technical capacity at a local level, both in relation to DRR and for general government duties;
- good levels of financial resources generally, and also a mechanism for ensuring that DRR funds are not diverted to other areas;
- high levels of civic education and public awareness about DRR; and
- strong national government leadership and enforcement mechanisms.

If most of these conditions are not in place there is little reason to expect decentralization to improve DRR (Scott and Tarazona, 2011).

Coordination mechanism and budget allocation issues are both belonging to the priority area of HFA1 which has four tasks (Tasks 1-4). In the result of the 20 tasks survey for Makati Group, Task 4 is regarded as the highest relevant and second highest priority by Makati Group. On the other hand, non-Makati Group did not have Task 4 listed within five most relevant nor five highest priorities shown in Table II. This high priority and relevance attached to Task 4 is interpreted as one of the most positive aspect for Makati Group. Considering the above suggested elements for decentralization which can strengthen DRR, the active function of the Makati City DRR Council as a coordination mechanism contributes to these elements and led the development of MAP. The Makati case demonstrated that having a good coordination mechanism support addressing the challenge of budget allocation issues.

As pointed out within the above fifth element, it is needless to say that national government supports for these efforts at local government levels are important. A local DRR is more likely when there is a strong national entity playing an oversight and enforcement role (Scott and Tarazona, 2011). In the Philippines, 2010 Philippines DRR and Management Act makes capacity strengthening of its most decentralized administrative units a state policy (IFRC, 2011). This provides a positive ground for a Makati City which is active in taking actions on DRR. For the process to develop local DRR capacity, phase approach is important, considering the point that the presence of decentralized governance systems does not automatically lead to participatory DRR. Effective decentralization of DRR can be constrained by low capacity at a local level (Scott and Tarazona, 2011). A number of European countries noted DRR efforts at the local level going back generations. Those countries with more years of work on DRR were seen to be significantly more advanced in decentralizing local action on DRR, possibly indicating a phased process whereby DRR was first addressed at the central level and seems to have been applied in an institutionalized way at the local level only later (Jackson, 2011). A possible "phased approach" from national to local level of HFA implementation was also mentioned during some of the HFA mid-term review workshops (UNISDR, 2011b). According to the mid-term review report, it noted that there is a process in the making in applying HFA guidance whereby several governments had recently approved, or were in the process of doing so, DRR national policies and/or frameworks, in which decentralization of DRR to the local level was an important component that would logically follow in the implementation phase. This is consistent with the observation that the HFA has brought about positive changes within national institutions but the process is still very much in the making, as would be reasonable to expect for a framework five years into its implementation (Jackson, 2011).

A platform of multi-stakeholders serve as an advocacy and coordinating tool of DRR in the local context. It facilitates coordination and participatory process engaged in problem solving based on evidence. Resources from various areas will be combined. Also, it streamlines the planning process so that DRR can be accepted as a public value and be mainstreamed into city plans as well as day-to-day operations of constituted authorities and businesses. A "local platform" is required for engaging actors in developing DRR strategies, capable of deciding what new instruments are needed to deal with local demands and needs, and to support new kinds of interactions and communication channels between relevant stakeholders (UNISDR, 2011b). In particular, a local platform is required for engaging actors in developing DRR strategies, capable of deciding what new instruments are needed to deal with local demands and needs, and to support new kinds of interactions and communication channels between relevant stakeholders. Such a platform, if well designed, could also support social learning by the creation of a "collective memory" based on the accumulation of knowledge and lessons learned from past disaster experience into preventative strategies (Serra and Chibay, 2011). In order to enhance local capacities as well as to foster both vertical (from the national to local level) and horizontal (among relevant branches of local governments and also with communities and civil society) communication to deal with DRR, resources should be devoted not so much to technical means, but to long-term institutional innovation and learning. Establishing a local platform on DRR among relevant multi-stakeholders and fostering its functions should present a set of solutions to address these interconnected issues on coordination mechanism, budget allocation, priority and decentralisation issues in an integrated manner.

6. Conclusion

The analysis of the 20 tasks survey demonstrated the current situation of Makati City in terms of its perception towards comprehensive DRR actions by revealing most relevant tasks and highest priority tasks, and also less relevant tasks and less priority tasks. The result was useful to understand the current situation, and provided a comparative reference for analysis on the action plan developed by Makati City.

The result of the 20 tasks survey revealed that HFA4 needed more focus and attention by Makati City. However, looking at the MAP developed; this need to focus on HFA4 has been already recognized by Makati City and being addressed by the largest number of planned actions (48 actions) developed under HFA4 within the MAP. Through the process of MAP development, the Makati DRRCC played the important coordinating role. Members of the Council got together to develop these actions by referring to the guide. The process of MAP through the Makati DRRCC demonstrated a practical case for an effective function of a local platform on DRR.

Reviewing further the results of the survey with the MAP developed by Makati City can show if MAP is trying to address these existing gaps properly or if gaps are still left out. Through the comparative analysis, Makati City is suggested to come up with more actions under HFA3 and HFA2, considering the fact that less relevance and less priority are observed in these two areas. Also the numbers of developed actions are only six actions under HFA3 and ten actions under HFA2 within the MAP. HFA3 has the lowest number of actions developed among HFA five priority areas, regardless of the gaps under HFA3 identified as the result of the survey. The importance of the area of HFA3 (knowledge and education) goes along with one of the elements of decentralization which strengthen DRR is high levels of civic education and public awareness about DRR, as discussed under Section 5. Makati City is suggested to follow up these action plans and also to check the progress in a cyclic manner to monitor the progress. By doing so, the gaps and necessary actions will be further identified towards scaling up their capacities on DRR. These continuous and sustainable efforts are important and this process is only effective through an active coordination mechanism, Makati DRRCC.

In order to build local DRR capacity, it is important to increase the capacity of local governments by themselves and also to increase the society's resilience through measures taken by local governments (McBean and Rodgers, 2010). A local platform like Makati DRRCC is well-positioned to meet this purpose of increasing its capacity by a local government itself. Social resilience is important that effort is put into building capacity in these regions. Society's ability to use their internal resources and competencies to respond to demands, as well as their learned resourcefulness, will work in tandem with the emergency services, to ensure that there is a measure of social preparedness and an adequate ability to respond and recover. In addition to allowing quicker recovery and minimizing loss, creating this type of resilience prevents against greater damage caused by further breakdowns of different systems or additional hazards. This is especially important given that a break down in a city or region will cause faltering decision making and slow responses, making communities more vulnerable to disasters (McBean and Rodgers, 2010).

As argued at the beginning of this paper, the literature review supported the importance of DRR at local government levels. At the same time it identified major obstacles in terms of the limited capacity of DRR by local governments, and raised the question on how these can be overcome. These challenges for the limited capacity such as budget allocation, effective decentralization, and coordination are the key areas. The HFA provides a set of recommendations to address these challenges by taking comprehensive DRR measures according to these five priority areas. Local platform plays an important role for coordination and for collectively solving these challenges, together with the phase approach supported by a national government.

For the purpose of building capacity on DRR by local governments, implementing HFA at local government level is relevant and crucial approach. Especially, HFA1 is addressing the priority areas of coordination mechanism and budget allocation issues. An effective local platform and efforts on DRR budget allocation provides an important basis for DRR actions. Establishing a local platform should be recommendable to other local governments. As discussed in Section 5, the phase approach should be combined with these efforts through a proper national support to the proper decentralization. The deconcentration of functions without wholly devolving authorities and budgets can be a pragmatic first step towards full decentralization. Twinning of capacity-rich municipalities and regions with poorer or more risk-prone ones, and strategic partnerships between technical centers and civil society organizations, further complement incremental devolution (UNISDR, 2011a). In this context, a local platform on DRR also has a potential to facilitate a strategic partnership for incremental devolution working together with other local governments in a country.

Makati City uses the HFA as a central guiding tool to implement comprehensive DRR actions, combining the use of the guide which facilitated their consultation and action planning. Makati City case demonstrated a case of a local platform for DRR, through MCDRRCC, which provides a basis for accelerating local DRR actions and a venue for collectively addressing challenges by ensuring vertical coordination among relevant divisions and stakeholders. The case of Makati City provides an on-going model process of a local platform on DRR which can be leant by other local government for possible replication.

References

Christoplos, I. (2003), "Actors in risk", in Pelling, M. (Ed.), *Natural Disasters and Development in a Globalizing World*, Routledge, New York, NY, pp. 95–109.

Gupta, S. and Leung, I. (2011), *Turning Good Practice into Institutional Mechanism: Investing in Grassroots Women's Leadership to Scale Up Local Implementation of the Hyogo Framework for Action*, Huairou Commission and Groots International, Brooklyn, NY.

Jackson, D. (2011), *Effective Financial Mechanism at the National and Local Level for Disaster Risk Reduction*, United Nations Capital Development Fund, New York, NY.

Kyoto University and UNISDR (2010), *A Guide for Implementing the Hyogo Framework for Action by Local Stakeholders*, available at: www.preventionweb.net/english/professional/publications/v.php?id=13101.

Kyoto University, CITYNET, UNISDR, and UNU (2009), *City Profile: Climate and Disaster Resilience*, available at: www.preventionweb.net/english/professional/publications/v.php?id=8168.

Kyoto University, CITYNET, UNISDR, WB TDLC, SEEDS (2010), *Climate and Disaster Resilience Initiative – Capacity-Building Program*, available at: www.preventionweb.net/english/professional/publications/v.php?id=16723.

McBean, G. and Rodgers, C. (2010), "Climate hazards and disasters: the need for capacity building", *Wiley Interdisciplinary Reviews: Climate Change*, Vol. 1 *No. 6, pp. 871–84.*

Matsuoka, Y., Sharma, A. and Shaw, R. (2009), "Hyogo framework for action and urban risk reduction in Asia", *Urban Risk Reduction: An Asian Perspective*, Community, Environment and Disaster Risk Management, Vol. 1, *Emerald Publishing, Bradford, available at: www.emeraldinsight.com/books.htm?issn=2040-7262&volume=1.*

Nagamatsu, S., Hayashi, H. and Kawata, Y. (2005), The Problem of Disaster Management Policy and Local Plan for Disaster Prevention, pp. 1-10.

Scott, Z. and Tarazona, M. (2011), *Decentralization and Disaster Risk Reduction, Study on Disaster Risk Reduction, Decentralization and Political Economy Analysis for UNDP Contribution to the GAR11*, UNISDR, Geneva.

Serra, A. and Chibay, I. (2011), "Assessing the role of vertical and horizontal communication in disaster risk reduction learning and planning: the case of the Spanish Tous dam-break, 1982", Integrated Risk Governance Projects, Barcelona.

UNISDR (2005), *Hyogo Framework for Action 2005-2015: Building the Resilience of Nations and Communities to Disasters*, United Nations International Strategy for Disaster

Reduction, Geneva, available at: www.unisdr.org/eng/hfa/docs/Hyogo-framework-for-action-english.pdf.

UNISDR (2007), *Words into Action: A Guide for Implementing the Hyogo Framework*, United Nations International Strategy for Disaster Reduction, Geneva, available at: www.preventionweb.net/english/professional/publications/v.php?id=594.

UNISDR (2010), *Information Kit for ISDR 2010-2011 World Disaster Reduction Campaign*, United Nations International Strategy for Disaster Reduction, Geneva, available at: www.unisdr.org/english/campaigns/campaign2010-2011/documents/campaign-kit.pdf.

UNISDR (2011a), *Global Assessment Report on Disaster Risk Reduction 2011*, United Nations International Strategy for Disaster Reduction, Geneva, available at: www.preventionweb.net/gar.

UNISDR (2011b), *Hyogo Framework for Action 2005-2015 Building the Resilience of Nations and Communities to Disasters, Mid-term Review 2010-2011*, United Nations International Strategy for Disaster Reduction, Geneva, available at: www.preventionweb.net/english/professional/publications/v.php?id=18197.

Further Reading

Kanagawa, K. and Togo, H. (2010), The Changing Local Governance Triggered by the Great Earthquake, Toulouse, France.

Kazama, N. (2008), "Japan's disaster reduction policy", *Public Policy Studies Association Japan Annual Report (1998)*, Disaster Reduction and Human Renovation Institute, Key Points in Disaster Countermeasures of Local Governments, Disaster Reduction and Human Renovation Institute, Kobe, pp. 1–25.

Matsuoka, Y., Sharma, A. and Shaw, R. (2011), "Linking resilience planning to Hyogo framework for action at local level", *Climate Disaster Resilience in Local Governments*, Community, Environment and Disaster Risk Reduction, Vol. 6, *Emerald Publishing, Bradford.*

Pelling, M. (2007), "Learning from others: scope and challenges fro participatory disaster risk assessment", *Disasters*, Vol. 31 *No. 4, pp. 373–85.*

Suganuma, K. (2006), "Recent trends in earthquake disaster management in Japan", *Science and Technology Trends*, Vol. 19, *pp. 91–106.*

UNISDR (2009), *Global Assessment Report on Disaster Risk Reduction 2009*, United Nations International Strategy for Disaster Reduction, Geneva, available at: www.preventionweb.net/english/hyogo/gar/report/index.php?id=1130&pid:34&pih:2.

United Nations (1999), *United Nations General Assembly Resolution A/RES/54/219*, available at: www.unisdr.org/eng/about_isdr/basic_docs/GA-resolution/a-res-54-219-eng.pdf.

United Nations (2001), *United Nations General Assembly Resolution A/RES/56/195*, available at: www.unisdr.org/eng/about_isdr/basic_docs/GA-resolution/a-res-56-195-eng.pdf.

Wamsler, C. (2006), "Mainstreaming risk reduction in urban planning and housing: a challenge for international aid organisations", *Disasters*, Vol. 30 *No. 2, pp. 151–77.*

Wisner, B. (2003), "Disaster risk reduction in megacities: making the most of human and social capital", in Kreimer, A., Arnold, M. and Carlin, A. (Eds), *Building Safer Cities – The Future of Disaster Risk*, The World Bank, Washington, DC, pp. 181–96.

Printed and bound by CPI Group (UK) Ltd, Croydon, CR0 4YY

15/09/2026

14962372-0001